A GANGSTER'S LIFE

SELECTED BOOKS BY PETER EDWARDS

Lytton: Climate Change, Colonialism and Life Before the Fire
(with Kevin Loring)
(2024)

*The Wolfpack: The Millennial Mobsters Who Brought
Chaos and the Cartels to the Canadian Underworld*
(with Luis Nájera)
(2021)

*Hard Road: Bernie Guindon and the Reign of
the Satan's Choice Motorcycle Club*
(2017)

Bad Blood (first published as *Business or Blood:
Mafia Boss Vito Rizzuto's Last War*)
(with Antonio Nicaso)
(2015)

*Unrepentant: The Strange and (Sometimes) Terrible Life
of Lorne Campbell, Satan's Choice and Hells Angels Biker*
(2013)

*The Bandido Massacre: A True Story of
Bikers, Brotherhood and Betrayal*
(2012)

*Delusion: The True Story of
Victorian Superspy Henri Le Caron*
(2008)

*The Encyclopedia of Canadian Organized Crime:
From Captain Kidd to Mom Boucher*
(with Michel Auger)
(2004)

*One Dead Indian: The Premier, the Police
and the Ipperwash Crisis*
(2003)

A GANGSTER'S LIFE

WAR AND ADDICTION IN THE NEW UNDERWORLD

PETER EDWARDS

WITH SHANE TIMOTHY DANKOSKI

RANDOM HOUSE CANADA

PUBLISHED BY RANDOM HOUSE CANADA

Random House Canada, an imprint of Penguin Random House Canada Limited
320 Front Street West, Suite 1400
Toronto, Ontario, M5V 3B6, Canada
penguinrandomhouse.ca

Random House Canada and colophon are registered trademarks of
Penguin Random House LLC.

The authorized representative in the EU for product safety and compliance
is Penguin Random House Ireland, Morrison Chambers, 32 Nassau Street,
Dublin D02 YH68, Ireland. https://eu-contact.penguin.ie

Library and Archives Canada Cataloguing in Publication

Title: A gangster's life : war and addiction in the new underworld / Peter Edwards.
Names: Edwards, Peter, 1956- author.
Description: Includes index.
Identifiers: Canadiana (print) 20240414470 | Canadiana (ebook) 20240418441 |
ISBN 9781039009707 (hardcover) | ISBN 9781039009714 (EPUB)
Subjects: LCSH: Dankoski, Shane. | LCSH: Gang members—British Columbia—
Biography. | LCSH: Gangs—British Columbia. | LCGFT: Biographies.
Classification: LCC HV6439.C32 B7 2025 | DDC 364.106/6092—dc23

Cover design: Matthew Flute
Text design: Matthew Flute
Typesetting: Daniella Zanchetta
Image credits: (clouds) Xuanyu Han/Getty; (silhouette) Руслан Галиуллин/
Adobe Stock; (city) GoToVan, Knox Mountain Park, Kelowna city view 2017:
https://commons.wikimedia.org/wiki/File:Kelowna_city_view_2017.jpg.
This file is licensed under the Creative Commons

Printed in Canada

10 9 8 7 6 5 4 3 2 1

Penguin
Random House
RANDOM HOUSE CANADA

To the late Michel Auger. Mentor and friend.

—PETER EDWARDS

To my wife Alesia and my children Jayden, Jordan, Jaida, and Jayla,
without whom this book wouldn't have come to life.
I know, and you're lucky you're still here! 🛡️ *—C.R.*

—SHANE DANKOSKI

CONTENTS

Author's Note   xiii

Chapter 1   Home Front   1
Chapter 2   Role Models   8
Chapter 3   Young Thugs   17
Chapter 4   Gangcouver   26
Chapter 5   Gangster Tools   41
Chapter 6   Moving Up   50
Chapter 7   Stranger and Stranger   61
Chapter 8   Gurmit's Gone   77
Chapter 9   The New Normal   88
Chapter 10   Real Hectic, Real Quick   102
Chapter 11   Kill Site   114
Chapter 12   Full Bore   125
Chapter 13   Closing In   137
Chapter 14   Borrowed Time   146
Chapter 15   Funeral Tears   158
Chapter 16   Manny   166

Chapter 17   Alone   178
Chapter 18   Rock Bottom   192
Chapter 19   No Turning Back   200
Chapter 20   The Deal   210
Chapter 21   Collaborators of Justice   223
Chapter 22   Strike Three Crew   240
Chapter 23   Killing Time   250
Chapter 24   The Trial   260
Chapter 25   Reminders   267
Chapter 26   Another Chance   279

Chapter Notes   285
Bibliography   290
Index   305

BRITISH COLUMBIA LOWER MAINLAND AND VANCOUVER ISLAND

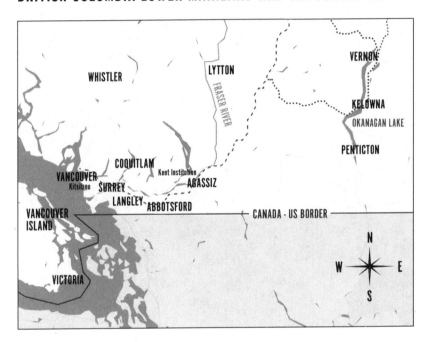

- - - COQUIHALLA HIGHWAY (HWY 5)   ······ HWY 97

Do you know what it takes to be a gangster in this day and age?

—SHANE TIMOTHY DANKOSKI

AUTHOR'S NOTE

THIS BOOK IS REAL. Over the past few years, though, I often found myself wishing that Shane's real-life story was fiction, or a bad dream.

It's not. It's a story from inside the underworld. Deep inside.

The story that plays out in these pages describes a millennial gangster's life in today's emerging, tech-savvy, internet-driven, multi-ethnic, multi-national underworld. It's an evolution of sorts from what we've grown accustomed to thinking of as "typical" gangsters and crime families. It's not as neighbourhood-based as what we might have seen in headlines from the mid- to late-twentieth century, or in classic gangster movies like *The Godfather* or *Goodfellas*. It's more mobile, winding across Canada, down to Mexico, and overseas to Dubai. It's a shiny new underworld of gold and diamonds, drugs and short life spans.

It's a story drawn from thousands of pages of official documents on former gangster Shane Dankoski. This includes Shane's prison records, the court and parole records of his associates and former enemies, and official records obtained under the Freedom of Information Act. More important, it draws from hundreds of hours of conversations with Shane over the course of four years.

This book is painfully factual. Shane has been as open as possible. A couple of identifications have been blurred for legal reasons or so that people can get on with their lives. The locations of some characters have been kept secret for safety reasons, and dates may appear vague on occasion. We didn't want to re-victimize victims or violate court orders. That said, nothing has been made up.

It didn't take any convincing to get Shane to work on this book. Quite the opposite. It was his idea, and he worked hard to make it happen.

I was initially curious but doubtful about the project. Lots of people say they want to write a book and then back out when the painful questions start. It takes courage to honestly tell your story. At the start, I gave Shane a few conditions that would have to be met in order for this book to go ahead with me. One: he could proofread drafts for accuracy, but he couldn't order me to delete any passages or change a word. I had to believe everything in these pages. I do. And two: if he ever lied, I would be obligated to point that out in print.

He agreed without hesitation to these conditions, and he never tried to change them. He told raw, pure stories, adding negative things about himself that I had not come across in my research. He was unflinchingly forthcoming, even when it made him look bad. I didn't have to prod him to work or tell the bad stuff. He was enthusiastic and didn't grumble.

"I can be a lot of things, good and bad," Shane told me. "Everyone is entitled to their own opinion. But if there's one thing nobody can question, it's my loyalty and honesty. I don't bullshit, I've never been a liar. I don't like liars."

Shane is not a liar. After more than four years of almost constant contact with Shane, I can agree that he tells the truth.

I was drawn to Shane's story in part because of the deep respect I have for how he shook his drug dependency. I cannot imagine how difficult that must have been. I was also attracted to his story because he reminds me of a modern-day Joe Valachi, the mobster whose life was chronicled in *The Valachi Papers* by Peter Maas back in 1968. Shane also brings to mind

Salvatore Bonanno, whose life is profiled by Gay Talese in his 1971 book *Honor Thy Father*. Maas and Talese are two of my early journalism heroes, and their books continue to influence and inspire me. Decades ago, Peter Maas even let me into his home to help me with my first book, *Waterfront Warlord*, back when I was just starting out. I am forever grateful.

Maas and Talese each chronicled life in the underworld, from the inside out, without trying to justify or glorify it. There is something raw and historic about their work. I was eager to attempt to follow in their footsteps with Shane's story, which tells of the underworld today.

In so many ways, Shane is the perfect subject for telling an honest, current, inside story of organized crime life in the early twenty-first century. What follows is a brutally honest story about an often brutally dishonest world.

"Do you know what it takes to be a gangster in this day and age?" Shane asked me once, and then went on to answer his own question in depth.

A couple of themes naturally presented themselves in my many conversations with Shane. Sometimes they are overt. Sometimes they're bubbling just under the surface.

There's brotherhood—a sense of belonging. Where do we look for it if we can't find it within our birth families? How much do we owe those we consider family? What happens when the people we want to love don't love us back?

Another recurring theme is redemption. It's front and centre throughout these pages. What does it take to truly escape our past? Is it even possible? Shane certainly hopes so—and his desire to embrace a fresh start was a big part of why it turned out to be a good time for us to connect. He felt he had to deal with his past before getting on with the present and the future, and he was ready to take responsibility. "Everything that I talk about is my own fault," he told me. "I don't blame anybody."

Shane told me he realized he needed to change his life when he was locked up in Kent Institution in Agassiz, British Columbia, the only maximum-security prison in the Pacific Region of Canada. He often spoke of those days when he sat in a segregation cell alone, thinking of the type of person he wanted to be, if he ever got the chance to walk free again. "You just have time to think, and that's what I did. You're in that cell. I really thought long and hard about who I was . . . and why."

This book was written as Shane faced a tough reality. He had moved past living on myths and hope, past the idea of any kind of "gangster code." He understands now that "real is real. Fake is fake. White is white. Black is black, and there's no in-between." And even though what he spoke to me about was often painful or embarrassing, saying it out loud was therapeutic.

"I've had to bottle in all of this without talking," Shane said. In the end, overall, it felt good to get it out, to talk it through, to get it down so it can be properly remembered. "It got feeling like somebody had just lifted a thousand-pound bag off of my back."

On several occasions, he described living on what he felt was borrowed time. He displayed a sense of wonder over the fact that he is even around and breathing to take part in a book. "Every day I put my shoes on could have been my last," he says, speaking of the life he lived before he left it behind. "How the fuck did I get here? It just all happened so fast. On any given day I could have been killed, or we could have killed somebody. But back in the day I genuinely felt untouchable."

Shane knows now that that was never true. No one is untouchable in his old world. He hopes to be able to do something positive with whatever remains of this time he's been granted—to show people that real, positive change is possible, and to change some lives in a good way. He hopes to be able to stop at least one person from entering the gang life. "If it [my story] can save somebody, it's worth it." He didn't sound preachy when he said that, just hopeful.

He also wants to show that you can quit drugs. It's brutally hard but it can be done. For Shane, the temptation to use is still there, but he fights it—and wins—every day. "It would just be so much easier to start using again. To just numb it out," he says. "You keep moving and you have to.

It doesn't mean that you don't have bad days or you don't go down those bad roads. Every day is a battle, but here I am. You have to be committed. You can't be one foot in and one foot out."

Shane also set a goal that startled me. "I can't wait for a normal person in society to say nice things to me. When a normal person says a nice thing to me, that means I've made it."

Despite the grim subject matter, I find myself surprisingly uplifted as this book is completed. I believe more than ever that people can change, but I also know that most don't. Shane has.

When the deal for this book was reached, Shane texted his thanks to me and my business partner/agent Juliet Forrester of Top Left Entertainment and our acquiring editor, Craig Pyette. Shane was thrilled to be part of a team again. "I'm trying to be as open as can be, because that allows you to be able to do your job the best you can, which is great for everyone," he said.

For years, I have thought that if journalists want a friend, they should get a dog. Somehow, however, I came to see Shane as a friend. "I value our friendship," Shane said at one point. "Like you once said, this links us forever, and I'm good with that, because we really will be friends for life. After life, well, depends which elevator you get on, my friend— ha ha. I think my button's already pushed."

What's next for Shane in this life? I do fear for his safety. Many of the people who hated Shane are either dead or in custody, but some are not. It takes only one person and one gun and one weak moment to ruin things forever. Shane knows that as well as anybody.

That said, Shane totally kept his word on committing himself to this book. He hasn't flinched. Instead, he has been grateful to us. In one message, he added, "I'm more thankful than you'll ever know. I really mean that."

I am grateful too.

—Peter Edwards, January 2025

CHAPTER 1

HOME FRONT

"Most of the people that I hung out with are dead or in jail."
—SHANE DANKOSKI

SHANE TIMOTHY DANKOSKI was almost eight years old and living in New Westminster, British Columbia, when his aunt Kathy met him at a Dairy Queen and handed him a white cardboard box. It was close to Shane's birthday, so he assumed he was getting a cake. "I was super excited," he recalls. "I rode home with it bouncing off my handlebars."

But when he got home and opened the box, it wasn't a cake he found inside but a clear plastic bag. A tag attached to it read, "DANKOSKI, Tim."

Inside the bag were ashes and bone fragments—all that remained of Shane's father, who'd died after strangers beat him to death in the hallway of his apartment building with a baseball bat.

"I just sat there looking as my mom cried," he says.

It wasn't a total surprise that Shane's dad died a hard death. He'd lived a hard life, too. Drug dealing, thefts large and small. He'd probably ripped off the wrong person one time too many. Shane didn't know all that at the time, but he knew enough. Enough to know that something was

1

horribly wrong when he came home one day, not long before the meet-up with his aunt in that DQ parking lot, and saw blood smeared in the lobby and on the walls of his family's apartment complex in a tough neighbourhood in British Columbia's Greater Vancouver Area.

In short order, Shane was driven to the hospital with his mother and sister by Audrey Green, the mother of full-patch Hells Angel Bob Green (Shane's family never had vehicles of their own, and there were always people connected to various gangs hanging around). The adults waited in chairs in the hallway while Shane sat on the floor directly in front of the door of his father's room, bawling his eyes out. A hospital worker came out and showed Shane a picture of his dad in his current state, to prepare him for what he was about to see. His dad had two black eyes, and half of his head was shaved.

Then Shane was allowed inside. His father lay motionless with a gauze patch on his head, stained with blood. Tubes ran down his throat and up his nose. His tongue was pressed up against a tube, and his mouth looked dry. "I remember pinching his arm as hard as I could, saying, 'Dad! Dad!' and trying to wake him up. I was hoping with everything I did that I would see his tongue move."

There was no movement.

Shane's parents weren't legally married, and his mother wasn't listed in the hospital files as a contact for his father, so it fell to a blood relative to make the decision to discontinue life support.

"That was it," Shane says. "They ended up pulling the plug. They never even talked to my mom about it."

Looking back on it now, Shane can see that there were plenty of reasons why things turned out badly for his father. "My dad's dad was left on a train station in Poland when he was a baby. He grew up there. He fought in World War II, and then took a ship over to Canada, is how I under-stand it. He had seventeen kids—my dad had fourteen brothers, two sisters. All of those kids were beaten. He used to beat my grandma too."

Life was rough and violent from the start for Tim and his siblings, as they grew up in New Westminster, BC. And for many of them, things didn't get any better. Shane's aunts and uncles had almost uniformly sad ends, including suicide, murder, fatal drug overdoses, and life prison terms. "They're all dead or in jail except my two aunts, and maybe three of my uncles," Shane says.

Shane's mother, Darlene, had a similarly unsettled childhood. Her father was nicknamed "Ron the Junkie." Ron wasn't a real junkie; he just dealt in scrap metal through his junkyard. While he didn't have a drug problem, he was a violent alcoholic with a controlling personality, a fact that his wife and kids couldn't escape. He was friendly with some of the neighbourhood gangsters and bikers. When Shane was an infant, it was Ron who obtained permission from the local Hells Angels for Shane to be outfitted in a "HELLS L'IL ANGEL" T-shirt.

Shane's parents met in 1982, after his mother moved from Montreal to Vancouver to be with her sister Donna following the death of their mother. Tim had originally been Donna's boyfriend, which made things awkward when they split up and he shifted his attention to Shane's future mom. Shane was born on Mother's Day in 1985.

Shane's parents didn't talk much about those early days of their relationship—about the things that drew them to one another. But if there was ever a bright patch in the union, Shane didn't see it. What he did see was his father taking out his frustrations on his mother, the same way his grandfathers had beaten his grandmothers. That was already underway when Shane's mother was pregnant with his older sister, Christina, and it carried on throughout their relationship, from as early as Shane could remember. His father smashed his mother's furniture, ripped up her family photos and clothes, and beat her regularly and severely, tearing her ear in one attack. And once, one of Shane's uncles also joined in, punching and dragging his mom.

"I remember watching my dad beat the fuck out of my mom on a regular basis, and beat her bad. We were always trying to hide from him," Shane says, recalling that she wouldn't take off her sweater and jacket in the family home for fear that Tim would call her fat.

No matter how bad the beating, though, Shane's mother avoided seeking medical attention. And she would always take Tim back, choosing to believe him when he said things like "I was just having a bad day," or "I'm sorry, I love you," or "You know I'll never do that again."

"He was really fucked up on dope. He was really fucked up," Shane says. "But I don't give him a pass for beating my mom."

Violence was just a way of life as Shane and his sister, two years older, grew up—a way to relate, a way to solve problems. Shane and Christina often fought. She was older but he could be merciless; he would punch her, pull her hair. Once he even stabbed her in the face with a fork.

But they were both fiercely protective of their mother. Shane remembers Christina sometimes biting their father to get him to stop beating on his mom. Sometimes, Shane would join in. "Me and my sister used to be hanging off his back. My mom would be in a turtle position. My dad would be over her, punching her, punching her, punching her. We're trying to get him to stop."

There were plenty of rides in emergency taxis—paid for by social services—that brought Shane, his mother, and his sister to battered women's shelters in the middle of the night. Other times, they slept on the couches of friends and relatives. And through it all, Tim kept reappearing and promising to make things better, for real this time.

While Shane had plenty of aunts and uncles and cousins, he had limited contact with them while growing up, and no role models to speak of. His mother was on social assistance her entire adult life, with no job skills to draw on. And his father only ever worked as a criminal. "I'd literally be with my dad when he was robbing people."

Family moves came every three months or so, when the rent was past due and the eviction notices arrived. The new apartments were invariably cramped one-bedroom units. Shane would get a large closet, while his sister got the bedroom and his mother slept on the couch.

A constant in Shane's life was the dull humiliation of welfare, along with the fading hope that things would get better this time around. His mother never found a job or trade. She was too caught up in day-to-day survival. "It was just a vicious cycle."

Somehow, there were also occasional flashes of joy. One day, Shane's dad picked him up in a truck—stolen, Shane later found out—and took him for a ride. Tim had been smoking crack that day, which wasn't a shock, and he had a handgun under the seat. That wasn't a major jolt for Shane either.

As Shane waited in the car, Tim pulled up to a variety store run by an Asian family and went in with the gun. A few minutes later he came back holding a box of chocolate bars. "He throws the gun on the seat, the chocolate bars on the floor," Shane recalls. Tim had stolen money for himself, but he grabbed the chocolate bars for Shane as a fatherly treat.

An hour or so before the beating that led to his death, on May 5, 1993, Tim Dankoski visited Shane at his aunt Donna's house while Shane's mom was off at bingo. Shane desperately wanted to believe in his dad— to believe that life would get better—and Tim seemed to want to be seen as a hero in the eyes of his son. That day, the last day of his life, Tim called his son over: "Hey, come here, buddy."

Tim had brought a plastic bag full of oranges and he gave them all to Shane. Then he pulled out a watch with a Michael Jordan logo on it. "He was super happy," Shane remembers. "'Here you go, buddy. Here's this watch for you.' He strapped it on my wrist. He was smiling."

Then his dad proudly pulled out three hundred-dollar bills from a wad of money he had folded up in his sock. "He got down on one knee . . . He grabbed my foot, put the bills in my sock, and pulled my sock up. He had a smile, but I feel he was stressed."

"This is for your mom," Tim said. "It's her rent money."

He didn't say where he'd gotten the money, and Shane didn't ask. Better not to ruin the mood.

Tim had wanted to take Shane back to his place, but Donna told Tim to fuck off, literally. So Shane's dad walked home through an alley alone. He ran a bath, and the water was still running when the strangers arrived, at least one of them carrying a bat. "The bath in the house was overflowing when the police got there. He went to run out the front door and they got him in the hallway."

The authorities never solved the murder of Tim Dankoski, and the media didn't bother much with it either. But Shane often wonders what would have happened if he'd gone with his father that day, if Donna hadn't stopped them. "Would those guys have done that? Maybe they'd think differently."

Or maybe they would have killed Shane too. Who knows.

"I always thought to myself, *What if?*"

Shane's mother never found another partner. And Shane never found a male role model who could teach him about life or take him fishing, or camping, or to hockey. Or tell him not to stab his sister. "We didn't even live anywhere long enough for me to have friends."

With each move to a new home came a new school. Shane remembers being hungry in class, and gulping air to try to fill his stomach. He remembers that many of the other kids were in the same boat. He remembers that kids sometimes made fun of him. He also knew his teachers were frustrated by his attitude. He didn't strive to be teacher's pet. Far from it. If a teacher asked Shane to do something, there was a good chance he would reply with a hearty "Fuck you."

"I'd flip my desk over at nine years old."

Shane's attendance had never been good, even though one of his schools was just across the street from his apartment complex. Occasionally Shane would go home for lunch and not return. Other times he wouldn't show up at all, taking three or so days off in a row.

Teachers often gave up on him, sometimes getting him to just sit at his desk and colour pictures rather than do work like the other students.

"Teachers didn't want me in their classes. I would fight, swear, not listen. And so I was basically pushed ahead every year without truly doing work," he recalls. "When kids in my class were taking math or spelling tests, the teachers would bring me paper and crayons or markers and I would colour or draw. The only award I ever got in school was in grade two for drawing skeletons."

School officials tried talking to Shane, and even threatened to call in a social worker. His mother had heard plenty of troubling predictions about her boy's future, was told again and again that he would "grow up and be just like his dad." (And they were right, Shane says now. "I had no respect for authority.") But she told them all that there wasn't much she could do, that her son wouldn't listen to her either. By that point, Shane had already beaten up a boy at the school, breaking his nose and a tooth, and punched a girl named Patricia in the face. He responded to the threat about calling in a social worker in his usual way—by telling the principal to fuck off and pushing him up against a wall.

Police and social services were called, and Shane found himself expelled from the school and banned from the school district. He was sent to a form of "kids' jail" for five months. Things were regimented there, and Shane was bused to yet another school, this time in White Rock. That didn't last long.

Shane was eleven when he quit school for good. He had completed grade five after attending sixteen different schools. And through it all— through the violence and the poverty and the moves and the turmoil— he grew to respect his mother's strength and count on her love.

"My mom is the only person in the world who didn't give up on me."

CHAPTER 2

ROLE MODELS

"I really looked up to Oddy Hansen.
He was so ruthless and everybody feared him."
—SHANE DANKOSKI

WHEN SHANE WAS ABOUT TEN—not long before the end of his elementary school career—he sometimes amused himself by catching frogs from a pond near his home in Surrey on 140th Street and 96th Avenue. He would also scoop up snakes from a nearby field.

Shane's family moved from New Westminster to Surrey, about a fifteen-minute drive away. Surrey was home to Shane's aunt Donna, his mother's older sister. Shane and his mother and sister all settled in a second-floor apartment in Mayfair Garden, a grandly named "little ghetto-ass building."

One day, a boy about eighteen months younger than Shane rolled up on a bicycle. Adam Lam lived a couple of blocks away from Shane. His family was Vietnamese and they had been displaced by the Vietnam War.

The day Shane and Adam met, Adam had a pail and a can of hairspray.

"We started talking about catching the frogs and the snakes," Shane recalls. "He's got a bucket full of frogs."

As Shane looked on, Adam sprayed the frogs with the hairspray, lit a match, and tossed it into the bucket.

"They're like jumping fireballs then. That's how I first met Adam Lam—lighting frogs on fire."

Adam was close to Shane's age and he lived in the neighbourhood, so Shane tried to be his friend. The boys sometimes rode bikes together, but Shane quickly realized that there was always the chance something would set Adam off.

One day, Adam accidentally left the lid off his frog bucket. When the captives hopped to freedom, Adam blamed Shane for his own mistake.

"What the fuck, man!" Adam shouted. "You let my frogs out!"

Shane told him to calm down, which went over about as well as you'd expect.

"Fuck you! Fuck you!" Adam screamed.

The next day, Adam rode up again. This time he had a knife and a friend. "He pulls a knife on me about his frogs!" Shane says. "This is no joke. He wouldn't let it go."

Adam also raised the spectre of deadly connections. "You don't know who my brother is," Adam said. "My fucking brother will fuck you up."

Adam had five siblings, so Shane had plenty to consider. "I ended up just fucking running away from him. After that, I was kind of scared of him. Every time I would see him, he would start problems with me. He would not let it go, and it all stemmed from those fucking frogs."

Shane's time at Mayfair Gardens was marked by several interesting relationships. In addition to his sort-of friendship with Adam, he got to know a single mother who was nineteen or twenty, and lived nearby. The young mother also had a roommate.

Shane would babysit when the roommates headed off to bars, and then make himself scarce when the two returned with young men (a regular occurrence). Soon enough, though, Shane wasn't making himself scarce at all. Despite a sizable age difference—the mother was almost twice his age—Shane's relationship with her turned sexual. It was eleven-year-old Shane's first sexual experience. His new lover also let him drive her car, an added bonus.

"She told me she loved me. I'm a kid. That was the first girl that I really loved. I think I loved her," Shane recalls, aware now that the relationship was far from appropriate. At the time, though, he didn't have any reservations. "I had a girlfriend with a car . . . By no means am I playing victim. I wanted that to happen. Believe me, there was no victim shit."

The connection lasted a couple of years. When it ran its course, his attentions shifted to an eleven-year-old girl who lived in the same building. Perhaps she was attracted by his slightly advanced age, or maybe it was how he seemed so determined to take care of himself. Whatever the case, by the time she was twelve, they were a couple.

Shane was indeed determined to make his own way in the world, now that he was no longer in school, and he knew that would have to start with earning some cash. While there weren't a ton of legit opportunities for kids his age, there were nevertheless a few ways to put dollars in his pocket. "I see my friends and they're selling a little weed, and I think *I can do that too*," he says, adding that car theft was another early career option. "My friends were little car thieves. We'd strip them in the middle of the night."

And so life fell into a rhythm. Average days consisted of hanging out with his buddies, selling weed, and cruising around in cars—even though most of them weren't old enough to have a learner's permit.

"That was my life as a teenager," he says. "Deeking and dodging from the cops."

Not surprisingly, Shane saw the cops as a negative force in the community, as barriers standing between him and his ambitions. Police wanted to catch you and lock you up, and you had to watch out for them. "They're just bad. They wanted to make charges."

—

By the time he was twelve, Shane was selling weed at the Surrey Sky-Train station. It was 1997, nearly two decades before marijuana was legalized in Canada. Much of Shane's supply came from older guys who robbed grow ops, dried the weed out themselves, and sold it for half the going rate.

For an investment of $150, Shane could turn a profit of $690, which wasn't bad for a kid who couldn't even call himself a teenager yet. "That would just give me the want to do more and bigger. It made me think, *What can I do with coke?*"

With thoughts like this running through his head, it was only a matter of time before Shane ran into trouble of his own. He was finally arrested when he was fifteen. He was in Whalley in a stolen car at 3 a.m. with his friend, sixteen-year-old Jimmy Reynolds. "We thought we were so cool. We were fucking around listening to 'Boot Scootin' Boogie' by Brooks & Dunn, and then the red-and-blue lights come on and we were like, *Oh shit!*"

Jimmy ran one way and Shane ran the other. One of the cops went after Shane and caught him.

Shane's mother was upset but, once again, helpless in the face of her son's choices. "My mom never encouraged me to do bad things. She also couldn't stop me. She did the best that she could," he says, adding that unlike some of the other moms in the neighbourhood, she never had an addiction. "My mother was a great mother for what she had. She was a single mom on welfare. She didn't have any control of me."

After the arrest, she pleaded with him to smarten up. "Jesus Christ, Shane. What are you doing? You're going to end up in jail."

Shane's mother had legal custody of Shane and his cousins Sheldon, Nikki, and Melissa—Donna's children—when they moved into a bungalow at 140th and 96th Avenues in Surrey. Their new next-door neighbours were the Hansens—eight of them in a two-bedroom house. It was tight quarters for some very large, very unpredictable men.

Not long after Shane moved into his new home, there was a knock on his door. It was Duane Hansen, better known in the neighbourhood as "Big Duane." His nickname was no mystery. Big Duane stood about six foot six and weighed in the vicinity of 280 pounds. His nephew was Little Duane, "a stocky little fucker" who was around six feet tall and 240 pounds.

Big Duane's voice wasn't easily forgotten or ignored, nor was it suitable for bedtime stories. It was like the voice of doom rumbling up from a mine shaft or an unfilled grave.

"Hey kids, how are you doing?" Big Duane asked at the door that day, not waiting for an answer. "You ever heard of the Hansen brothers?"

"Yeah."

"I'm Duane Hansen. I live next door."

Then Big Duane laid down the law. It was fairly simple and left no room for negotiation or interruption or appeal: "No funny business. No drugs and no gang shit."

Big Duane Hansen's siblings included Airell Dale and Lance Tracy, better known as "Oddy." All the Hansen boys were born and raised in Whalley, and there were also Hansen uncles and a nephew and nieces. There was no proud father in sight.

Shane quickly decided he shouldn't aggravate his new neighbours. "You do not fuck with the Hansen brothers," he says. And you particularly did not fuck with Oddy. "He was the man back in the day. I really looked up to him."

One day, when Shane was sixteen, he noticed a half-dozen Honda Civics parked outside the Hansen home.

Teenagers were milling about on the driveway, shirts off, when a bare-chested man in jeans with long hair and a bandana came running up. The man darted through a hole in the fence and through Shane's backyard.

The shirtless runner was Al, a.k.a. "Screwy," and he was Oddy Hansen's close friend.

An instant later, a police dog tore up the driveway in hot pursuit. Hustling along behind the dog and Screwy was Constable Chris Williams of the RCMP.

Screwy was arrested in Shane's backyard, where the police dog tasted his leg before Williams took him into custody.

Shane got into the mood of the event, telling the cop, "You're a piece of shit."

"Pardon me?" Williams replied.

"You're a scumbag," Shane said.

Three months later, Shane and Williams met again—when Williams arrested Shane for car theft. "He remembered me from the driveway that day," Shane says.

By this time, Shane was well versed in the ways of auto theft, and capable of generating plenty of trouble in other ways too. Occasionally, when he was pulled over by the police, Shane was behind the wheel of a 1987 black Buick Grand National, which had been stolen and expertly "re-vinned," or given a new Vehicle Identification Number (VIN).

In theory, VINs are permanently attached to vehicles, an anti-theft measure that can be used by buyers to check the ownership history of a used vehicle. When a vehicle is re-vinned, the old identification number is removed and replaced with a number from another vehicle, which looks the same.

"That was a VIN swap," Shane says. "It's so easy to re-VIN a vehicle."

Shane's circle now included a man considered the undisputed king of the province's auto thieves, who ran up more than forty convictions and four years in custody.

It was a simpler time for auto theft, before Canada became a hot-spot for the overseas trade of stolen vehicles. Today, criminals use high-tech devices to mimic electronic key fobs and steal cars—many of which are exported to overseas markets through the Port of Montreal.

"It's sophisticated now," says Shane, "not like the olden days. A flat-head screwdriver and away you go."

No one was better at it then than the king of auto theft who lived nearby. "Started and gone in less than thirty seconds," says Shane. "I'm not kidding."

The auto theft king was a grade-eight dropout and a runaway who slept in parks before learning the secrets of auto theft. Now, he was able to steal semi-trucks and trailers with relative ease.

"I remember one time [he] stole a semi and the trailer was full of boxes of cartons of cigarettes. Another time he stole a trailer full of flats of beer. I'm talking literally thousands of cases of beer. I wasn't friends with him by any stretch—he was like thirty, and I was sixteen or seventeen . . . And I had my licence, so I would drive him around stealing cars, usually Mustangs, and for doing that he would give me the stereo and subwoofers."

Always looming in the background of Shane's world were the Hells Angels. They had structure, with definite ranks, and tradition that dated back to American servicemen returning from World War II, looking for brotherhood and adventure. They also had scope, with charters across Canada and around the world.

Oddy wasn't overly impressed by any of it. He didn't appear bothered by the fact that he'd fallen into disfavour with Hells Angels prospect Randy Potts, who was connected to the East End Vancouver chapter. There are four steps to becoming a Hells Angel, and Potts had reached the second—the hang-around stage. That meant he was allowed to wear a vest but nothing with the club's copyrighted "Death Head" patch of a winged skull.

The Downtown Eastside chapter is one of the club's richest charters in the country, and even on a good day they aren't "turn-the-other-cheek" folk. They don't take insults or challenges lightly, regardless of whether they're made against full-patches or fringe members like Potts.

But Oddy didn't care. He made a move on Potts's girlfriend, who was said to have once appeared in a *Playboy* centrefold.

Not surprisingly, the biker didn't take this well. Also not surprisingly, Oddy responded by beating Potts and stealing his vest.

Oddy had now insulted the entire chapter. Potts was ordered to "get rid of him," according to Michael (Big Mike) Plante, a long-time friend of the chapter. And "get rid of him" meant "kill him."

Big Mike looked like just the right man for the job. His nickname was "Sherman," as in Sherman tank. He was a bouncer and biker bill collector who weighed 250 pounds and could bench-press upwards of four hundred pounds with the aid of steroids.

What the Angels didn't know was that Big Mike was also a police agent. Big Mike was feeding his police handlers information on an incoming cocaine shipment from Colombia. Big Mike stood to make $500,000 from authorities in a police operation called Project E-Pandora, with another $500,000 if he hung in through the trials that the operation would generate. That earned him a nickname: the "Million-Dollar Rat."

Shane was eating Chinese food at Oddy's house one night when a knock sounded on the door. On the other side was Big Mike, with an Uzi submachine gun in one hand and a .38 handgun in the other.

"Shane, you want to go get the door?" Oddy said.

Shane went to the door and opened it, but could see no one outside. So he returned to his Chinese takeout. A moment later, another knock.

"I'll get this, okay?" Oddy said.

There was a field of waist-high bush across the driveway from Oddy's house. There were two strangers at the door; the man who knocked and another man with a balaclava who ran out of the field, right through Oddy's front door. The masked stranger fired five bullets into Oddy's chest and then fled. His identity wasn't clear.

Oddy was still alive when the gunfire ended, and neither of them had gotten a good look at the gunman. "[Oddy] was wearing a bulletproof vest," Shane recalls. "The vest was heating up."

Oddy spent the next five months in hospital. As a show of bravado, he saved one of the bullets that was cut from his body, encased it in gold, and put a diamond on it. It became a medal of honour of sorts. "He used to wear it around his neck."

Despite the flashy gesture, Oddy was never the same after the hit. "He was just so different," Shane says. "He talked different. He acted different."

CHAPTER 3

YOUNG THUGS

"In this life, that's the way it goes. Ratting is ratting. You don't talk to police. You don't give them names, and you certainly don't call them. That's a thing you can't do when you're in this life."
—SHANE DANKOSKI

SHANE WAS OUTSIDE one day, on the steps of Oddy's house on 140th, when Adam Lam rolled back into his life. Adam had moved on from his bicycle-riding and frog-burning days. He was now driving a BMW X5, and he had four or five stumpy but tough-looking associates in tow.

Adam was fifteen and didn't have a driver's licence. He wore a North Face puffy jacket, sweatpants, flip-flops, and a tough-guy expression, doing his best to look like a gangster. He was smallish and had two handguns tucked into the waistband of his sweatpants, for easy access with either hand.

Adam was still easily irritated and "dangerously, scary stupid," just like he'd been when he and Shane first met. Adam gestured towards a Honda sedan in Oddy's driveway that belonged to a local resident named Dustin.

"Is that Dustin's? Is that Dustin's?" Adam asked.

"No, no."

Shane had learned enough from the people he hung out with to know that you don't give up information, especially about anybody in your circle. Adam didn't bother arguing with him.

"You fucking tell Dustin Adam Lam's looking for him."

Oddy wasn't fazed when told of Adam Lam's visit, but then again, Oddy wasn't fazed by much. And Shane wasn't inclined to give the incident much more thought. Adam was just being Adam, and the days when the two of them had considered each other friends of a sort were long gone. Shane had new friends now, real friends.

One of Shane's homes in his late teens was behind a Chevron gas station at 128 Street and 96th Avenue in Cedar Hills, Surrey, which was a popular hangout for everyone who was anyone in his world. Shane was fifteen in 2000 when he met his lifelong friend James (Fitzy, Fatty, Fitz) Fitzgerald there. Fitzy was from a financially comfortable home— his dad ran a dump truck company—but soon after they met, Fitzy and Shane were selling weed together for ten dollars a baggie.

Shane was still living with his mom and sister, and it was no secret that he was selling pot. But there also wasn't much they could do about it. His mom had long since given up trying to steer her son in the right direction.

Also hanging out at the Chevron were Manny Hairan, Stevie Leone (aka Tucker), and Thomas Mantel.

"We were like original brothers, from fourteen, fifteen on," Shane says. "We were brothers from our crew."

And then one day a new black Lincoln rolled into the neighbourhood. Behind the wheel was eighteen-year-old Sukh Singh Dhak.

"It was one of the best cars around then," says Shane, but Sukh acted as though he had every right to be driving the exclusive ride. "He was just cocky."

Sukh gave off an air of danger, even though he stood just five foot nine and weighed about 145 pounds. "He walked around like he was six foot two, 220. When he was drunk, he walked around like he was six foot six, 290." And then there was the impression he left you with that he needed control. "When the guy had his hooks in you, he had his hooks in you."

Shane didn't know it yet, but Sukh would eventually change his life. The young hot shot already knew Fitzy—and valued him because Fitzy was good with numbers, which was a prized trait for a drug dealer. And the connection between the two young men was clearly paying off. Fitzy loved to put his new earnings into low-rider cars. Everyone in their little social circle was getting nice cars now, but Fitzy's were always the best. That included his 1993 Fleetwood Cadillac, ridiculously outfitted with nine TV screens—attached to the roof, headrests, mirrors, and even the steering wheel, "anywhere you could think of," says Shane.

Fitzy loved to cruise the White Rock downtown strip, by the Pacific Ocean, and attend auto shows, where he was a minor celebrity. "He was known for having these sick fucking low-riders and stuff."

When cruising the White Rock main drag, Fitzy would show off how the engine made a low roaring *vroom* that seemed worthy of a race car. There was also the Fleetwood's illegal but impressive hydraulics system, which allowed its driver to do things like dip one side of the car down to the pavement while raising the other high in the air. "While he's doing this, he's smoking a blunt. He was notorious for having a big huge cigar that he'd cut open and fill with weed."

Fitzy may have loved his Caddy, but Shane was sticking with imports, like Honda Civics. "Like I was in one of the *Fast and Furious* movies," he says. Behind the wheel, he could almost imagine he was a character in the wildly popular movie franchise and not an anonymous kid.

Around this time, Shane also occasionally bumped up against various members of the Alkhalil family. Manny Hairan—one of the Chevron station crew—was about sixteen and already working with local gangster Mahmoud (Mac) Alkhalil, whose family was rising fast in the underworld. There were five Alkhalil brothers in all and for a time the whole crew lived in an apartment building near Shane in Surrey's Holly Park neighbourhood.

Holly Park had a reputation. "We called it the ghetto," Shane says. "Everybody in these buildings would have been on welfare."

The Alkhalils lived together on the first floor of their building. Rabih (Robby), the youngest of the brothers, often hung out at the soccer field by the apartment buildings. A box lacrosse area was right next to it, but everyone seemed drawn to soccer.

"He was just one of the little kids at the park," Shane says.

There was a dead-end street near the park—a laneway, really, with yellow cement barricades. "You did not want to walk through Holly Park on a Friday or Saturday night," Shane recalls.

At the back of the park were the Iranians and Iraqis, including many Alkhalil relatives. They were known in the neighbourhood as "the Iraquians," and they never seemed to leave the laneway. "All of their cousins, all of them, would hang around there. They would sit there, all fucking day, all fucking night."

Shane understood that the brothers presented a united front. "You fight with one brother, you fight with them all."

The Alkhalils were Palestinians, whose family had fled from modern Israel to a refugee camp in Lebanon during the 1948–49 Arab-Israeli War and who were deemed stateless after moving again to Saudi Arabia. All the brothers were born in Saudi Arabia: the eldest, Nabil, in 1976, and down through Khalil, Hisham (Terry), Mahmoud (Mac), and finally Robby in 1987. The family arrived in Canada on December 12, 1990, saying they sought to escape the Gulf War and provide education for their children.

If you managed to pass through Holly Park in one piece, you would get to the Gianis' side, which was equally tough. "They would jump you if they saw you going through that neighbourhood and they did not know you."

At the time, Shane was hanging out a lot with the Gianis side and not the Alkhalils. But they all knew each other. "The gangster world is small. We all go back to being kids together . . . It's funny, because any one of us could have been on either side. We were all little kids together. It's crazy to think of all of us as kids, hanging out. We knew each other and then grew up to be rivals. There's an explanation, though: greed."

Kyle Gianis was particularly good at spending money. "Kyle was a winer and a diner with girls. He loved to play the part."

For a time, his brother Nick Gianis hung around outside a convenience store with Mac and Nabil Alkhalil and a group of Iranians. "It was like the spot to be. Nick was a baller on a short schedule," Shane says, going on to explain that in gangster talk a "baller" is someone who makes lots of money and is flashy, and to be on a "short schedule" means he's in a hurry.

Back then, teenage Mac Alkhalil could often be seen riding about in the passenger seat of a green Mustang convertible belonging to Nick Gianis. It was a fine car, with a retractable roof and white leather seats. Worthy of a baller.

"They were like brothers," Shane says.

Then, something went horribly wrong.

At four in the morning on August 18, 2003, nineteen-year-old Mahmoud Alkhalil was murdered at the Loft Six nightclub in Vancouver. The club was packed when the shooting started. Two people were killed and five wounded. Some of the victims were mobsters, others bystanders.

Nick Gianis was there that night, and the Alkhalil family blamed him for what happened.

Sensing the danger, Nick Gianis went on the offensive. One day, he showed up at Terry Alkhalil's place, banging on the door and demanding to be let inside. He brought a gun, and Terry was understandably concerned.

"He calls 911," Shane says.

"In this life . . . ratting is ratting. You don't talk to police. You don't give them names, and you certainly don't call them. That's a thing you can't do when you're in this life."

That was one thing everyone could agree upon, regardless of affiliation. Part of the screening to get into the Hells Angels, for example, was to ask candidates if they had ever called police on anyone, for anything. If the answer was yes, the interview was over. "If you've ever done that in your life, you can't be a Hells Angel."

That's why the lips on the Hells Angels winged skull logo are sewn shut, and blood red.

In the fall of 2004, a woman in a hijab with a ponytail emptied a .40 clip into Nick Gianis in a McDonald's drive-through, telling him, "This is for Mac's death."

It seemed like an ugly end for Nick. Everyone expected him to die from his wounds.

But then Nick Gianis did something shocking: he survived.

Nick Gianis was a 'roided-up six-two/280 when he went into hospital. He left the hospital at 150 pounds, with dangerous enemies and frayed nerves.

"Nick was so paranoid after he got shot. They were blaming him for Mac. Everywhere we went, Nick had a gun."

One night, Shane went with Nick to a beautiful high-rise condo overlooking Stanley Park. Nick was trying to re-establish himself after the shooting and needed product to sell. In one of the units they met a man who stood about six-six and weighed around 320 pounds. The huge stranger sported a gold-and-diamond neck chain and a tight white T-shirt.

Shane watched as the goliath opened a safe with about twenty kilos, or "birds," of cocaine inside.

Bro, this guy is a baller, Shane thought.

The man agreed to front Nick a couple of kilos, with no money down, because Nick had been good to him in the past. "Pay me when you get back on your feet," he said.

Shane and Nick departed together and made their way to a rub-and-tug massage parlour. They were considerably more relaxed a few hours later when they finally drove away with the cocaine. Nick rode shotgun in the front seat with a .45-calibre handgun.

They hadn't gotten far when a Vancouver city cop pulled them over.

"Are you doing alright?" the cop asked. "Are you scared for your life?"

The cop was just having fun—all of them knew who Nick was—and to Shane's great relief, he didn't bother to search the car. "I'm like, *Holy fuck. Did we get lucky here?*"

Nick's plan was to connect with a buyer in Edmonton and sell the drugs there. He rented a Chevy Trailblazer for the trip.

Mixed in with the cocaine were hundreds of thousands of caps of ecstasy. Shane had never seen so many in his life. Some of the drugs were expertly packed into family-sized, sealed boxes of Cheerios. "I have no idea how he did it."

Those boxes were tucked in among real packets of noodles, Kraft Dinner, and other groceries. Cocaine was also hidden in panels of the rental car, which meant Shane had to take extra care while driving. "You don't want to get stopped and they see the panel has been fucked with."

Shane also brought a fully packed hockey bag, so he could say he was on his way to a tournament, if police asked.

They left Surrey for Edmonton around 1 a.m. It was December and blustery when they hit Crowsnest on the Rogers Pass. The road was super slippery and visibility was close to nil. Shane handled the driving, with Nick sound asleep in the front passenger seat, which was dropped back all the way. The CD player had an Akon rap album with the song "Ghetto" on repeat, but it wasn't helping to keep Shane awake. "I'm nodding off at the wheel," he recalls.

Shane wove in and out through a web of a half-dozen tunnels. "You can't even see. There's so much snow."

It was around 3:30 a.m. when Shane saw a cop at the side of the highway. Not long after that, he hit black ice and began a 180-degree slide. "It keeps spinning and spinning and spinning. I'm now going backwards into oncoming traffic."

The Trailblazer just missed a transport truck, then flipped onto its side in a snowbank. Three windows were shattered and an airbag was deployed.

Shane thought back to the cop they had just passed. Would he rush to help them and then discover the drugs?

Luckily for Shane, a trucker came to the rescue first, pulling the Blazer upright and back onto the road. They were in Edmonton for just an hour, swapping the drugs for money and then planning the trip home. Nick announced he wanted to take a flight back, saying, "Bro, I can't go through that again."

"Are you kidding me, bro?" Shane replied.

In the end, Nick flew home, leaving Shane, who hadn't slept, to head back to BC alone—with $300,000 in cash and two guns hidden in his skates.

The drive couldn't have been much worse. The Blazer was missing a mirror and had three shattered windows, but the CD player was still cranking out Akon into the frigid air. Somehow, Shane made it home in one piece.

Not long after returning from Edmonton, Shane and a group of his gangster buddies were out for dinner one evening, decked out in their gold chains and diamonds. Gone were the days of selling baggies of weed. They still dealt weed, but in much higher volume. More significantly, they were now dealing cocaine as well.

A server arrived at their table to take the drinks order. Shane recognized him as a classmate from back in grade three. His name was David, and he was sporting the same mushroom-style haircut he'd sported then. Back in those days, David had stood out as the best basketball player in their class. He'd been one of the winners; Shane had not.

"Is your name David?" Shane asked, and then followed up with, "Do you recognize me? I'm Shane."

He couldn't help but think about how the tables had turned. Now Shane was wearing $300,000 in jewellery while his old classmate was serving him for minimum wage, plus tips. "These kids would make fun of me for being a bad kid, always in trouble, while barely ever being at school."

"Shane?" David replied. "Yeah. Holy . . ."

"He got a pretty good tip."

CHAPTER 4

GANGCOUVER

"It was an instant beef that never went away.
There was a lot of bad blood."
—SHANE DANKOSKI

THE MURDER OF Mahmoud (Mac) Alkhalil sent ripples out into the lives of Shane and his friends. None of them had been anywhere near the Loft Six club on August 18, 2003, but that hardly mattered. The events there that night made Vancouver a far more dangerous place for everyone in the underworld.

In the aftermath of Mac's death, Shane became increasingly aware that he was one small part of a big-time organized crime ecosystem. As he moved deeper into Sukh Dhak's orbit, Shane had become affiliated with the United Nations—a multi-ethnic umbrella group that took in the Dhak brothers—Sukh and his older brother Gurmit—and many others. The UN had plenty of enemies, but their main rival was the Wolfpack Alliance, founded in 2010 by Hells Angel member Larry Amero and now home to big-time gangsters like the Alkhalil brothers and the notorious Bacon brothers—Jonathan, Jarrod, and Jamie.

Even before Mac's death, something unique and powerful was underway in Vancouver. The gang activity in British Columbia's Lower Mainland was different from what you'd see in movies like *The Godfather* or *Goodfellas*. It wasn't as white or as neighbourhood-based, and it reached across borders with the internet. Some wag even came up with a nickname to describe it: Gangcouver. It was very real, and very west coast, and very dangerous—especially for those who dared to switch sides.

Shane's friend Manny Hairan had worked for Mahmoud Alkhalil, but his connection to the family snapped with Mac's death. Now, Manny was feeling the pull to work for the Dhak brothers. "Sukh was coming around," Shane recalls. "We were hanging around Sukh quite a bit." Gurmit, too, got involved, making it clear to Manny that he was working for them now.

It was natural for the Dhaks to want Manny, who was a big earner in the drug trade. Shane was doing well, but Manny was moving about three times the volume. "Manny was known as a guy who moved a lot of dope. He knew all of the crackheads. He brought all of those customers with him."

Looking back, Shane considers Mahmoud's death and Manny's shift in loyalty as the starting point for much of the animosity that would follow. The Alkhalils were infuriated by Manny's switch on both a personal and a professional level. It was easy to imagine them thinking, *Our brother gets murdered and now you're going to someone else?*

"It was an instant beef that never went away," Shane says. "There was a lot of bad blood."

When the Alkhalils realized they couldn't win Manny back, they came up with a plan B: they would kill him so he couldn't work for anyone. His death would be a powerful statement about the costs of betraying the Alkhalils.

Manny knew he was in trouble. "Manny did not want to run into those Alkhalils anywhere, and they would be everywhere," Shane says. "Everywhere you went, they were there."

United Nations or Wolfpack, it was all connected—from the brutal world of ambushing and killing someone over a drug deal to the nicer things like high-end cars and white gold, rubies, and bracelets.

For the United Nations, the latter came from a shop in a mall that Sukh and Gurmit frequented, which meant good business for the jeweller, who would make them $100,000 necklaces and diamond earrings that could run $30,000. Most important of all were the white-gold bead bracelets he would craft. They cost $6,000 or so but were priceless in Shane's gangster world. They signified membership in the United Nations, and like Hells Angels patches in the biker world, the bracelets could be worn only by the chosen few. For Shane, getting one was a goal—something to aim for.

Police started noticing the United Nations gang in the late 1990s. At first, the UN was called the Global United Nations Syndicate, which had a cool acronym (GUNS) but was also a tongue twister. Over time, it was shortened to the "UN gang."

The UN name highlighted the gang's pronounced cultural inclusion, and also took a dig at the Hells Angels, on the Wolfpack side of things. The Angels had only slowly been diversifying after their lily-white beginnings. In contrast, the UN had a certain aggressive wokeness. Members could come from any culture, as long as they were criminals. Many leaned towards eastern symbols, which appeared on jewellery and clothing, often marked with the motto "Honour, loyalty, respect." There were also special rings for some members and bosses, which were made at the jewellery shop Shane's group frequented. Rings were earned for things like dramatically improving business, or for pleading guilty to a serious charge like manslaughter without giving up any information or names to authorities.

The UN had no supreme leader or boss, just a collection of bosses of different groups, based on ethnicity, geography, and contacts. The sudden growth of the internet made geography less important than in the days when gangs were defined by—and named after—neighbourhoods. Shane's associates in the Dhak group didn't have a gang name either. "Everybody just knew us as Sukh's guys."

The United Nations was a powerful umbrella. Aside from the Dhaks, the UN included what insiders called the "Iraqi Kurds," the "City" guys from Vancouver, the "Valley Side" from the Fraser Valley, and the "FOB [fresh off the boat] killers," who were often Vietnamese immigrants. Gurmit Dhak was friendly with their leaders. "They were no joke," Shane says. "They were mostly gangsters. Some just drug dealers. But they had shooters, and Sukh dealt with them a lot."

You needed a sponsor to get into the broader UN group, and for Shane it was a gangster named Jason. Jason had been one of the top guys for Clay Roueche, the founder of the UN. "We worked together, spent every day together. He sponsored me. We were really close for a long time."

Jason was already a five-year member when he became Shane's "sponsor/big brother," and to Shane he seemed like a winner. "He was a good guy, a good money-maker, moved a lot of keys of coke. I loved him so much, like a real brother."

Connecting with Jason felt like joining a real family. And for a kid who'd lost his dad at an early age and whose home life had been anything but stable, that was the best feeling in the world.

The work wasn't bad either. The real gangsters in the UN didn't work nine to five or take orders from anyone outside their world. "No one had straight jobs," Shane says. "None of our crew. But they had businesses."

Sukh's businesses included something called Luxury Holdings in Surrey, while Manny Hairan had M and H Ltd. Gurmit didn't have a business of his own, but he helped his parents with their laundromat and with some apartments they owned.

For Shane, being seen as a gangster seemed like a higher calling. He felt he was doing better than his father and gaining real control of his life. "A gangster is what we were," he says.

When you are a gangster, you live by the code, which I did through and through. Not fake. I was 100 percent loyal. Honesty. Honour. Respect. Your boss comes first. Period. You don't betray him. You don't talk to police, and you're always down for whatever he needs you for, whenever. And I was and I did all that. A lot of guys . . . in the life, they play the part. But when it comes down to real life and death, sitting in that interrogation chair, most are fake. I was really about it. Really about that shit.

There's a big difference between a drug dealer and a gangster. Just because you're a drug dealer doesn't make you a gangster. A gangster is the full deal. You live by the code. You could set up hits. You could possibly do hits. You've got it all. You run shit.

Just being ruthless didn't make someone a real gangster either, even if you were a reliable killer. "Somebody who just takes a contract to do a hit isn't a gangster," Shane says. True gangsters are all in, with a readiness to do whatever is necessary. Killers in the UN weren't paid for contracts. It wasn't an extra job; it was just part of the overall life.

True gangsters also kept time in a different way. Five minutes for a gangster could mean five minutes or it could mean three hours. It was whatever a gangster decided it should be. "We call it dealer time," Shane explains. "If someone's waiting on drugs and you're going to bring them to them, you're, 'I'll be there in five minutes.' That could mean an hour or it could mean three hours. The dealer has all the power. But when dealing with high-level guys, buying or selling kilos, that's when you're on time.

"When you're dealing with drugs, everything is five minutes," he continues. "A drug addict wants drugs now. You don't even want to wait two minutes. Two minutes feels like a lifetime. If you want a fix, you want it now. You never tell anybody more than five minutes when you're a dealer."

Time was also measured differently for meetings with other serious bad guys, especially when they were from an opposing group. "If you're going to be meeting other bad guys, then you're four hours early." Being early gave you time to scope out the meeting place and see if a trap was being set for you. Or to see if you could set a trap. "Gurmit would say, 'Don't ever have anyone wait for you. Make sure you are there first.'"

As Shane moved up in the gangster world, he started to take his watches seriously, although they were often more for show than actually keeping time. He bought a high-end Breitling, with diamonds and eight-carat gold, valued at $35,000.

Sukh had multiple Rolexes, with the best valued at about $70,000. But that seemed frugal when compared with Gurmit's best Rolex, slathered in gold and diamonds, worth $130,000.

Manny never got into the watches, even though he definitely had the money. He had his beads, a diamond chain worth $80,000, $75,000 earrings, and a diamond-and-white-gold ring that must have cost $40,000. "He wasn't a jewellery guy, lol. Funny that someone with a quarter million dollars in white gold and diamonds wasn't much of a jewellery guy."

Despite the bling, Shane and the guys in his crew knew that being a true gangster wasn't just about being flashy—rocking sleeves of tattoos and hundreds of thousands of dollars' worth of jewellery. Flashy people who live to be impressive in bars are "going to flip in half an hour" at a police station, Shane says. Being a true gangster involved connections and reach. In this way, Sukh and Gurmit Dhak were part of an emerging trend in organized crime, spurred on by the connectivity the internet provided. That connectivity was noted in an organized crime overview released in 2024 from the Royal Canadian Mounted Police think tank, the Criminal Intelligence Service of Canada:

77% of [organized crime] groups have reported collaborative links to others, either directly or via common associates. As in prior years, the 3 most interconnected criminals networks include outlaw motorcycle gangs [OMGs], mafia groups, and street gangs.

84 OCGs [organized crime groups] assessed in 2023 maintain collaborative criminal associations with 5 or more other groups. Of these, 24 have an international scope and 22 had an interprovincial scope. The combination of broad established networks and geographic scope of criminal activity enhances the threat that OCGs present in the national and international landscape. Many of these and other OCGs are also involved in diverse criminal enterprises, building extra revenue streams and redundancies in their operations.

Being a gangster was also about entitlement. And there was certainly something righteous and entitled about Gurmit and Sukh Dhak. When the Hells Angels tried to tax their illegal earnings, they simply refused.

The Dhaks knew it took muscle to act this way, and they had that too. Gurmit could kill without losing his temper, like a farmer ending the life of a chicken or a steer. That made him particularly dangerous and effective. "He was always respectful, very humble, nice, yet dangerous and very feared. A true legend in that world. For real. Gangsters don't mind being called gangsters."

Aside from his own abilities, one of the reasons Gurmit could pull off the entitled act was his connection to another Jason, killer Jason McBride. McBride was one of the first in Shane's circle to get United Nations beads. He was a hard man to deny, and a major reason the Dhaks were feared. He was the gangster other gangsters were afraid of.

McBride was about a dozen years older than Shane, with a criminal record that included break-and-enter, possessing break-and-enter tools, and robbery. He also had a ten-year firearms prohibition, put in place in 2005, after police found a .40-calibre semi-automatic Glock handgun in his Lincoln Navigator. McBride was a major drug dealer too, one who moved kilos of cocaine. But the main reason he stood out was his capacity for violence.

"He's a tough guy," Shane says. "He's rowdy. He's down to fight. He'll shoot. He'll stab. He's no joke. He's a serious guy. Around women he would smile and stuff, but no, he was a serious dude."

McBride sported a "gangster fade" hairstyle: a full head of hair on the top and a close shave on the sides. He stood just under six feet and weighed a solid 210 pounds or so. "He was good-looking and the girls loved him. Pretty boy."

McBride attended parties, but also held back. "He just kept to himself. He wouldn't go out of his way to go up to another table to talk to us."

Despite his good looks, McBride actively stayed away from cameras. Everyone in Shane's circle knew this. "No pictures of him. I'd be shocked if anyone had one, other than a mugshot. You could not take pictures in his presence."

McBride didn't speak about his family or background, and Shane certainly didn't ask. You could be around him a lot and not really know much about him, except that he was extremely dangerous. That was how he preferred things.

"I know him pretty well and I barely knew him," Shane says.

When with his associate Viet "Billy" Tran, McBride shifted into a very low-key, all-business mode. He became "really quiet. Really really observant," says Shane. And extremely dangerous. "I never seen him without a gun. Ever."

McBride didn't seem to have any boundaries, even around cops, says Shane.

We were once at a hall in Burnaby. Our whole crew and Gurmit's entire crew. It was a closed party obviously. At 3 a.m., we had the music so loud that the cops showed up—two guys and a woman.

They came inside and Jay fucking sucker-punches the guy cop. Drops him. Then out of nowhere another guy drops the girl cop. The third cop comes in and then, boom, he gets knocked out too.

Imagine being the third cop to come in. He didn't know the first two were already knocked out when he went in through the door. And then to come in there . . . Seriously, imagine.

Everyone's leaving. I'm standing at the doorway, and as guys are running out, everyone's throwing their guns in the garbage can, one after another. I had never seen anything like that, as far as assaulting cops. It's one thing to resist arrest or run away, but to actually knock a cop out cold . . .

They were throwing their guns in the garbage can so they don't get pulled over and caught with a gun. There was no garbage in the can, so you could hear the sound of guns hitting the bottom of the can. By this time, lights on, music off, people running. I did not have a gun.

McBride didn't even pretend to have a legitimate job. "He never worked a day in his life."

Known as "White Boy," McBride seemed to be constantly travelling back and forth between Vancouver and Toronto. There were whispers he was responsible for fifteen killings during his travels, and that he sometimes ventured into Quebec for wet work, or murder.

For Gurmit and Shane's group, McBride's very presence was an unspoken threat. "He was a stone killer," former Vancouver police officer Doug Spencer says. "When you look into a person's eyes and they're two pieces of coal, that's McBride."

Also wearing United Nations beads was Sandip (Dip) Duhre, who was a very different type of gangster.

The Duhres grew up in North Vancouver, where Sandip was known for his brains and his quick sense of humour. He was influenced in the 1990s by Indo-Canadian gangster Bindy Johal. Then Johal was shot dead on the dance floor of Vancouver's Palladium nightclub on December 20, 1998, and Dip was on his own.

Dip had also once been close to the Bacon brothers of Abbotsford, but that ended with a resounding crash. When Dip's cocaine bills weren't paid, he took it as nothing less than an attack on his honour. It was as if the Bacons were saying, "What are you going to do about it?"

Dip always impressed Shane. "I loved Dip. I considered him a good friend. The knowledge this guy had, the way he thought about things, how he handled himself, how he handled business. I learned a lot from Dip, and a lot of guys did in our crew. You would be hard pressed to find a better guy in the life. He was so humble. He had such a presence, too. He really was intimidating if you didn't know him, or even if you did, if that makes sense."

Dip's younger brother Balraj was wounded in a shooting attempt in 2003 in Surrey and wounded again when he was shot in a Vietnamese restaurant in Vancouver in 2005. And Dip himself was the target of an attempted hit in May 2005 at a Surrey convenience store. That shooting took the life of his friend, Egyptian-born Dean Mohamed Elshamy.

Three months later, someone opened fire in East Vancouver on Dip and Balraj as they rode in a bulletproof BMW. Again, they survived.

In October 2010, Abbotsford police chief Bob Rich told a public forum that the Bacon brothers had been replaced at the top of the drug trade in the Fraser Valley. Now it was run by the Duhre brothers. "We are going after them," Rich said.

For all his notoriety, though, Dip didn't have much of a criminal record—just convictions for uttering threats and possessing a weapon for a dangerous purpose.

Shane answered directly to Sukh and Gurmit, but Dip still had influence. Shane quickly learned that Dip wasn't shy about correcting what he thought was foolish behaviour. He often did this with terse text messages. "He would zap me," Shane recalls. "He would zap Fitzy. He would zap anybody. He would just say, 'This needs to stop.'"

By the time he reached his mid-thirties, Dip was a wise old man of the Vancouver underworld. He had the stature to act as a peacemaker, and could approach outlaw bikers because they respected him. Dip's general approach when facing a problem was: "This is not happening. This is what should have happened, and this is what we'll do to get things better."

For Dip, violence was a credible alternative, but he preferred to solve things in other ways. He wanted his four children to have a father. "He always looked at the big picture," Shane says. "Dip would sit there and listen to what everybody had to say. At the end, Dip would speak. He was very level-headed and he was respected and he would never say he would do one thing and then do another."

Dip was a valued man in Shane's world. Despite all the attempts on his life, Dip didn't shy away from meeting with dangerous men. "He went by himself. Nothing happened. This is all from years of trust."

The Dhak–Duhre side of the United Nations gangster world was now Shane's home, so to speak. But there was another side—run by UN founder Clay Roueche. Although they all worked under the same umbrella, Shane seldom saw the man. This was in part due to the fact that Sukh wasn't wholly comfortable with Roueche, and cautioned his men to keep a safe distance from him and his men.

"These guys brought on so much heat, Sukh was just telling us to stay away," Shane says. Clay seemed to preen for the cameras, as if he was a little John Gotti, the flashy, camera-friendly New York mobster. "I didn't hang out with him a lot, other than a few meetings and a few dinners. But he was nice, respectful. He was smart. He put thought into everything he said before he said it."

Like Gotti, Roueche didn't hide his wealth. He drove a Maserati, a BMW 750iL, and a Lincoln Navigator—and he wore two UN diamond rings.

Shane and Roueche had very different backgrounds. Roueche came from an upper-middle-class family in Coquitlam in the Fraser Canyon.

His father Rupert (Rip) made a good living running a car-crushing business. He had a girlfriend whose father was in the Big Circle Boys Asian gang. Roueche found this fascinating.

Roueche fancied himself a Renaissance man of sorts. Police bugs picked him up discussing a variety of topics, including Armani fashions, hot yoga, home decor, and Botox for men. He said he had a black belt in taekwondo, and he liked to burn incense and smoke pot. He was also captured speaking of wide-reaching drug connections that wound through China, India, Mexico, and South America. Under Roueche's guidance, UN gangsters funnelled large shipments of cocaine from Mexico throughout BC's Lower Mainland and interior, as well as Calgary and the United States.

Although Roueche owned a shiny new condo in Coquitlam, he seemed to always be out of town. On the few occasions he was around, he fretted about police surveillance. "I know he was very paranoid about cops," Shane says. "I remember being out for dinner and probably in that hour and a half he brought them up five times. 'I bet that guy's a cop.' 'When they seat us, we're going to move to that table that I pick. I bet that table's wired.' Shit like that."

Roueche may have been paranoid, but he wasn't hostile like Sukh. "I never seen him yell or get mad at anybody," Shane says, recalling that Roueche was also capable of saying things that could make someone scratch their head. His words of wisdom included "Don't let anyone touch your head," "Don't walk under a clothesline," "Don't drink out of someone else's glass unless you wash it first," and "Don't eat dog, cat, or snake," although pork was fine. He also believed that symbolic beads shouldn't be worn to funerals, since that would somehow suck the energy from them.

The Dhak–Duhre side of the UN was tougher, and proud of it. "We were more gangster, more down to handle shit. Probably more violent. We were street guys. We took pride in that," Shane says. Sukh or Gurmit would make the calls on drive-bys and hits, after assessing the possible consequences. "If something needed to be handled, it would go through us. If there was going to be a shooting or something had to happen, it was going through our side . . . Gurmit would have to sign off on it."

Sukh combined a sense of theatre with paranoia—in stark contrast to Roueche's laid-back approach. At one point, Sukh had his security guys hanging out at bus stops, dressed as old men, with guns in paper bags. They included Thomas Mantel, who wore a latex mask.

Although Sukh might not have wanted to admit it, his boss was his big brother Gurmit, who had no boss. In turn, Sukh was Shane's boss, while Shane had a dozen or so guys under him, including someone to manage his phones and money. "Every guy had their own little circle."

They didn't have titles, like in the Hells Angels and the Mafia, but they did have varying levels of power and influence. Shane was senior, above Thomas Mantel but under Manny Hairan. Newcomer Jujhar Khun-Khun was also under Shane in the pecking order. The most powerful people were those who were closest to Sukh and Gurmit.

Doug Wheeler brought a fearful intensity and a chilling lack of fear. He had hardened himself during a seven-year stretch in Kent Institution after committing a litany of crimes for the Bacon brothers, including home invasions and weapons offences. Wheeler looked the part of an enforcer with his cauliflower ears and football lineman's physique. Khun-Khun made a far different first impression, but was also intense. He wore a turban. "He kind of looked like a nerd."

Sukh had reasons for allowing both of them inside his circle. Sukh would quickly weed out guys who were just talk. He wanted people around who were money makers or good at protecting him. Loyalty was huge. "Sukh was a really smart guy. He really was . . . Eventually he would see your true colours. If you tell Sukh that you're down, he's going to put you to the test," Shane says. "I think Sukh always felt he was safe with me."

Shane didn't plan to join Sukh's crew. He just did. "It just happened organically."

Over the years, he rose to become Sukh's right-hand man. There was something empowering about it—the respect paid to him by others, the better chances at earning—but there could be something degrading about it too.

Sukh walked about as if he were a little prince. "Sukh didn't carry anything. When you were with Sukh, Sukh didn't have hands."

Shane was once at a spa with Sukh and his driver/bodyguard, Thomas Mantel. As a female attendant handed out towels, Sukh nodded to Shane and Thomas, a wordless command for them to handle it: he wasn't about to carry his own towel. Shane and Thomas weren't surprised in the least. "He didn't open his own doors. The guy literally didn't do anything for himself, ever."

When Sukh took off his jacket, he expected someone to immediately take it for him. At the Pacific National Exhibition Playland, this left Stevie Leone (aka Tucker) carrying his jacket for an entire day. When Sukh won a stuffed animal there, an underling got to carry that for him too. And when Sukh had leftovers from a restaurant, of course someone in his group was expected to carry them. "He wouldn't even carry his own food," Shane says. "We literally did everything for this fucking guy."

Sukh did use his hands for driving, but he did that badly. His driver's licence was suspended after he ran up a string of unpaid tickets for things like improper lane changes and not signalling before turning. That meant he relied on Thomas even more heavily.

Sukh had no qualms using his hands to strike others. He knew that the far bigger men in his circle wouldn't dare to hit him back. He had a certain relentless quality that transcended his small stature, and it was easy to conclude he was jealous of his big brother Gurmit and his natural grace.

Sukh didn't appear to be mellowing as he approached his thirties. In fact, he seemed to be getting worse, which raised troubling questions. If he couldn't get along with his own group, what would he do with his rivals? Could he ever negotiate? Was war inevitable? "In the beginning he wasn't like that," Shane recalls. "When it was just me and him, he was nice. Enter a third person, he's a dick. I can't tell you how many times Sukh punched me in the face. It didn't hurt physically. It hurt me mentally."

Despite the challenges that came with working for Sukh, Shane knew his boss respected him on some level. Sukh appreciated Shane's attention to detail, which included a knack for spotting vehicles that might be driven by undercover police officers.

He also appreciated Shane's commitment. Life in the gang came ahead of everything else; there was no work-life balance. Shane had been with his girlfriend from Mayfair Gardens since his teens, and his gangster life wasn't good for their relationship. "I loved her dearly. I loved her to death, but I was always cheating on her," he admits.

As Shane rose in the gangster world, it was far easier to pick up strippers. His $100,000 diamond necklace, $30,000 earrings, and nine-carat white-gold-and-diamond ring worth more than $20,000 announced that he was a somebody. And being recognized as a gangster came with other perks, like not having to endure lineups to get into bars. "We'd typically walk up to the front like we owned the place and they'd let us in, every time."

Something about such special treatment left an odd taste in his mouth. "I started to feel that everybody in my life was fake. Not a true friend."

Once, Shane was in a mall when a young man asked him an odd question: "Do you know Shane Dankoski?"

"He fucking used my name when I was standing there. I didn't even know him."

CHAPTER 5

GANGSTER TOOLS

"Those closest to you are the most dangerous to you."
—GURMIT SINGH DHAK

SHANE WAS MOVING UP FAST in the gangster world. Proving himself useful to Sukh meant more responsibility. In fact, it meant more of everything. More work, more money, more influence—and more stress.

If the UN had had an organizational chart, by 2008 Shane's name would have been sitting higher than Fitzy's and way higher than Khun-Khun's. "I was right there with Manny," he says.

Others could sense Shane's upward trajectory. "You get more pull. I don't need Sukh's approval for everything. Guys know who I am." There was a sense of, "You know who I am, it goes without saying."

Those new responsibilities gave him a crash course in "the life," including lessons on the math, the lingo, and the tools that millennial gangsters used on a day-to-day basis.

No one had warned Shane that being a gangster involved so many numbers. And yet there it was—all day every day, as Shane and others whose eyes would have glazed over in math class at school had to meticulously learn the unforgiving math and science involved in cooking cocaine for market.

The first time Shane ever bought a kilo of cocaine it retailed for $19,000, and the last time was for $58,000. The market was ever-changing as prices and expectations kept rising.

Early on, Shane learned of an ingredient called "super buff," which could be mixed with cocaine to dilute it and jack up profits. Baking soda would do in a pinch, but it didn't work so well with crack cocaine. "It leaves white stuff in your pipe," says Shane, and it tasted bad, too. "It's called soda dope. The whiter the dope, the shittier the dope. You want your crack cocaine to be yellow. People don't want baking soda in their crack. Super buff is the only fucking thing. You can cook it up in your crack and it looked just like crack."

That's where the math came in. An ounce is slightly more than twenty-eight grams, and so when Shane got an ounce of high-grade cocaine, he would immediately cut it down to twenty grams. "I would take eight ounces right off the top. I've got eight ounces' profit off each kilo."

The super buff was added to make up for the missing grams of actual cocaine. If the cocaine was particularly high-grade, Shane could take fifteen grams off the top, making up the lost weight with super buff. "My dope from Sukh was so good I could two-to-one it," he recalls, adding that the super buff they used was actually a form of bird medication that someone in Sukh's group got through a veterinarian. "People were smoking that. Imagine."

The mixing process involved putting the product in a bin, crushing it, beating it with a hammer, and then mixing it well. "As the prices go up, you've got to add more buff. But you've still got to sell good-quality coke."

The bedrock of the drug trade is the twenty-dollar crack rock. It has to pack a buzz or customers will go elsewhere. "At the end of the day," says Shane, "you have to be able to sell a twenty-dollar crack rock."

As super buff grew in popularity—the UN weren't the only ones using it—the price shot up from $500 to $5,000 a kilo. "People started buffing super buff. Adding anything you can to it. It started turning into its own little market. People start asking, 'How pure is your super buff?'"

Manny and Sukh were big on adding buff. "We used to call Manny 'Soda King' and Sukh 'Buff Bagwell.'"

But there was a serious drawback to relying too heavily on buff. "A wise man once told me, 'Good product sells itself. Keep your product as pure as you can and you will always make money off of it. If you buff it, you will make more now. If you don't, you make more in the long run.' That wise man was Sandip Duhre. And he was right. I always kept that with me. You can use it in life too."

When it came to moving the drugs that Shane and his associates took such care in cooking, as well as the money they earned for doing so, hidden compartments in vehicles were the way to go. Cash from each worker was vacuum-sealed in a plastic envelope and then gathered together into another plastic envelope, which was also vacuum-sealed.

Shane and Fitz routinely sent $100,000 or so to Sukh each week, which eclipsed what other members of the group were paying.

Shane's job also involved directing shipments of cocaine. The cartels down in Mexico often sent the product to California, where it then became the buyers' job to bring it into Canada. That final leg—considered to be the toughest of the journey—was called "the ride," and it often involved stashing the coke in a hidden compartment of a semitruck. The driver might get $250 or $300 per kilo for a load. A good driver might deliver a load every couple of weeks, and was worth more than his weight in cocaine. "Sandip [Duhre] had the same driver for ten years," Shane says.

There was also the guns—plenty of them, as it turned out.

"It was nuts. Anytime, anyplace, anywhere—if somebody had a gun for sale, Sukh was ready to buy it."

A good Glock handgun might cost $4,000 or $5,000, and Sukh bought them from fellow gangsters, bikers, and Tom Gisby, a wealthy business-man with wide connections. Sukh bought them in bulk whenever pos-sible. A typical purchase might be in the order of thirty Glocks and fourteen AK-47s.

Sukh's interest in acquiring firepower seemed excessive to Shane. "I don't know why he bought all of this shit. I don't know why he needed that much."

Guns, cocaine, and money were stashed throughout Vancouver in safe houses. "Every safe place that we had, every condo, Sukh would have his cache of guns." To get a gun, a crew member just had to mes-sage Sukh and say words to the effect of: "Hey bro, I need a strap."

That was just one example of how millennial gangsters like Shane and the Dhaks and Roueche tweaked the language they spoke to keep up with their lives and business. Some of these tweaks were inspired by the internet and the ever-increasing role it was playing in their lives. To "buzz" someone meant to contact them on an encrypted BlackBerry. Having "eyes" meant surveillance, which was aided by planting GPS tracking devices on vehicles. "Setting the record straight" meant set-tling a debt and getting vengeance. This could include murder. Kilos of cocaine were called "birds" because they came up from the south and moved everywhere, the way birds seem to do. Picking up three kilos of cocaine could be expressed as picking up "three turkeys."

People were referred to in a gangster shorthand as well. Wolfpack and Hells Angels member Larry Amero was referenced with one hand mim-ing revving up a Harley and the fingers on the other hand shaped into an L. The Bacon brothers were the "Bacons," "Pigs," "Porks," "Porkx," and "goofs." Shane and his UN associates also used hand signals when discussing the brothers, in order of age: one finger for Jonathan, two for Jarrod, and three for Jamie. (Despite being in custody since his April 3, 2009, arrest for his role in BC's worst gang slaughter, Jamie remained an underworld force. During that hit, rival drug dealer Corey Lal was slain, along with five others, over Lal's refusal to pay $100,000 in "tax" to the Bacons. The incident became known as the Surrey Six massacre.)

Coded language like this was useful whenever Shane and his crew were in a space they thought could be bugged, and especially useful when talking about a hit. But shorthands and nicknames weren't safe enough. Pretty Good Privacy (PGP)–encrypted communication systems were the norm now.

"We had our guy and when we would meet him, I would bring one of my workers, so he never saw my face," Shane says. "I would give my worker the cash, usually $25,000 for ten BlackBerrys, with a subscription for six months. When we would get the ten Berrys, each one would already be set up with an email. Sukh would put them in a pillowcase and we would draw them at random, and that would be our new handle."

Even with those precautions, you had to be careful. Shane remembers Sukh and Gurm always saying, "Never talk about hits on these. Never talk people's names. Use them for work [drug dealing] only." Even so, he would never message Sukh about dope. "I would only talk to him about money."

When a hit happened, there was a plan in place. "Sukh would send out a message to our entire crew, and it would say, 'Shut off Berry. They're getting wiped'—meaning some shit's been talked about on them, someone got hit, they all have to go—and then I would send my workers around to collect them all from everyone near me. Our Berry guy had the main server in Vietnam, so that they [the cops] could never get a warrant for it, but the backup server was in Langley, BC. This one could basically do everything the main one could, but it could be cleared and erased right away if ever seized."

Shane handled the business with four different phones, including one that was just for high-volume customers. One phone, on a bad day, handled $4,000 of business and often cleared $15,000. There was a separate BlackBerry for Sukh, who couldn't stand to be kept waiting.

Shane regularly switched up his phones so the police couldn't get a handle on what he was doing or get warrants for certain numbers. It could be confusing and physically uncomfortable. When sitting in a restaurant, it was common for a troop of gangsters to each have four or more phones on the table in front of them.

Not surprisingly, given the intense rivalries at play, surveillance was also getting more and more sophisticated. GPS tracking devices were now essential. They allowed gangsters to learn where rivals slept and ate and hung out, and they also made it easier for hitmen to swoop in on them, should the need arise.

The Dhak group used GPS to keep tabs on their enemies, so they had to assume their enemies were keeping track of them this way too. "Sukh was definitely aware of them. We would literally have to crawl under his vehicles to make sure there wasn't one on his car," Shane says, recalling that when he first started using GPS trackers, they were maybe the size of a cassette tape; by the last time, they were about half that. "We also had a guy who would come check our cars out regularly for bugs. He would hook up this equipment and look for frequency."

The driver's main vehicle would always be kept in a garage, says Shane, but even that wasn't foolproof. "We had guys break into garages to put them on, so really, if you're gonna be tracked, you're gonna be tracked."

GPS devices were often attached to vehicles in mall parking lots. "It can happen in seconds, and timing is everything," Shane says. "You would park in front of the vehicle, your hood up like you're adding washer fluid. And you'd get down and clip it on. No one blinks an eye."

Gurmit stressed that all this security wasn't just about cars, guns, and electronic devices; it was about staying alert to people around you. "Those closest to you are the most dangerous to you," he said.

This, then, was the life. The day-to-day of being a gangster. And for the most part, Shane was happy. He was quickly making a name for himself in the Dhak–Duhre group, and the money and everything else that came with it was good. The only tricky part was Sukh—and his total disregard for boundaries. "That guy rode me so hard. It could be Christmas Eve, and Sukh would be, 'I need you to drive to Vancouver Island to pick up two keys of coke,'" Shane says. "Sukh always wanted me to do everything."

Or maybe it was Shane's birthday, or three hours before a family Thanksgiving dinner, with twenty guests gathered at Shane's home. It didn't matter. Shane was still expected to do Sukh's bidding—immediately. Which didn't help Shane on the home front. His longtime girlfriend, as well as his mother and his sister, made no attempt to hide their annoyance whenever he had to run off in the middle of some occasion or another.

But Sukh "didn't care about that shit." And that took its toll.

Shane's drug use went up accordingly. His drug of choice was always a downer, something to take the edge off. Often, at three or four in the morning, he was still wound up from a stressful day, so he would pop thirty or forty Percocets. "I used drugs to numb myself."

Despite the stress, though, Shane never thought of getting out. He still got grubby jobs from time to time, but he "enjoyed being a street guy"—even when others suggested he shouldn't be "driving around doing this shit." Being a gangster meant being part of a family—not a family you were born into, but one you chose. A family that—for a time, at least—seemed to live by a code.

"You don't talk to police," Shane says. "You respect everybody in your circle. Your honour is the biggest. You never sell out on your own guys. If you got yourself into a situation, you got yourself out."

Shane added his own personal rules to that list:

Don't talk on the phones or do dumb shit.
Always assume everything around you is bugged and tapped.
Assume there are cops out there trying hard to catch you.
It's your fault that you got caught.

—

Some of the rules Shane lived by were even inked on his skin. He loved tattoos, and by his late teens his arms were tatted out from shoulder to wrist. On his chest were tattoos of his father, and another one of Jesus and the devil arm-wrestling (neither good nor evil wins). "FEAR NO MAN" also appeared, in all caps, a motto for the way he tried to live his life, every day.

And then there was this one: "Lord protect me from my friends. I can handle my enemies."

"Turned out to be the realest tattoo I'd ever get," Shane says. "In the end it's your fucking friends. Your friends are the most dangerous. They know the most about you. They're the closest to you."

Shane wasn't targeting anyone with the comment; he just liked the sound of it. "At the time when I got that there was no significance to it. None of my friends were dangerous to me."

And yet the ink ruffled feathers. Manny seemed particularly offended. "Not us," he said. "We're a fucking crew. We're fucking bros." Sukh wasn't a fan either. "Why would you get that?" he asked. "Bro, your friends are your bros."

Shane's inner circle had a rule that they couldn't see police alone— another part of the code. It was intended to cut down on snitching and rumours of snitching. "That way, everything was up and up." There was also a rule about meeting someone new. "If you don't know him, just think he's a cop. I'd tell all my workers that."

Sometimes, Shane liked to tease Manny that he must be snitching since he didn't ever seem to get busted. Manny laughed it off, most of the time. Other times he offered a defence of sorts for snitches. "Manny said to me, 'Bro, look at some of the biggest gangsters in the world who have snitched,'" referencing Sammy "The Bull" Gravano from the Gambino crime family in New York City.

Belief in a gangster code—and belief in the strength of your relation- ships with your friends—felt good, just like it feels nice for children to believe in Santa Claus or the Easter Bunny. In reality, though, Shane's world was governed by jungle law. Perhaps there had once been a code, but if so, it was long dead.

"Money did destroy the code," Shane admits. While Shane and everyone in his circle seemed to be getting richer and richer, it never felt as if it was enough. "It was just fucking brutal. Then it became a competition: Who can sell the best dope for the best prices? That's where this shit got bad. That's when all of the murders went haywire. When the prices of drugs started to rise everybody started to get greedy. That's when the code left the game."

CHAPTER 6

MOVING UP

"I'm dating strippers. I'm buying girls fake boobs, thinking I'm the man."
—SHANE DANKOSKI

THREE HOURS ON the Coquihalla Highway gets you from Surrey to Kelowna in the lush Okanagan district. Kelowna is British Columbia's third-largest urban area, perched in a prime spot to capitalize on markets in the province's interior, as well as in Alberta and across the American border. The mother of his girlfriend at the time was going to school in Kelowna, studying to be a nurse. Shane's girlfriend went with her, which meant that Shane had been making the drive out there every weekend to see her.

Shane may have looked at Kelowna as a place to spend time with someone he loved, but when Sukh Dhak looked at it, he saw dollar signs. Aware of the area's potential, he was eager to get a drug-selling business in play. A crackdown on law enforcement in the Lower Mainland also bolstered Kelowna's appeal; it was a rich market with, hopefully, fewer police eyes.

Convincing Shane to make the "beautiful, amazing, one-of-a-kind" city his home in 2005 wasn't a tough sell. Shane loved living five minutes from Okanagan Lake, which was great in the summer, and thirty minutes from the mountains and all they offered during the winter. "You've got boating, or snowboarding . . . women everywhere . . . you can't keep enough cocaine on hand for the city of Kelowna . . . Kelowna was the place to be."

Shane knew it was a positive move, career-wise, even if Sukh wasn't the kind of guy who would come right out and say so with a feel-good talk. Shane's new territory also included the nearby cities of Vernon and Penticton, and in trusting him with it, Sukh was basically saying, "Hey, look, you can be your own guy, you can be your own boss. I think you're responsible enough. I think you've shown me enough. I think you've got this. It's freedom, right?"

Except it wasn't really a totally feel-good situation, or total freedom, given that Sukh was still involved. "Sukh wanted to be in the know on everything. Everything," says Shane. "This fucking guy wanted to know everything."

As he prepared for and made the move, Shane felt he was constantly being spied on by Sukh. Sukh pushed the idea that he had eyes and ears everywhere—and he certainly did have Fitzy and Wheeler and others in Kelowna. He could grill his men and compare notes, compare stories, and suss out who might be lying or holding back.

With that kind of system in place, it felt dangerous—it *was* dangerous—to hold secrets. You never knew if or when Sukh's questions were a test: Did he already know what he needed to know? Was he waiting to see if you were keeping something from him? It was nerve-racking, and on top of all the new responsibilities, it added another layer of stress in Shane's already stressful life.

When Shane arrived in Kelowna, he rented a high-end condo to use as his base. The condo was in a new building, with a spacious pool and barbecue facilities. It was a great spot from which to launch his first new business—a dial-a-dope line. Shane and his workers would drive around, on the lookout for potential customers. When they found some, they'd hand out free cocaine and crack, along with a phone number and the promise of quick delivery.

The payoff was quick and large, and it helped with the finances when, in early 2008, Shane and his girlfriend moved from the condo to a house: a $900,000, 3,300-square-foot house on Sunview Drive. It was a well-heeled subdivision of Kelowna, with a scenic view of the mountains. This was nothing like the apartments he had lived in while growing up in Surrey, when he'd had to sleep in a string of closets. The new place had a big basement with a $10,000 pool table, an infrared sauna, and a hot tub. There was a forty-inch plasma TV in a bathroom, so he could keep an eye on anything his security cameras were picking up. One of his next-door neighbours was a doctor. It was, says Shane, "your average nice rich guy's house" in a neighbourhood of "doctors, lawyers, gangsters."

By this time, Shane was a known commodity to police. He knew them and they knew him, and he knew they were constantly on his tail. "Sukh used to say, 'Don't get mad at them. That's free security. Do you know how much money that security would cost?'"

If Shane's new neighbours had any sense of what he did for a living, they didn't mention it outright. But it was obvious he had money. His driveway was a revolving showroom for his vehicles; a Cadillac Escalade, a Jeep Cherokee, a Corvette, a Navigator SUV, a Mercedes sedan, and a $100,000 boat were on display at various times. There was also a four-by-four quad and a trailer with an $18,000 Sea-Doo, not to mention the 2007 Harley-Davidson FXR in the garage. The latter was white with a blood-red Death Head on either side of the gas tank and "Hells Angels" painted on the rear fender.

Shane also announced his wealth with a hot tub big enough to seat fourteen, with plenty of extras. "Stereos built in. Pop-up speakers. Lights everywhere." The hot tub had become available when the driver of a semi-truck—also a regular customer—asked him, "Do you need a hot tub, buddy?"

"What do you want for it?" Shane asked.

They agreed that Shane would pay for the tub in dope, which turned out to be a pretty good deal given that he paid about $30 for cocaine that was worth $300 on the streets. Which is how Shane managed to scoop up three hot tubs that would have cost $13,000 each for about $500 apiece. He gave one to Sukh, another to Manny, and he kept the third for himself. "We all had sick hot tubs, man."

Getting the thing installed was quite a production. Shane used two cranes parked in the middle of the street to hoist it into place as neighbours stared out their windows.

The hot tub itself was pretty conspicuous, but Shane's guests for hot tub parties were also worthy of a second glance. They included Hells Angel Norm Cocks, who showed up wearing his patches. Cocks loved his Angels gear. Aside from the obligatory Angels tattoos, he sported sunglasses, key fobs, and anything else he could find with the Death Head logo. "Everything this guy wore was Death Heads."

Members of the United Nations also enjoyed the backyard spa. "Me and Doug Wheeler would have naked girls in there," Shane says, noting that he only did this when his girlfriend wasn't around. "That was all kept secret from her."

The party continued down on the waterfront, where there was valet parking for Shane's new boat. He'd do deals on the water while popping Percocets, surrounded by girls. During daylight hours those girls would be wearing bathing suits; at night, they'd be naked.

Somehow, the parties and the girls and the drugs didn't seem at odds with Shane's personal life. He was still with the same girlfriend he'd had since he was fourteen years old, and in early 2009 they were expecting their first child. This was a good time for the couple: money was coming in, and there were trips to Mexico, Vegas, Los Angeles, Anaheim, and Hollywood.

"She kind of just grew with it, with me," he says. And although she'd watched Shane evolve as a criminal, it wasn't something they talked about. None of his friends discussed their jobs—or their crimes—with their girlfriends or wives. "None of that's talked about with your girlfriend. I'm not going to her asking for permission," he says. And besides, "They get the perks of it." That meant Gucci bags, expensive dental work, fake breasts, and riding in the passenger seat of a Corvette. "It was just a gong show, brother. At the time, this was just my normal life."

Normal for Shane's world, maybe, but a far cry from normal for everyone else. One morning, Shane came bombing up the street in his dark-blue C6 hard-top Corvette with the music blaring. He had just been out with strippers all night and pulled into his driveway as a firefighter neighbour hauled garbage cans to the curb.

He stared at Shane and put his hands on his hips. Then he shook his head, saying, "The good life, eh? The good life. Have you ever had a job?"

"No, I never had a job," Shane replied. "I don't think I'll ever have one."

The firefighter shook his head in disgust.

Shane didn't tell the firefighter how he felt oddly trapped in his life. "It wasn't even that it was good. Regardless of how good or bad it was, I didn't have a choice," he says. "There wasn't an option."

His girlfriend had told Sukh that it might be time for Shane to move on from the life, now that they were expecting their first child. Sukh's answer was quick and blunt, as he leaned against their pool table. "The only way he's leaving me is in a body bag," he said.

Shane became a father on October 16, 2009, the day Jayden made his entrance into the world.

"It was the happiest day of my life. I got to cut the cord. It made me cry. It was so emotional," he says, recalling the explosion of emotions that went through his head. "It makes you think of everything."

Holding Jayden for the first time made Shane think of his own father, and how he must have felt the same euphoria when Shane was born. Shane ached to think how wonderful it would be if his dad could share this moment and hold his grandson.

And then there were all the predictions Shane had heard when he was growing up—about how he would wind up just like his dad. That was always meant in a bad way, as people anticipated trouble with the police and drugs and violent death.

As he looked at his newborn child, Shane convinced himself that things would be different this time.

"Most people don't get a second chance in life. I remember thinking, *I'm going to be there for my son.*"

That meant taking responsibility so he could be around as this tiny perfect baby grew up. Before Jayden's birth, Shane had thought of life in six-month chunks. It seemed ridiculous to plan for any longer than that since the risks of sudden death or jail time were so high. Now, Shane wanted to be present for all the time, and for everything. "I need to be around for this kid."

Shane felt he already had something to build upon. He had come so far from the days when he'd slept in battered women's shelters and was grateful for stolen chocolate bars. He was making ridiculously good money, so anything seemed possible.

Sukh and Manny and Fitzy came by the hospital to share the joy and held Shane's baby son. "Sukh was, 'That's nice. You've got a kid. This show has got to go on.'"

Despite all the joy, Shane remained tethered to Sukh. Sukh was his pipeline to money and possibilities his father had never experienced. And it was a huge amount of money, so much that he needed a counting machine to tally his cash, which came to $150,000 or so a month. Shane was able to announce his financial success in true millennial gangster fashion—by wearing a $100,000 necklace and $30,000 earrings and driving a Mercedes S550 AMG. He didn't consider his jewellery expenditures to be excessive. "It isn't a lot. Not in that world," he says. "I wasn't much of a jewellery guy."

He also didn't worry about robbery. "Come for my chain, you're probably getting shot."

The flood of money from Sukh meant that Shane could quietly take care of his mother, and his sister's education. It also meant he could invest in what appeared to be legitimate businesses, including two tanning salons. One was beside a gym. Shane had tanned there himself and was eager to buy in when a buddy told him he was selling it. "Bro, if you want to buy this place, I'll give you a crazy deal," he said.

There were three different membership plans, as well as a drop-in rate of ten dollars a tan. Most of the customers didn't ask for receipts, which made it extra easy to toy with the reported cash flow.

There was also a whole ecosystem of profits waiting for him in the tow business. Some of the money was made towing cars to yards that were in business with Shane, where they could charge $180 within four minutes just for hooking up with a vehicle. A gate fee added $200 for an impound after 6 p.m. There were also kickbacks from physio clinics and body shops as well. "There's so much money in it, it's ridiculous." There was money for steering work to physio clinics and a body shop, and there was money for helping them defraud insurers into paying for non-existent work.

The investment was fairly low. Paying off a cop who alerted them to calls cost fifty bucks or so, and that was money well spent. Shane also invested in a police scanner to monitor the action to make sure his drivers would be first on the scene to get the hook.

On top of that, tow trucks provided the perfect cover for moving drugs. If a tow truck driver was stopped by police, he could claim ignorance of whatever was found in the vehicle he was hauling. How was he supposed to know there were drugs in the car?

Shane recalls a driver who'd parked illegally freaking out when he saw his car being towed. Manny was with Shane that day. The driver shouted, "Why don't you get a better fucking job? You guys, what do you do that for? Ten dollars an hour?"

"I'd be thinking, *Buddy, you have no fucking idea.* Tow trucks at that time . . . it was the best-kept secret . . . It's legalized money laundering."

And it didn't stop there. Shane and his buddies would buy cars at auctions for a few hundred dollars, and a friend would register them under random peoples' names. The auto auctions also allowed the guys to have a bit of R and R.

I used to take my workers and my cousin, who was my manager, and the five of us would go to the auction in Kelowna. The undercover drug cops would be there watching me bid on these cars. I'd buy three at like $600 or $500 each.

The cops thought they were being sneaky watching, and that they now knew the work cars my guys would be using to drive around the city selling dope. But they were wrong. I'd buy them and put day permits on them. We drive them away, and then we'd take them to a place called Postill Lake. We would play demolition derby, and smash into each other, all fucked up on Percocets, doing jumps, and then we would put them in the lake or light them on fire when we were done playing bumper cars.

The cops would be like, "What the fuck is he doing buying all these cars? We're not seeing them on the roads."

Business opportunities abounded in Kelowna for Shane to keep making money for his young family. Aside from the dial-a-dope line, the tanning salon, and all the car-related revenue streams, there was sports memorabilia. Shane had a eureka moment on this front when he reconnected with an old acquaintance at a Kelowna Rockets Junior A hockey game.

The man ran a sports memorabilia store where you could get everything from autographs to what he said was the puck Bobby Orr shot to give the Boston Bruins their first Stanley Cup in twenty-nine years with an overtime goal against the St. Louis Blues on March 10, 1970.

"Man, you've got some pretty nice shit," Shane said.

"Hey man, I also do autograph signings," the memorabilia man said, explaining that he often flew sports celebrities and up-and-coming National Hockey League stars to sign autographs. He'd pay the athletes for the signatures, and turn around and sell the signed items for more. He was looking for someone to invest with him.

"That's music to my ears, bro," Shane said.

Shane was always eager for places to wash his money so that he could explain to Revenue Canada why he had what he had. "It was really, really, really perfect."

Shane started with an investment of $15,000, which netted him $22,500 within a month or so. After a couple more deals like this, Shane decided he couldn't keep the opportunity to himself. "I let Manny in on the secret. This was a good gig going on."

It turned out Manny couldn't keep it a secret either. "He tells Sukh about it. He tells Gurmit about it."

Soon enough, Shane was called in to meet Gurmit. Jason McBride and Billy Tran were also in the room. "If I give you $150,000, what can I get back?" Gurmit asked.

Shane told them about an opportunity that would pay twenty-five NHL draft rookies $10,000 each to sign cards. The cards would then be sold for a markup to sports fans at the store or through other brokers. When the wheeling and dealing was done, the net profit was staggering. Shane quietly scooped off $30,000 for arranging the deal, leaving Gurmit with a cool $320,000 profit.

It seemed too good to be true, and maybe it was. The payoff was supposed to come in a month, but it didn't. "When the thirty days were up, [the memorabilia man] started giving me the runaround."

Gurmit may have been the calm Dhak brother, but he wasn't a pushover. He was also the brother who was closest to Jason McBride, easily the most frightening member of their circle. Not surprisingly, Shane was worried about how Gurmit would react to the delay.

When it became clear the buddy-buddy approach to collecting payment wasn't working, Shane went to the memorabilia man's office wearing his UN shirt. "I don't think you have any idea who they are. If you fuck around, they will kill you," he told him.

"He kind of got all scared. About another week went by and he paid it."

Shane delivered the profit to Gurmit, who surprised him by quickly saying, "Let's roll it again. What can he do with my 320K?"

For a time, Shane was "killing it," making a profit off Gurmit's investments and Manny's as well. But then Sukh started to quibble over the business relationship. Sukh couldn't handle the fact that Shane was making money off the transactions. He made Shane give him the memorabilia man's contact information and began dealing with him directly.

Meanwhile, the memorabilia man was spinning out of control. "He started fucking around more and more and more," says Shane. When it came to payment, there was always an excuse: "Oh, I'm meeting with a guy" or "These cheques have got to clear."

But excuses meant nothing to Sukh. He expected Shane to make sure he was paid. It didn't matter that Sukh had horned his way into the deals; he would just revert to the attitude of "I don't give a fuck. He's your guy."

At this point, the memorabilia man owed Gurmit $400,000, Sukh $350,000, and Manny and Shane $200,000 each. And yet he didn't seem to fully appreciate that owing gangsters over a million dollars was a dangerous, even deadly, state of affairs.

Shane didn't need the money, but he wanted it—big time. He kept a safe downtown, in an apartment above a strip club. The safe was full of cash, guns, and dope. Even so, Shane had no thoughts of letting the memorabilia man off the hook. He planned on getting richer, and that meant collecting his debts. He was a somebody, and the memorabilia man could respect that or pay the price.

Shane thought back to how people had predicted he would turn out like his father, broke and murdered. He wasn't about to let that happen. No way his life was going to end up like his father's. Shane expected better.

"He wasn't a drug dealer," he says. "I was a successful drug dealer. I'm proving everybody wrong."

CHAPTER 7

STRANGER AND STRANGER

"One of our guys is ploughing a cop's wife?
That's hard-core, man."

—SUKH SINGH DHAK

THINGS KEPT GETTING stranger and stranger, like the day a man in his early twenties rode into Shane's world in Kelowna in a jacked-up truck. The truck was a gift from his family, but he said he'd cut off all connections with them. From the sound of it, his family was nice enough, but the newcomer still had some serious issues with them. Those issues weren't explained, and nobody cared enough to probe. The newcomer seemed fine to work Shane's dope phones, selling crack, and Shane was a drug dealer, not a family counsellor.

Shane got the newcomer set up in a condo so that he could focus on business. Soon, the newcomer was working sixteen-hour days moving dope.

"I liked him," Shane says. "He was a good kid. He was honest and he worked his bag off for me." On an average day, Shane's phone that the newcomer worked did $10,000 in sales, and on welfare days it could hit $25,000 to $35,000.

The newcomer's family issues stayed in the background as he moved the crack. On Christmas Day there were sad messages on Facebook from his family, asking where he was and how he was doing. The newcomer ignored them, and just kept working. He was making $2,000 a day in profits for himself, and he saved all his money.

Around this time, his girlfriend was friendly with a woman whose husband found a job driving a tow truck for Shane. The driver's ambition was to become a cop, and he was accepted into the RCMP depot in Regina for the intense training. He had to know what Shane did for a living, but he didn't really seem to care. Their widely different career goals didn't appear to faze him in the least.

As the former driver trained to be a cop far away in Regina, his wife stayed home in Kelowna, driving a Ford Escape registered in her husband's name. Before long, she and the newcomer began having an affair.

The newcomer wasn't the only one taking advantage of the prospective Mountie's absence. Shane had started moving dope from Surrey to Kelowna in the cop trainee's Escape, hiding it in side panels. Shane reasoned that police were unlikely to pull over and search an SUV registered in an officer trainee's name.

Even so, Shane knew he couldn't keep it going for too long. The prospective Mountie would soon be a full-fledged cop, carrying a taxpayer-funded gun. And then there was the fact that the newcomer, his worker, was "still fucking his wife."

On top of that, the newcomer's work on the dope phone was slipping. Shane sometimes called him when he was supposed to be working and got no answer. He left messages like "Where are you? Get the fuck out of that bitch's house," and heard nothing back.

Somewhere in all this, the newcomer had clearly crossed a line or two. Not only was the situation costing Shane money, but it was getting out of control. "It's a cop's wife," he says. "You're fucking the cop's wife in the cop's bed with his picture by the bed."

When Sukh heard of the situation, he took a different view. He was impressed with the newcomer. "One of our guys is ploughing a cop's wife?" he said. "That's hard-core, man."

It was, until it wasn't. When Sukh noted the newcomer's drop in production, he too wanted things fixed.

"I have to beat him up," Shane said, adding that he'd already warned him that "next time, I'll break your fucking hands."

Shane couldn't stop thinking about how her husband was going to be coming home soon with plenty of police training and a gun. He couldn't be expected to react well. "It was a big fucking headache."

Then local police raided the newcomer's condo. "He lost every fucking dollar."

Even then, he didn't fall into line. He kept sleeping with the cop's wife in the cop's bed when he was supposed to be selling dope for Shane. "He wouldn't listen," Shane says. "I ended up beating him up again a couple of times. It was really starting to take its toll. He would not stay away from her."

When Shane called the newcomer on his encrypted BlackBerry, he discovered that the newcomer's phone had been shut off again.

Shane asked his cousin Sheldon to check in on the newcomer. "He's gone, bro," Sheldon reported. "He fucking left."

The newcomer had bolted, ripping Shane off in the process.

Making things worse, Shane learned that Sheldon had helped the newcomer move out. He'd even helped him load his U-Haul.

Now Sukh was ultra-involved—and very far from amused. When Sukh found out that Sheldon had helped the newcomer, Sukh figured it was necessary to murder Sheldon to make an example of him.

Shane protested and Sheldon was spared, but just barely.

As for the newcomer, he was nowhere to be found.

If some parts of Shane's life were getting increasingly complicated, one place he could always count on feeling comfortable was the Ellis Street property of the Kelowna, or "K-Town," Hells Angels. Their clubhouse was in a renovated home, hidden behind bushes and cut off from the street by a gate. Visitors had to buzz and speak into an intercom to get inside. If they were approved, they were allowed in through the double front doors, which were reinforced with metal supports. The doors opened outwards because that made it harder to bash them in.

The property included a combination garage and guest house. The garage had a huge tool box chock full of crazy-good and pricey equipment for vehicle repairs. The upstairs bedroom was for out-of-towners.

The K-Town Hells Angels had just gotten full club status in 2007, and their pride was prominently on display. The walls of the main house were lined with Death Head symbols and memorabilia. "You couldn't spread your pinky finger and your thumb without touching Hells Angels memorabilia on walls," Shane recalls.

To the left of the front door was a huge bar, stocked with expensive alcohol. Farther inside was a dining room, with a large table loaded down with pizza, snacks, pop, and fresh ice—supplied by prospects. There was also a rotating hot dog machine. The entire downstairs was open concept, with a leather couch and a big-screen TV behind the bar. A pool table stood ready for anyone wanting to play.

The top floor was supposed to be for members only. On the stairway was a built-in safe, with a Death Head logo on the front. Club meetings—called "church"—were held at a round table on the second floor.

Tommy the Prospect was in charge of music. He liked club dance music, and loved Rihanna's "We Found Love." Its seemingly endless chorus about finding love in a hopeless place was practically inescapable, and usually everyone would be singing along. Tommy would say, "When I become a patch this will be the song I think back on."

The TVs in the clubhouse were controlled by a full-patch member named Richard, who liked a constant stream of news.

The food was often barbecue or pasta. Once a week, Tommy distinguished himself with his take on spaghetti and chicken fettucine alfredo.

Even though Shane was part of Sukh's group—and by extension part of the UN—his association with the bikers felt natural enough. Looking back, Shane remembers being impressed with what he saw as the club's organizational skills and close brotherhood. Some of his childhood friends had gone on to be Hells Angels, and it didn't hurt that when Shane was a toddler, he'd been dressed up by his grandfather in an Angels-approved "Lil Hells Angels" outfit. Rather than acting like rivals, Shane and the Hells Angels actually enjoyed each other's company. "The Kelowna Hells Angels had so much love and respect for me," Shane says.

It was particularly nice when he would chill in the hot tub and be called "bro." That meant something to Shane, who had no blood brothers of his own. "I don't take that word lightly at all."

In Shane's world "goof" is the worst insult you can hurl at a man; by contrast, "bro" is the highest compliment. Tommy the Prospect didn't seem to understand that. "One of my friends used to call me bro and he would do that in front of other Hells Angels. They would be like, *What the fuck?*" In the Angels' universe, the word "bro" was pretty much reserved for other Hells Angels, and it had to be earned. Shane had seen visitors put in their place for using it to refer to club members. "Don't call me bro," a biker might say. "I'm not your bro."

It wasn't just the Angels who took the word seriously. "Sukh would only call you bro if you were in his inner circle. It was serious. You don't just call anybody bro."

One of the Angels who owed Shane $50,000 went even further than that:

He ended up giving me his pearl-white Harley-Davidson FXR with a blood-red Death Head on each side of the gas tank until he could pay me. The cops were so confused. You shouldn't be riding a bike that's all Hells Angel'd out if you're not a member. You can't even if you're a prospect.

So one day [senior Hells Angel] Dave (Gyrator) Giles sees me on it, doesn't say a word. The next day at the clubhouse in front of all his members, he says, "You need to cover up the Death Heads. Just put paper over them until you get it painted." So I taped a piece of loose-leaf paper over the Death Head. Soon as I got on the bridge they flew off. They never said another word.

It was crazy fast, very nice-looking bike . . . You'd be stopped at a light, people staring, big white guy, full-sleeve tattoos, and diamond watch, wearing a UN T-shirt, on a bike that said Hells Angels all over it. Must have been weird to see.

In 2010, Shane and a group of Hells Angels went out for Halloween, along with fellow Hells Angel Norm Cocks and Shane's cousin Sheldon. "The four of us went out in downtown Kelowna to the bars dressed up, dark-blue pants with yellow stripes, black leather gloves, fake bulletproof vests that said 'Gang Bang Task Force,' instead of 'Gang Task Force,' and then we each carried a box of Timbits . . ."

The big kicker was that they all also wore plastic pig noses. At least some of the downtown police seemed amused by the costumes, which had been made by Shane's sister. Some of the local cops even had their pictures taken with Shane's group (those photos became instant collector's items). "I had my long-sleeve United Nations shirt on."

The police joked about it for weeks, Shane remembers, saying, "Hey, Shane, heard about your costume."

And then there was the time a cartel guy from Mexico showed up for one of the Tuesday poker nights at the Ellis Street clubhouse. He stood about five-six and weighed maybe 130 pounds. He was clean-cut, with short hair and a thin moustache and no visible tattoos. He looked to be around forty-five or fifty.

It wasn't that unusual to see someone from a Mexican cartel interacting with a Canadian criminal inside Canada. A 2010 study by the Washington-based Center for a New American Security found that Mexican drug cartels had set up "branches" in the United States and Canada, including at least 235 sophisticated distribution networks throughout North America.

The cartel worker arrived at the Kelowna clubhouse in a Shelby Mustang. Shane got there in his Corvette.

There were plenty of members at the clubhouse that night, including some from the Southland chapter in Edmonton. "It was a packed house."

The cartel guy could barely speak English.

"He's really close with El Chapo," Shane's friend said, referring to Joaquín Archivaldo Guzmán Loera of the Sinaloa Cartel in Mexico, considered one of the most powerful drug lords in the world. There was apparently a picture of the visitor with El Chapo, which supported the belief that their guest was a big deal.

"No way," Shane said.

"Yeah."

There had been reports of a boat sinking with 1,500 kilos of cocaine on it, and that apparently had something to do with his visit north. He needed to sort out what had happened.

The cartel guy went outside for a smoke. When he returned, he had a question. "Hey, my friends. Whose Corvette is that? Nice Corvette."

Shane let him know it was his.

"That's my Mustang. You want to race?"

Shane wanted to race.

Shane had bought the 'Vette from Manny, who liked to dump crazy amounts of money into his vehicles to torque up things like the cold-air intake and make them super-fast. "He added a bunch of horsepower," Shane says. "It was fast as fuck."

The next question was how much they wanted to bet on the race. They started with a $500 wager, which quickly hit $1,000 and then $5,000.

"Everyone started yelling. Everyone's making side bets on who's going to win this bet. Everyone piles outside."

The clubhouse backed onto a fruit juice and snack factory by the train tracks, and that's where the race was to happen. The workers on the plant's night shift got wind of what was going down and came out to watch. Some of them appeared to be taking bets too.

The race was about a quarter kilometre, and about a quarter of the way in, Shane pulled ahead of the cartel member, who was looking down as he shifted gears. "I beat him by about half a car length," Shane says. "It was crazy. It was so loud. It was a good show."

And it was all in good fun. "He laughed his ass off. He started cracking jokes on himself and his driving. He paid me. We drank all night together."

It was in the same Hells Angels clubhouse back in 2007, that Shane had first met Larry Ronald Amero. They shook hands. Larry shook hands with a lot of people, and he always seemed genuine. "He always had a smile on his face. It was real. It was like a perma-grin."

It was impossible to be big in the drug trade in the Lower Mainland and not know about Amero of the Hells Angels and Wolfpack Alliance. Amero was a full-on millennial biker. He was born June 1, 1977, and was a full-patch member of the White Rock charter of the Hells Angels, with a tattoo on his lower abdomen that read "Hells." When Shane first saw him, Amero was about 260 pounds and jacked from plenty of work in the gym. "He was a big boy."

With that kind of build and credibility, Amero could easily have been a bully, but instead he had a very different reputation. "He wasn't known to shake guys down and muscle people. From all accounts, he was a really great guy. He didn't big-time anybody. I like that about people."

Amero managed to seem humble yet important, the way true leaders do. "I guess you can say people kind of flocked to him," Shane says. And even though he was a big deal, Amero didn't give off the "Who are you to talk to me?" vibe that Sukh and Manny often exuded.

Amero had a union card as a longshoreman and a young son to support. He moved large quantities of drugs and was connected to wealthy, efficient people. When Tom Gisby said things like, "I'm doing work with a friend of mine," he really meant, "I'm moving drugs with Larry Amero."

Gisby knew it was dangerous to work for both sides in a war, but it also paid well. "He was on the fence," says Shane. He was also trapped. "If he cut Sukh off, Sukh would have had him killed."

Amero had plenty of associates outside the Angels, including Randy Naicker of the Independent Soldiers gang, whose criminal convictions included kidnapping and extortion. Shane wasn't impressed with Naicker. The guy was "cocky, arrogant, rude, mouthy," he says. "Thought he was better than anyone."

The authorities certainly knew about Amero. In December 2002 he was found guilty of possession for the purpose of trafficking and production of a controlled substance. He got off lightly: just a one-year conditional sentence, to be served in the community, followed by a year of probation.

Amero grew to be a priority customer of the cartels, and Gurmit sometimes grumbled things like, "We didn't get our load on time, but Larry got his load on time."

Amero announced his success by driving high-end vehicles like a BMW M5, a Cadillac Escalade, a Chevrolet Silverado, and a Porsche Cayenne. And while he looked like a jacked-up UFC fighter, Amero never actually fought—at least not that Shane heard of. He likely had bigger things on his mind, like bringing massive amounts of cocaine up from Mexico.

It was to the cartel's advantage to support a certain amount of instability in Canada's underworld. They didn't want any one of their buyers to rise high enough to start making unreasonable demands. It was best to spread things around and keep them all a bit subservient and needy. That meant charging different prices to different buyers working the same market. And that, in turn, meant it was natural for the Canadians to get jealous of each other, even though they were all making huge amounts of money.

It was also potentially fatal.

Tensions in Shane's tense world began to pick up in early 2008, with twenty-two targeted gang shootings in the Lower Mainland in less than a month.

Gangster Barzan Tilli-Choli of the United Nations was in his Lincoln Navigator on the night of Friday, February 15, 2008, when he got a text from a woman at a strip club in Surrey.

"That guy is here," she messaged.

That guy was Tyler Willock of the Red Scorpions, a west coast gang on the Wolfpack side of the underworld split.

Tilli-Choli messaged Aram Ali of the UN that he was needed immediately. He also told him to wear black clothing. Ali told Tilli-Choli that he planned to hit Willock "in the head."

"Shoot him all over his body," Tilli-Choli replied. "Put your window down and keep your arm in the car."

Ali's SUV pulled alongside Willock's Range Rover at an intersection near a strip club on East Whalley Ring Road shortly after midnight. The blast of gunfire caught the driver in the shoulder, but the three passengers, including Willock, were spared.

There were plenty more people the UN wanted shot, including former member Kevin LeClair. LeClair was what cop-turned-academic Keiron McConnell calls a "choice gangster," who had plenty of alternatives in life besides crime. The Bacon brothers and Clay Roueche also fit into that category of kids from comfortable homes who chose to be gangsters. "LeClair is the quintessential BC gangster in that he came from a good home, with a nurse for a mother and a police officer father," McConnell writes in *Vancouver Gang Violence: A Historical Analysis*. "He is a classic example of a 'choice gangster.'"

Shane's group had a different term for LeClair. They called him "traitor" after he left the Roueche side of the UN to team up with Jamie Bacon. Traitors like LeClair were particularly dangerous in Shane's world, as they knew the names, home addresses, and habits of UN members. A $15,000 bounty on LeClair's head was soon increased to $50,000.

Two hitmen opened fire on LeClair with high-powered rifles outside an IGA supermarket in Thunderbird Mall in Langley around 4 p.m. on February 6, 2009. LeClair had just left a nearby pub, and there were plenty of bystanders in the mall parking lot when the gangsters with at least one AR-15 military-style machine gun arrived. McConnell notes that "several slugs were pulled out of a car's child seat."

"The mother had just dropped the baby off at home because her husband was home sick for the day and available to babysit; otherwise, the baby would have been in the car and would likely have been a victim of collateral gang violence," McConnell writes.

On February 15, 2009, twenty-three-year-old mother-of-two Nicole (Nikki) Alemy was shot to death while at the wheel of her Cadillac, which crashed into a tree. Her four-year-old son witnessed the murder of his mother from the back seat, screaming in horror as she died. The killers thought one of Alemy's relatives was connected to the UN gang.

Gangsters Ryan Richards and Sean Murphy had planned to switch from the Bacon side to the United Nations, but were shot dead hours apart on March 30, 2009, in Abbotsford.

United Nations gunmen waited for Randy Naicker of the Independent Soldiers to return to a Vancouver halfway house on Cambie Street on September 29, 2009. They killed bystander Rajinder Soomel by mistake.

Not surprisingly, given the rising levels of violence, the Dhaks were extremely guarded about their personal information.

Shane was trusted enough to visit the home of Sukh and Gurmit's parents in the Greater Vancouver Area. There was high-end marble and granite throughout, including on the floors. "It was one of the most beautiful homes I've ever been in. It's just a beautiful huge luxury house," he recalls.

There were also plenty of security cameras on the huge white house, which was big enough that the three-car garage in the back didn't seem out of place. The basement, says Shane, could have housed a separate family.

The address was carefully guarded from the Wolfpack.

"Larry knew they always were at their parents. I remember someone sent Dip a PGP message, from Larry Amero, saying he would pay 25K for the address confirmed!"

Gurmit lived in a new house on a cul-de-sac in the Newton area of Surrey, off King George and Highway 64. "Nobody knew where Gurmit lived. It was top, top secret."

Gurmit's hideaway was pleasing to the eye and looked like the type of home a top surgeon or a CEO might own. It was also protected with high-end security cameras and reinforced doors.

Sukh had a condo in the Whalley neighbourhood of Surrey and a gated townhouse nearby. The condo was more of a hideout than a show home, with paper cups from McDonald's scattered throughout. Its best feature was a sixty-inch TV. "It was just a little dive."

Sukh had a third place under construction—and that was the one that really mattered to him. It would be his statement that he too had arrived. The lot was about a five-minute drive from Gurmit's mansion in Surrey. "Every day me and Sukh would go to check on the guys building the house," Shane says. "He designed that new place."

Plans called for the new property to be rimmed by cedar trees and a metal gate. There would be a guest house in the back and a basement suite, with a glass fireplace and autographed sports jerseys on display from the memorabilia shop in Kelowna.

One day, Sukh called with an order. "He said, 'Come to the property. Come to the property.'"

Sukh summoned a whole gang of United Nations members and supporters that day, including Tucker, Fitz, Manny, and Mantel—about thirty guys in all. Their collective job was to hoist a wall that was about fifty feet long and fifteen feet high.

Anyone helping lift the wall was highly trusted. No one but the absolute inner circle knew the address. "In the height of the beefs, cars were driving around looking for Sukh every day to kill him. We were right under their noses. Right in Surrey, right in Whalley."

The escalating war brought Shane and Sukh into constant contact. "Sukh was my go-to guy. My boss. I was in contact with him not just every day but twenty times a day."

As the hit crews searched for Sukh, he and Shane sometimes dined out, right under their noses, in the food court of the Surrey Place Mall. And they were busy conducting their own searches too. There were no time outs in the hunt for humans.

"Our crew was literally out hunting for these guys," Shane recalls. "Christmas Eve, Christmas fucking night . . . Those guys were probably doing the same thing."

They collected licence plate numbers and vehicle descriptions, which they fed to Manny's ex-girlfriend, who worked in the insurance industry and had remained friendly with the UN. Her job allowed her to check addresses of gang rivals, which helped hit teams do their grim chores.

"We'd sit in these vehicles eight or ten hours, pissing in bottles. That's called homework," Shane says. "We would do that . . . That's the only way to do a proper murder."

Without going into detail, Shane admits he did horrible things.

"I was a monster."

—

Sometimes during these years, Shane's mind drifted to the murder of his father. Nobody had ever been convicted for the crime, but as Shane's stature in the UN grew, details began to fall into place.

One of Shane's uncles used to tell him when he was growing up that he knew who killed Shane's dad. "One day, I'm going to tell you so you can handle it," he said. Then, one day, he told Shane how he had been drinking in a pub a few days before the murder with two men who talked about killing Shane's dad. "Why he never said, 'Don't do that to my brother-in-law. He has kids,' I don't know. I loved him but he too was an alcoholic."

The story emerged that Shane's father had ripped off an after-hours booze-can drinking spot that had been under the control of legendary BC gangster Bindy Johal. Tim had stolen a pound of marijuana from it.

Dip Duhre had risen up under Johal, which meant that Shane was working with the men who had murdered his father—two brothers who had worked for Johal back in the day. He could understand the reasons Tim had been killed, but family was family.

Dip asked around a bit for Shane but didn't get anywhere. And so Shane and Manny set out to avenge Tim Dankoski's murder on their own—or at least give it a good try.

The time seemed ripe. Johal was long gone and no one else in their circle would be particularly upset if they settled the score by shooting the brothers. Shane and Manny heard they lived in the Fraser Valley community of Chilliwack, and decided to hunt them down.

Manny was enthusiastic about getting some level of justice for his friend, saying, "Bro, I'm going to kill these guys who killed your dad."

Once in town, they stopped a lot of people, asking if they knew where to find them. They learned that one of the killers had already been murdered and the other was a hopeless junkie, killing himself on the streets. The life had already taken care of them.

It was taking its toll on Shane and Manny as well. Shane was trying to be a gangster and a family man, but with the stress and tension of his daily life, it was getting hard to keep things together. Drugs offered an escape. "The drugs had taken over. I was so fucked up on drugs."

He and Manny were leaning more heavily towards Percocets and OxyContin. Shane had been popping Percs since his early twenties, and his abuse was escalating. The downer, which had once brought a nice mellow feeling, now also made him numb and vulnerable. "You start to lose your sharpness," he says.

For a time, Sukh was unaware of Shane's increasing drug abuse, but soon enough "he started to pick up on little things: forgetting who owes us, when I said I was going to come down, exactly how much product got paid."

Once, Sukh showed up uninvited at Manny's place, coming in through the garage. He found Shane and Manny in the basement, watching a movie with three open bottles of Percocet and almost $800,000 on a nearby table, next to mounds of cocaine.

"Me and Manny were so fucked up. Tongues hanging out of our mouths. Literally drooling."

Sukh was disgusted at the sight of them. He called them junkies; he called them goofs.

Another day, Shane, who was sick with strep throat, got a message from Sukh. "He says, 'Come down.' I don't even know what it's for."

Saying he felt sick would have gotten Shane nowhere with Sukh, so he drove from Kelowna down to Surrey, "pulling over every twenty minutes to puke." When he got to Sukh's, Shane quickly realized why he'd been summoned. Sukh spoke about Shane's health and Manny's— and not with the concern of a friend. His words sounded more like a warning.

"This is what's wrong with you and Manny," he said. "You're fucking junkies." He let Shane know that he wasn't fooling anyone. "You're a fucking junkie."

Shane knew his boss wasn't wrong. He knew he was slipping. Back in 2009, he'd been fully involved in the birth of his first son, and fully committed to being a good father. Three years later, when his second son arrived, he would be having trouble holding things together. The uncertainties of his life weighed on his mind.

Would his boys face the same situation he had faced, back when his father was murdered just before Shane's eighth birthday? "What if something happens to me? My poor kids. I worried about them having to grow up with no dad. I also worried about something happening to me at my house when I'm there. I loved my kids more than anything, but sadly I put the life over them and I put my addiction over them. I always knew you don't last long in the life."

CHAPTER 8

GURMIT'S GONE

"That was the day everything changed."
—SHANE DANKOSKI

THE TEXT CAME on October 13, 2010, when Shane was in Kelowna and Sukh was in Surrey.

"Yo," Sukh texted.

"Yo."

"Come down."

"What's up?"

"Gurm's going out."

Shane knew exactly what that meant. If Gurm was going out, Shane was going out too. He was expected to immediately head down to Surrey from Kelowna. It didn't matter if he was putting his boat in the water or taking his family for an outing or just wanting to relax—Shane was expected to be in Surrey within hours. "I would literally drop everything I was doing. Jump in my car as fast as I could, for King Gurm to go out."

This time, Gurmit was attending a wedding, and Shane, Manny, and Tucker had been called in to do security, guarding the hall. That was a typical task for them now: to sit outside in rented vehicles to make sure

77

no one crashed the party. They had their gangster kits of GPS trackers, laptops, and guns, including an M-16 assault rifle, as they kept tabs on people in the area. Meanwhile, inside, Gurm was dancing the Worm in his Gucci and Louis Vuitton clothes to tunes like "Like a G6" by Far East Movement featuring the Cataracs and Dev. "Everybody just loved it," Shane says of Gurmit's moves.

There would be other gangsters inside, drinking only water and keeping watch from their own table close to Gurmit's. A couple more gangsters would be on the dance floor, close to Gurmit and packing Glocks. "We did it from our hearts," says Shane.

A few days later, on October 16, it was gang killer Jason McBride's turn to provide backup. Gurmit told McBride that he wanted to go shopping at Harry Rosen's, a high-end men's store. Gurmit's plan was to later meet up with his wife and twin daughters at a Build-A-Bear workshop in the Metrotown shopping centre, where they would make stuffed animals for the kids. His wife was pregnant and family time was particularly important. "It was Gurm's dream to have a son." When the shopping was done, they would drive home, separately. "Gurm never rode in the same car as his wife and his kids. Never, ever."

They also wouldn't walk in or out a door in public together. That wasn't considered paranoid; in fact, it was common practice in this life for people of Gurm's stature. They were just trying to protect their loved ones as much as they could.

Gurm was on his BlackBerry to Jay McBride shortly after 4 p.m.

"Okay, bro, I'll zap you," McBride replied, meaning he'd be in touch with a text message. He had given Gurmit a little space but was still regularly checking in.

There was no reply.

"Yo, bro, where are you," McBride texted again.

There was still no reply. It was 4:07 p.m.

At that moment, Gurmit's wife was putting her daughters into her Escalade. She heard several bangs nearby, in rapid succession. When the bangs stopped, Gurmit sat motionless in his BMW X5, with gunshot wounds to his face.

In Kelowna, Shane was loading gifts into his own Escalade following his son Jayden's first birthday party. The celebration had taken place at a nice hotel, and guests had come from as far away as Alberta. Shane was walking down a wheelchair ramp from the hotel when his phone started to buzz. But with his hands full with a kid-sized Power Wheels black Escalade, he couldn't immediately answer it. A few minutes later, when he finally got the box into the back of his vehicle, he looked at his phone. "In my head I knew it was Sukh."

He was right. A tearful Sukh was on the other end of the line. "Bro, they got him. They killed him."

"I knew exactly what he meant and who he was talking about."

"Get down here," Sukh ordered.

Gurmit Singh Dhak died at the age of thirty-two, three years after he survived being ambushed and shot at a birthday party at Quattro restaurant in the beachside Vancouver neighbourhood of Kitsilano. Shane believes he died at exactly 5:51 p.m. It was a mystery why he didn't return McBride's text at 4:07.

"He had been going back and forth with Jason McBride on the Berry, and his last out message was at 5:50, and there was nothing else after that," says Shane. "The reason we know is we were able to get the Berry guy to pull his Berry from the server. Then he duplicated it, and Sukh was able to go through and read every single email Gurmit sent and received for the past two weeks.

"I never left Sukh's side for about two weeks," Shane adds. "We barely slept . . . We were in that car maybe eighteen hours a day. I had never seen Sukh cry before. It was life-changing, actually. He was a mess."

It felt obvious that the attack was the work of the Wolfpack Alliance. Tensions had been rising with them, and who else would have the nerve to go after Gurmit?

"That's when it was go-time for us—the day they killed Gurmit," Shane says. "That was the day everything changed. I always thought nothing would happen to him. When it happened, every sense of safety was gone."

In those disorienting days after Gurmit's death, Shane and Sukh rushed to gather up Gurmit's jewellery, guns, drugs, and money before it fell into other hands. In addition to the Wolfpack and the authorities, they were particularly concerned about Gurmit's things being stolen by their own group. It was a sad but realistic fear. "We were worried about our own trying to steal. Your bros. And they wore the same beads as you on their fucking wrists."

In a suede box at Gurmit's house, there was more than $4 million worth of jewellery, including three gold chains with diamonds, each worth $150,000. "Sukh and Gurmit both had a sick, sick, sick attachment to diamonds," Shane recalls. "In this box was just pure diamonds." There were hundreds of them, ranging in quality from a quarter carat to three carats. There were also rubies, rings worth $20,000 and $30,000, and three Rolex watches, including the special edition gold one lined in diamonds. There was valuable paperwork as well.

"Scoresheets," Shane explains. "This is how we were able to see who owed him money, and how much, and where all the money was." No one knew Sukh had this information, which gave him and Shane an advantage. "He would go to guys and say, 'Hey bro, did you pay my brother his 200K?' And the guy would say, 'Oh yeah, bro. I did the day before he died.' And then Sukh would pull out the Berry and say, 'Then why was he asking you for the paper last night?' So a lot of shit like that happened."

Shane's crew scrambled to their "offices," gang-speak for apartments or condominium housing units where drugs, money, and firearms were cached. Gangs on the UN side often had trusted residents covering the rent, which lessened suspicion around the units. There were rules that these residents couldn't have visitors or use drugs in the apartments—a further guard against unwanted attention.

There were stacks and stacks of hundred-dollar bills, and plenty of fifties and twenties, to gather up. It added up to $4 million, which was enough to fill gym bags and Walmart bags and a wheeled suitcase.

One stop was in a luxury apartment overlooking Stanley Park, with no furniture except a single mattress on the floor and a TV on a plastic box. There were also two condo buildings in the old Whalley section of Surrey, in a rough downtown strip. Manny's former girlfriend had her place in one of them.

Hidden under the sink were guns and explosives. Zip-lock containers held grenades, as well as fifteen or so Austrian-made Glock handguns, which Manny loved. There were also a half-dozen or so AR-15 machine guns and some extended bullet clips. Shane, Manny, and Khun-Khun gathered up the weapons and put them into white garbage bags.

Khun-Khun peeked out into the hallway before announcing that the coast was clear. But as they stepped out of the apartment into the hallway, a woman appeared. "She looks down at the bags and she goes white as a ghost," Shane says.

Together, they rode the elevator down to the parking garage. They didn't want the woman to see their vehicle, assuming she would call the licence plate in to police as soon as she could, so they stood beside a random car until she left. Finally, they got into Shane's Jeep Cherokee and stashed their haul in its two hidden compartments.

As they drove along Highway 152 in Surrey, a police officer blew through a stop sign, almost T-boning their vehicle loaded with handguns, machine guns, and explosives. The cop had no idea what was happening under his nose, and was apologetic as he approached them.

"You guys all right?" he asked. "You guys okay?"

Shane, Manny, and Khun-Khun certainly weren't about to make a big deal of it. They accepted the cop's apology and drove on.

As the cleanup work continued in and around Surrey, Sukh remained uncharacteristically quiet. "It was just pure silence," Shane recalls. But that didn't mean Sukh wasn't feeling his brother's absence.

One day, Shane and Sukh went to collect Gurmit's laundry. Gurmit had loved his tailored suits, and there were plenty of them to gather up. An elderly Chinese woman at the dry cleaner asked about Gurmit. Sukh was clearly uncomfortable as he told her, "My brother passed away."

"What?" the woman said, and then started to cry. "I know Gurmit for more than twenty years."

She handed Sukh an armful of his brother's clothing, which he immediately passed over to Shane. Sukh's rule about never carrying anything—even if that thing had belonged to his recently murdered brother—was still in effect.

"When we left the dry cleaner, Sukh started crying," Shane says.

One day shortly after Gurmit's death, Shane was about to make the turn onto the highway from Surrey to Kelowna in his Jeep, with his longtime partner and their son Jayden, when his BlackBerry buzzed. He obviously didn't pick it up quickly enough, because the first words he heard were "Answer your fucking Berry." It had to be Sukh.

"Meet me at Washworld on 72nd," came the order.

As usual, Shane was expected to drop whatever he was doing, make a U-turn, and drive to the other side of Surrey. There was no consideration given to whether this would be inconvenient for Shane and family. None of that mattered to Sukh.

When Shane arrived at Washworld, Sukh wasn't there. A full hour passed before the bay door to the car wash finally opened and Sukh rolled up in Gurmit's old car, a Mercedes S550 AMG class sedan. True to form, Sukh didn't apologize for the inconvenience or for being rude to Shane in front of his girlfriend and son.

"All right, there's your new car," Sukh announced. "I need this Jeep, bro."

And that was that. No discussion permitted. Then and there, Shane had to take his son's car seat out of the Jeep and transfer it to the Mercedes. Sukh ignored Shane's partner and Jayden as he continued to give orders.

"He made me take Gurm's car," Shane says. "Think about that. Who does that? That Jeep belonged to my girlfriend. I bought it for her. No joke."

The Mercedes was worth $150,000, considerably more than the Jeep—and the discrepancy hadn't escaped Sukh's attention. "Okay, you owe me the difference," he told Shane.

Sukh's logic for the car swap was simple: Shane's Jeep Cherokee was brand new, and their enemies likely didn't know about it. The Mercedes, however, was on enemy radar.

To Shane, it seemed as if Sukh was spinning in the wake of his brother's death, his mind hopping from one thing to the next. First there was the car. Next up was the house. Sukh was haunted by the thought of some stranger living in Gurmit's home, so close to his own place, so he ordered Shane to buy it. Shane balked. "I was happy living in Kelowna," he says. "That was Sukh's way of bullying me." (Shane held his ground, and eventually Gurmit's house did go to a stranger.)

And then there was the boat. Around this time, Shane got a phone call from his sister, who was clearly upset. "Shane, what the fuck is going on?" she asked.

She wanted to know why Gurmit's forty-foot cigar-shaped racing boat, with three big engines on the back, had been left, without explanation, on her driveway. The hitch of the $150,000 boat spilled over onto the sidewalk, a bylaw infraction that had drawn a ticket from the city.

Shane called Sukh. "The boat's gotta be moved, bro," he said.

Sukh was indignant. "Don't fucking call me with this shit. Fucking figure it out."

Khun-Khun's dad moved the boat to a more convenient spot in front of Shane's sister's place, but it still straddled her front lawn and part of her driveway. "That's how it stayed for about a month and a half," Shane says. Once again, Sukh didn't apologize. "I don't think Sukh ever apologized for anything, ever."

Sukh may have been occupied with cleaning up the details of his brother's life, but he had much bigger things on his mind as well. The

Dhak group had heard of two brothers, nicknamed "the Cowboys," who were believed to have killed Gurmit. The Cowboys had a handful of close associates, including a Hells Angel and an early member of the Red Scorpions, in the Wolfpack orbit. "They wanted to kill Manny like you wouldn't believe," Shane says. "They were dangerous motherfuckers . . . These guys really had it out for Manny. Manny, Gurmit, Sukh, it didn't matter."

Sukh and the others knew there was no negotiating with the Cowboys—there was too much water under the bridge. And so, says Shane, "We were hunting."

One night less than a week after Gurmit's murder, Shane, Khun-Khun, and Manny met at Manny's house, where they spread photos of their enemies out on the kitchen counter. Manny flipped through them, wearing gloves. First on the United Nations' hit list were two Red Scorpions, who had moved with the Wolfpack against the UN as battle lines were drawn. One of the intended targets had a particularly tough reputation. "He was a dangerous dude." Shane knew the other intended victim by reputation as well. "Never talked with him. He was dangerous as fuck. He was a killer. Multiple hits. He also sold a lot of dope. He was an Independent Soldier . . . back in the day."

The two intended victims were fired upon on October 21, 2010, on Richmond Highway. Both survived—but the attempt was enough to further heighten tensions.

Shortly before his death, Gurmit appeared to have brokered peace between the Red Scorpions and the Dhak group in Surrey. Now, all of that was gone. The UN and the Wolfpack were both fully in hunt mode, and the stage was set for all-out war.

But first, there was a funeral to attend. Among Shane's crew, there was a protocol for member funerals. On the day of the event, they all went to the funeral home in the morning to wash the body from head to toe. After that, they had a break, and then they were the first ones back for the ceremony, where they stood at the front, by the casket. People would file up to them, shaking their hands and paying their respects.

By underworld standards, Gurmit's funeral was an epic event. He had been widely popular in life, and that was evident on the morning of Wednesday, October 27, 2010, at the Five Rivers Funeral Home in Delta. As Shane drove up with Sukh beside him and Manny in the back seat— alongside a large framed photo of Gurmit wearing a suit—there were law enforcement Tahoes on both sides of the road, lights flashing, along with minivans. As they got closer, there were also marked police vehicles and, circling overhead, a helicopter.

Across the road from the funeral home itself were command posts for the Delta and Vancouver police as well as the RCMP. Three dozen cops in anti-gang vests, holding AR-15 assault rifles, stood at attention. Occupants of every vehicle coming into the parking lot were photo- graphed and asked for identification. Guests included full-patch Hells Angels, even though they were supposedly on the other side in the tensions that had killed Gurmit. Dip Duhre was there too, keeping a low profile.

"The respect that the guys had for Gurm was tremendous," Shane says. "It was unbelievable. It was over-the-top, nuts."

The gangsters' wives and girlfriends arrived together, after meeting up at one of their houses. During the service, Sukh's partner sat with the wives and girlfriends who were comforting the new widow as she sobbed. Later, she told Shane she couldn't help but notice a grim pattern. Shane recalls, "At the previous funeral she'd seen me sitting with this guy, she said, and now we're burying him." She told Shane how painful it was to look at the men and wonder who would be next. "That really started to fuck her up. 'This is getting too much,' she said. 'When am I going to be one of these girls crying?'"

Shane told her the truth—that he didn't know.

Shane was a pallbearer, along with Sukh, who had clearly been changed by his brother's death. Shane was stunned to see him break down and sob. "I thought this man was stone cold to the fucking bone. I literally thought this man had no soul."

Gurmit's five-year-old twin daughters each carried the bear they had built with their dad on the final day of his life. They found some comfort in playing with them on the floor in front of his casket.

It was at Gurmit's funeral that many in his crew learned for the first time that his widow was expecting a baby. She had just a little bump, signalling the change underway. Gurmit had always said he wanted a son.

"It ended up a little boy," Shane says. "They named him Gurmit."

After the ceremony, police from the Combined Forces Special Enforcement Unit (CFSEU) covertly followed Jason McBride and several of his associates to Vancouver's Kensington Park. McBride was of particular interest to the anti-gang cops, as he had been close to Gurmit and was said to be a particularly enthusiastic killer. It wasn't a stretch to think he might have revenge on his mind.

Seven of them arrived in three vehicles.

They met on a baseball diamond, between home plate and first base.

When one of McBride's group saw police moving in, his expression shifted and he walked quickly towards the announcer's hut, hands still in his pockets. When officers checked that area, it took them just fifteen seconds to find a Ruger .40-calibre semi-automatic pistol in a box. It was wrapped in a Chinese-language newspaper. The gun was clean and dry. It was a restricted, fully functioning firearm loaded with eight rounds in a prohibited magazine. Its safety switch was off and it was half-cocked, ready to fire.

A tow truck was called to unlock a Jeep connected to McBride's group. A box of twenty rounds of .223-calibre rifle ammunition was found hidden far underneath the driver's seat. A rifle was tucked in a gap under the rear bench seat. As an officer pried the seat open, he heard a click, then saw a hidden compartment with two Colt AR-15 assault rifles and three magazines with twenty-seven, twenty-eight, and twenty-nine rounds of ammunition. The assault rifles had no manufacturer's mark or serial numbers. Each was capable of firing in fully automatic mode. Next to them were stolen licence plates with Velcro backing. On the rear seat were night-vision binoculars and a map book.

There was a second hidden compartment as well, in the middle of the Jeep's dashboard behind the display screen. Inside it were two bala-clavas, two pairs of gloves, and a GPS tracking kit in a hard plastic Pelican case with magnets.

When a BMW connected to McBride's group was searched, police found $20,000 in cash. There were also three identical photos of an enemy from the other side.

Funeral or no funeral, the hunt was still clearly on.

Several weeks after Gurmit's death, Sukh learned that a Hells Angels target would be attending a birthday party. It would be as good a place as any to kill him.

On the day of the attempted hit, a girl at the party texted someone what she thought was innocuous information that gave up the biker's location: a normally family-friendly restaurant on Oak Street in a nice neighbourhood in West End Vancouver. That tidbit almost got the biker killed—and it got the texter herself shot.

"The fucking girl that gave the information got her fucking leg blown off," Shane says. She was one of ten people injured that day by gunshots, including the biker.

Manny was part of the UN team who attempted the hit. It was an off-day for him: not only did he survive, but Manny wiped out on slippery grass while fleeing the scene, snapping the handle of his AK-47 as he fell.

But there would be other guns, and other chances to finish the job.

CHAPTER 9

THE NEW NORMAL

"Every day you have to put on the mask. It's just go, go, go.
It's a constant fucking battle."
—SHANE DANKOSKI

THE DAYS AND WEEKS after Gurmit's funeral were a crazy time. Sukh had started wearing Gurmit's white beads; it seemed natural to cling to anything for comfort.

"People were getting shot left and right and centre," Shane says.

He and his crew were now expected to sit in bushes and rental cars, stalking their enemies and pissing in bottles. A war zone stretched from Kelowna to Vancouver, and there was no room for pacifists in it. Business would have to wait. For the time being, the life wasn't about making money.

"Sukh knew this would cost him his life and it would cost us our lives," Shane says. "It was just fucked up."

In the midst of the chaos, though, time was made for mourning.

There was a little fence around Gurmit's gravesite, with "Dhak" on the gate. Marble benches provided a place to sit and reflect—and sometimes Gurmit's old friends would go there for a quiet sip from a sixty-ounce bottle of Crown Royal.

Everyone in Shane's crew seemed to appreciate that it was a special place. "It's a beautiful area," he says, explaining that it also became a common spot to hold bead ceremonies, which took place when associates were promoted to full membership in the United Nations.

It felt like a tribute for Shane to play "Steady Mobbin'" by Lil Wayne when he drove to Gurmit's resting place, to pay his respects. Shane would sometimes sing along, and one day he noticed Sukh glaring at him from the passenger seat as he sang the lyric about being the best at "never doin' shit."

"You don't be so disrespectful like that," Sukh snapped, as if the words were a direct attack.

Everything was personal now.

Shane, Manny, and Doug Wheeler liked to unwind at a Surrey strip club that was a popular spot for would-be tough guys who enjoyed strutting about in biker support gear. Even though Shane was still with his long-time partner, he got involved with the owner's girlfriend; the woman even tattooed his name over that of her boyfriend. "My girlfriend had no idea I was seeing other women and doing what I was doing. None," says Shane.

Shane's interactions at the club extended beyond those with the owner's girlfriend. His visits would often end in wild brawls with the poser tough guys. Glasses would be broken, pool cues would be thrown, and tables would be flipped over. "Nine times out of ten we would go fight with those guys."

Until Shane's group arrived, the room was controlled by characters with mobster-like names such as Ricky Rings ("He had rings on every finger") and Fat Jay, who wasn't in prime shape. Both Ricky Rings and Fat Jay were prospect bikers.

"The moment the real guys come, they no longer run the party," Shane says. "These guys know who the real guys are."

A man connected to the Hells Angels sat at a table in the back room, playing poker while sipping a glass of vodka and soda, when Shane's group walked in one night not long after Gurmit's murder. Shane didn't really like him to begin with and this was a particularly sensitive time. "[He] was a clown. A try hard." He was related to a member of the Independent Soldiers, in the Wolfpack orbit.

What Shane heard next was shocking.

"Sukh's a goof and so is Gurmit," the man at the table said.

That fact that Shane and his crew were still mourning made the comment all the more offensive.

"What the fuck did you say?" Shane asked.

Then he began to pound on the man at the table, knocking him out cold.

Shane helped drag him to the bathroom, where they resumed the beating, breaking a toilet bowl lid on him in the process.

"I fucking ripped his earrings out," Shane recalls.

When they were done, Shane zapped Sukh on his BlackBerry to tell him what had just happened.

"Sukh says he owes us 50K."

That was the penalty Sukh decided was appropriate for the words of disrespect. There was a meeting called for later that morning in the office of the strip club. There were ten men present, with equal representation from both sides. Some of the men from the other side were bikers.

"We're strapped up," Shane says, meaning his group was carrying guns.

The man who made the triggering comment about the Dhak brothers didn't look well.

"We can't even see his eyes. He's wearing a pair of sunglasses to hide his face."

The man in the sunglasses tried to explain himself, but Shane cut him off, saying, "Shut the fuck up."

He tried again.

"Shut the fuck up." This time it was Sukh issuing the order.

The man in the sunglasses tried yet again to talk, and Shane told him, yet again to "Shut the fuck up."

"This is my guy," Sukh chimed in. "If he's telling me something, it's the truth. I will never question it. It's as good as it gets."

The owner of the club tried to moderate, saying something about there being two sides to every story. Sukh was having no part of it.

"If [Shane] says that's what happened, that's what happened," Sukh said. "You guys owe me 50K for this. If you don't want to pay the 50K, then we'll fucking see what's up." He let this sink in for a few seconds and then continued. "You called me and my brother a goof. You're lucky I don't fucking do you. You've got twenty-four hours to pay me the paper."

The man in the sunglasses who made the offending comment that incited everything stood about six feet tall and weighed about 230 pounds, which made him considerably bigger than Sukh. That didn't matter in the slightest. "[Sukh] was the smallest guy in the room that day. He was the smallest guy in the room all of the time," says Shane. But Sukh was also clearly the most powerful and the most dangerous. He made his point and he made it quickly. "The whole meeting was twenty minutes."

The offending man paid the $50,000 on time, which didn't surprise Shane. "I can tell when a guy is real and when they're fake. I could tell by looking . . . that he's a bitch."

Nothing was fun after Gurmit's murder—not even hockey games.

In December 2010, two months after Gurmit Dhak's death, Shane and his club brothers were at a Vancouver Canucks hockey game, where they saw Chris Reddy and Larry Amero, and five or so other guys from the other side of the war, including an Independent Soldier.

The Independent Soldier "looks at us and he has a smile on his face." Then he ran his thumb across his throat. "Where's your bro?" he mouthed, clearly referring to Gurmit.

Sukh called over Manny, Khun-Khun, and Mantel. They had a straight-out, no-weapons brawl in which Reddy managed to get the better of Khun-Khun. They were about the same size, and Khun-Khun was a bit more jacked because of weightlifting, but Reddy got to him anyway.

"The fight was broken up by security and cops," Shane says. "I wasn't involved in that fight. When I came around the concourse, Khun-Khun and Chris Reddy were already on the ground, Chris on top."

Most hockey games weren't so eventful. Shane sometimes watched the Canucks from the Rogers Centre box that was originally owned by Gurmit and Tom Gisby. Everyone in the UN knew Gisby sometimes did business with their enemies in the Wolfpack Alliance, but the man somehow managed to stay on everyone's good side, more or less. Large, red-faced, and always hungry for approval—and more money—Gisby would feed information on bikers to the United Nations and on the United Nations to the bikers. "He was on the fence," Shane says.

Gisby's split loyalty was annoying, but Sukh still relied heavily on him for cocaine, especially after Gurmit's murder. Gisby was a big deal in his own right, although he didn't look the part. "Tom Gisby would wear a plain shirt, greenish grey, faded, frazzled around the neck, jeans, no jewellery, small-framed glasses on the top of his head," Shane says. "If you looked at Tom Gisby, you'd think he wasn't anything. Tom Gisby was a really big dog."

Skilfully playing all sides made Gisby rich. In fact, he'd reached that level of rich where he seemed to try to look poor, or at least didn't care. When Shane showed off a nine-carat ring he had bought, Gisby displayed his smaller diamond, proud that it was less eye-catching. "Less is more," he said.

Even so, Gisby clearly had more than most people. His heavy equipment shop in Fraser Heights in Surrey displayed an actual helicopter and a full-sized armoured tank, with mannequins of camouflaged soldiers climbing on netting. Preferred customers could drop off guns that had been used in killings and have them ground down to a powder. That powder would then be placed on an industrial pallet and dumped in the ocean.

Shane heard that Larry Amero had told Gisby to stop playing all sides, but Gisby ignored the Hells Angel. He just kept right on doing what he was doing.

The entire Dhak–Duhre group was eager to see the end of 2010. It had been a terrible year, filled with violence and death. Sukh even spent the last part of it in custody—held on breaches of release conditions from old charges that hadn't been resolved. "It was their [the cops'] way to keep him off the streets 'cause shit was getting crazy with all the shootings," Shane says.

Even with Sukh behind bars, New Year's Eve called for a celebration. Shane, Manny, and pretty well everyone else in their circle except Sukh were partying in Whistler that night. Sukh had demanded that Shane come down to visit him the next morning at 8 a.m. sharp, in the Surrey pretrial centre. The order didn't stop Shane from partying; it just prevented him from sleeping.

Shane's hands were purple from carrying around ecstasy tablets when he arrived the next morning to see Sukh. "I looked like a fucking mess."

"Happy New Year's Day, bro," Sukh said through the heavy security glass that separated them.

Then Sukh began writing messages out on paper in tiny letters and holding them up to the glass so that only Shane could see them. Once Shane got a look at a message, Sukh would pop it into his mouth and eat it. All that ink was giving Sukh's lips and tongue a bluish tint, a lot like what Shane had on his hands from the ecstasy pills.

Despite Sukh's paranoia, there wasn't anything too noteworthy in most of the eaten messages. They contained obvious orders like "Don't talk on phones," "Be careful," and "Don't trust anybody." But there was also "The cops know it's us."

Shane didn't need any reminders to be careful—he was already doing that—but the last message got under his skin. It was a hugely stressful time, and wondering if the cops were going to bang on his door any second, looking to connect him to any number of the hits that had taken place since Gurmit's death, didn't help. It was just stress piled on top of stress. And Shane coped the way he'd been coping for the last few years: by using drugs.

By early 2011, Shane was using $500 of heroin a day. Some weeks he would go from Kelowna to Surrey three times to drop off cash and get more drugs. And no one knew that one of the habits he was feeding was his own. "They don't know that I'm secretly hooked on heroin," he says.

There were constant talks with Sukh about moving drugs. Sometimes those talks would last an hour; other times Shane would stay in Surrey for a week. Sometimes he would get others to bring $100,000 or so to Surrey; other times he would just do it himself. He had an assortment of vehicles for transporting drugs and cash.

Drug problem or not, Shane was clearly a somebody now. He could walk into a strip club and leave with one of the dancers within ten minutes. He could also go for a meal and let business come to him. "As soon as you sit down for dinner, you've got a guy walking up to you. Saying things like, 'This guy, a guy owes me $50,000 and you collect it, you can have half.'"

Getting richer and richer was as addictive as the heroin for Shane. "You don't want to stop. You don't just stop. When is enough enough?"

Shane kept pushing ahead. "Every day you have to put on the mask. It's just go, go, go. It's a constant fucking battle."

That pressure, combined with Shane's increasing dependence on drugs, made for some interesting interactions. Early in 2011, for example, there was a stag for one of Manny's friends in Whistler. Several of the two dozen men present worked in real estate or selling cars, but there were also a half-dozen of Shane's crew, including Manny, Fitzy, Khun-Khun, and Doug Wheeler.

By the end of the night— after imbibing Percocets, ecstasy and alcohol—Shane and Manny were in rough shape. Somewhere along the line, the two had gotten the idea that one of the men in the party should die immediately. Nothing in particular had happened to make them feel this way; they'd just decided that he should die.

They let Khun-Khun in on their idea. He was religious and didn't use drugs or drink, but he did like a good murder plan. They got a carpet for wrapping the body and gasoline to help destroy it, before they threw it down a mountain. "Don't ask me why we were doing this," Shane says. "I don't know. There was no reason for it."

When they'd decided the time was right, they crept up the stairs to where the legit people were partying. The man they planned to kill was soon looking extremely uncomfortable. "He must have known we were looking at him funny."

Shane and Manny grabbed him in the kitchen and tried to pull him downstairs. "We have a full-blown fist fight at the fucking stag."

The intended victim fought hard, and the drugs had taken their toll on Shane's crew. In the end, the abduction plan failed, though no one seemed to care too much. "We laughed about it after for years."

Not all of Shane's mishaps were laughing matters, though.

A criminal with the unfortunate nickname of Matt the Rat was selling dope for Shane in Kelowna. He had been stuck with the label mostly because it rhymed and it was sort of fun to see how much it angered him. That said, there was a lingering suspicion that, just maybe, he would talk with the police. "He fucking hated it," Shane said of Matt the Rat's reaction to his moniker, adding that his anger wasn't something to be particularly feared. "He wasn't tough but he thought he was." Matt the Rat called Shane one night when Shane was driving from Surrey to Kelowna. He said he needed a couple of ounces of cocaine. "Bro," he said, "this guy won't stop bugging me."

There was an apartment in Kelowna where Shane knew he could access coke in the middle of the night. He paid the rent and utilities for a group of "safe, normal, beautiful girls" living there. In return, they let him keep a safe on the property.

Shane stopped by the apartment, picked up the coke, and brought it to Matt the Rat. When he arrived, he buzzed him on the intercom. There was no answer.

He buzzed Matt the Rat again. This time, a voice on the intercom asked, "Who is it?"

That seemed like a weird question. "What do you mean, who is it? Who else are you expecting?"

As Shane was getting buzzed in, he could see, in the reflection of the door, a man in a Seattle Seahawks jersey and a balaclava running towards him. "He's got a strap [gun] in his hand. My life is flashing before my eyes."

Shane pulled his knee to his chest and raised an elbow over his head in a defensive position. The man didn't shout anything as he charged forward. He just grabbed Shane and threw him down. Then, finally, the man shouted, "Police! Police!"

"I was kind of relieved that it was police," Shane says.

Suddenly, there were a dozen or so cops around him. "They're all over the place . . . When he got me on the ground he pulls out the four ounces of coke. In my other pocket, I've got ten grand. They took the dope. They took the ten grand."

In the ensuing search, they found a couple of hundred Percocets in Shane's new 2011 GMC—a metal-grey 2500 HD truck. The truck and his laptop were also seized.

Shane wondered about Matt the Rat's delay in answering the buzzer, and how odd it was that he'd asked who was there. "I thought Matt the Rat had ratted me out."

That particular interaction landed Shane in pretrial custody. For all his crimes, it was the first time he had been behind bars. He faced an assortment of firearms and trafficking charges, and his lawyer, Kelly Christiansen, beat them all.

"Kelly was really good at what she did," he says. "She beat lots of charges for me, from drug charges to traffic tickets and everything in between."

The arrest was a warning for Shane, who had let his guard down because of his addiction.

That luck couldn't last forever.

The "new normal" that was life after Gurmit's death got even more complicated when RCMP officer Chris Williams arrived in Kelowna to become the new head of the drug squad. The cop remembered Shane from back in the good old days in Surrey, when Shane was just sixteen and Williams had been chasing down Oddy Hansen's best friend—right through Shane's backyard. He wasted no time letting Shane know about his new status. "I'm the new sheriff in town," he told him, "and I'll be getting your ass."

"Fuck off, buddy," Shane replied.

Not long after that, there was a raid in which Shane's workers were arrested, but Shane wasn't present.

"I was hoping you'd be in the house when I kicked the doors in," Williams told him.

Despite the banter, Shane developed a real respect for Williams. "He was a really good cop. He turned out to be really fair."

Shane's reacquaintance with the police officer happened around the same time as Hells Angel Norm Cocks offered to sponsor Shane for membership into the outlaw biker club. That put Shane in the odd spot of being sponsored for membership in two sides of an underworld war. Both sides thought he was spying for them on the enemy. Both sides would kill him if they knew he wasn't totally on their side.

Cocks was formerly tied to the East End Hells Angels charter in Vancouver, but had moved to Kelowna when a clubhouse opened there in 2007. Cocks regularly bought cocaine from Shane, as the two men were friends. To get into the Hells Angels, you first had to be sponsored by someone who'd known you for at least five years, and Cocks looked like Shane's entry ticket. Cocks's name meant something in the club, and he had previously sponsored Randy Potts, the candidate who'd been soundly punched out by Oddy Hansen several years earlier.

Potts had gone on to get his full patch, later joining the club's "Big House Crew"—for members who were behind bars—after he pleaded guilty in 2010 to conspiracy to produce and traffic in methamphetamine, two counts of trafficking in cocaine, and unlawful possession of proceeds of crime, as a result of the undercover work of police agent Big Mike Plante.

As thrilled as Shane was with the news, he was concerned that he might have to undergo some sort of humiliating initiation ceremony to get into the biker gang.

"Bro, I'm not scrubbing toilets and washing bikes," he told Cocks.

"No. Never. You're basically trading your UN shit," Cocks said. "You've got to get on our side."

What Cocks meant was that Shane could make a largely seamless transition from the United Nations gang to full status inside the Hells Angels. The UN wouldn't like it, but that was life. He would have left their fold.

Shane was already a known entity in Hells Angels circles. "Four or five of them used to grab coke off of me," Shane says. "They all knew I was a money-maker. I was always at the clubhouse."

At least a half-dozen of his childhood friends and acquaintances had gone on to be Hells Angels and members of the Wolfpack Alliance, so it wouldn't be totally foreign turf. When Shane was around the bikers, there was always something fun and exciting about it. By contrast, there was something scary about Sukh. Nothing ever felt fun with Sukh, no matter how much money Shane made for him.

Any decision on Hells Angels membership needed the okay of Dave (Gyrator) Giles, the Kelowna charter president and a long-time outlaw biker. Gyrator had been a member in Montreal, Halifax, and Vancouver's East End before moving to Kelowna, and his contacts included Montreal Hells Angels president and convicted killer Maurice (Mom) Boucher.

In March 2011, Cocks prepped Shane for his meeting with Gyrator. Shane could expect to be asked why he wanted to join the club. His answer, Cocks said, had to be, "I want to be a fucking Hells Angel." That was what Norm had been told to say back when he got his patch, and it was now the thing Shane needed to say to get his.

Shane's next step was to talk with Sukh, who was edgy and paranoid at the best of times. But that conversation went surprisingly well. Sukh felt that Shane was doing it for him—acting as a spy for Sukh's group. "'We'll get so much information,'" Shane recalls him saying. "'We'll be able to kill these guys whenever we want.' That's really how this guy thought. That's not what I felt about it. A part of me really wanted to go that way and be a Hells Angel."

Shane met with Gyrator in an upstairs room of the Kelowna clubhouse. They sat at the round table, where Shane was asked why he wanted to join the club. "I want to be a fucking Hells Angel," Shane replied.

"He kind of smirked at me and was like, 'I like it, I like it.'"

"We've gotten to know you well," Gyrator continued. "You're always respectful when you're here." He then told Shane that "the patch doesn't make the man. The man makes the patch."

He asked Shane if he had a bike and told him it had to be a Harley-Davidson.

And with that, the rules changed for Shane. "You can come around here without Norm," Gryrator said. "You're welcome any time."

Shane let Gyrator know that he had heard the Angels could have a demeaning apprenticeship. "I don't want to give up what I have to scrub toilets and wash bikes."

Gyrator looked a little offended. "Everyone has to go through the program," he said. "No one gets a pass." He did, however, address Shane's concerns. "We don't make our guys scrub toilets," he told him, adding that Shane also wouldn't have to start at the bottom all over again. "Within six months I would get my bottom rocker and I would be a full patch within a year.

"Norm was super fucking happy. 'We're going to be brothers one day. We're going to be brothers,' Norm would always say."

Shane recalls being happy at this point in his life too. Despite the ongoing tensions in the aftermath of Gurmit's death, and his increasing drug use and often erratic behaviour, he was comfortable when he was with the Hells Angels. "I was hanging around with these bikers on a daily basis," he says. And no matter what Sukh thought, Shane didn't feel like a spy. Instead, he felt at ease, relaxed. "Wow," he remembers thinking, "this is really something that I want to fucking do."

The feeling didn't last long.

Just a few months later, in June 2011, Norm Cocks asked Shane to drive him to a bar in Kelowna, where Cocks had left his Jeep Wrangler YJ. As they drove, Shane noticed undercover cops following them. He drove to a baseball field, where Norm suggested they "get out and go have a talk."

"You don't bring your phone when you're going for a talk, and you don't talk about serious shit in a vehicle in case it's wired," Shane explains.

At the field, Norm filled Shane in on a recent incident involving a man named Dain Phillips—a fifty-one-year-old married father of three and a former semi-pro hockey player. On June 12, 2011, Phillips had died on a road outside Kelowna while attempting to peacefully resolve a dispute connected to his son and Hells Angels. The tensions began with harsh words on Facebook and quickly escalated to real-life insults and punches. Phillips and Cocks hadn't even known each other until the day in question, when Cocks used a ball-peen hammer to strike Phillips in the head while fellow Hells Angel Robert Thomas swung a baseball bat. At the end of the beating, Phillips lay dead.

The plan of Cocks sponsoring Shane into the Hells Angels was soon in the ditch. "Shit was like real hot around there for months," Shane says.

Cocks eventually pleaded guilty to manslaughter and was sentenced to fifteen years in custody. As Shane's sponsor went on ice, the push for Shane to join the Hells Angels fizzled.

CHAPTER 10

REAL HECTIC, REAL QUICK

"He just laid out the mother of my fucking kids.
He really changed the dynamic of things."
—SHANE DANKOSKI

IN THE SPRING OF 2011, as the Dhak–Duhre group continued to mourn Gurmit and as Shane's dreams of becoming a Hells Angel stalled, Shane had his eye on buying a black Dodge Ram Laramie edition truck, which had been used by a gangster who often made trips from the west coast across the prairies into Winnipeg. It was a special vehicle, with televisions mounted on the headrest and on the roof headliner. The ceiling TV was useful for the vehicle's owner. A gangster who had lost his licence, he could now lie back with his seat fully reclined and watch shows while he was chauffeured about.

There was also a hidden compartment for moving guns and drugs.

The gangster traded it for six ounces of cocaine, which cost Shane

$700 an ounce. It sold for $1,700 an ounce on the street, meaning its street value was $10,200. Making it an even better deal was the fact that Shane had buffed the cocaine down, so that the actual cocaine in the product was worth just $2,100. "That's a good deal for that truck."

The black Dodge Ram also caught Sukh's eye—and he got it for even cheaper.

"He just took it from me," Shane says. "He stole it from me."

There was still the small problem of mileage to sort out: the Dodge had 600,000 kilometres on it. Sukh didn't let that stop him. He got a crackhead to go to Enterprise and rent a similar truck with just 4,000 kilometres on the meter. The engines were swapped, and the crackhead returned the leased truck to Enterprise, now sporting a 600,000-kilometre engine.

Shane and Sukh used the truck to attend another Canucks playoff game in the spring of 2011. Attending in different vehicles were Manny, Khun-Khun, and Tucker. Also riding in the truck with Shane and Sukh was Sukh's girlfriend, the mother of his two boys. The others weren't allowed to bring partners, but Sukh could. "We didn't bring our girls with us ever, but Sukh could always have her."

Shane had known her even longer than Sukh. Their acquaintance went back to when they were in grade four, a couple of years before Shane quit school altogether.

The group drank particularly hard that evening, and Shane decided he should drive Sukh's truck after the game. If there was a DUI charge, Shane could absorb it. But Sukh insisted on driving. "When he got something in his mind, there's no changing his mind. Especially when he's drunk," Shane says. "On this night Sukh wanted to drive. He was piss drunk out of his mind."

Sukh was strict about his men drinking and driving, as it would be a major inconvenience if one of them lost his licence. But that rule didn't apply to Sukh himself.

"I'll drive. I'll take the DUI," Shane said.

"No, I'm fucking driving," Sukh replied, kicking Shane to the back seat, moving his girlfriend to the front, and cranking up the music so loud that no one could even hear themselves speak.

Sukh hit the gas hard. They passed other vehicles that were going a hundred kilometres an hour as if they weren't moving at all. Soon enough, Sukh and his girlfriend started to argue. The argument got worse, and then exploded.

"He's hammer-punching her," Shane recalls.

Sukh's left hand stayed at the twelve o'clock position on the steering wheel while he continued to punch her with his right. They reached speeds of 180 kilometres an hour as the punches continued and the truck swerved.

"Shane! Stop him!" she screamed. "How can you let him do this? I've known you for my whole life."

In an effort to intervene, Shane reached his hand between them from the back seat. It just made things worse. Sukh was livid that Shane had dared to touch him. "If you ever fucking do that again, I'll bury you in two seconds!" he said.

Then he continued to beat her. Sukh slammed on the brakes while grabbing her by the hair. He slammed her head into the dashboard and then resumed punching her.

"Shane, help me! Help me!" she screamed, as Sukh kept pounding.

Sukh beat her all the way to Surrey, and when they got out, he dented his truck's right fender with her face. "Her nose explodes with blood everywhere," Shane says.

The weather was nice that night, and people were out on the street. That meant several neighbours watched Sukh drag her out of the truck by the hair. He was still beating her as parents from neighbouring homes shooed their children into their houses.

"Not a person called the police."

For the next few days, Shane's phone wouldn't stop buzzing with messages from Sukh, but Shane declined to answer. "I kind of blew him off for a couple days. He's blowing me up, zapping me on the Berry."

On day three, Shane finally returned a zap.

"Come grab me, bro," Sukh messaged.

Shane said he'd rather just go hang out at Sukh's place.

"No, bro. You're not allowed here," Sukh replied, then refered to his girlfriend. "Bro, you can't come. She's really mad at you."

"Mad at me?"

"You should have stopped me."

"Come on, bro."

"She is right, bro," Sukh said. "You should have stopped me. This wouldn't have happened if you would have stopped me. It isn't right."

Shane may have been angry with Sukh—for beating his girlfriend and for ordering him to give up the black Dodge Ram truck—but there was still work to be done. Revenge for Gurmit's murder was never very far from the minds of UN members, and things amped up when the crew learned that several Wolfpack members planned to attend game two of the National Hockey League finals between the Vancouver Canucks and the Boston Bruins on June 4, 2011.

After the game, which the Canucks lost 3–2 in overtime, Shane and some of his fellow UN gangsters placed themselves outside the Rogers Arena, ready to kill Wolfpack members as they filed out. "We're all wearing Canuck jerseys. We're all wearing Canuck caps. We're all there with PGPs, with guns."

Ultimately, the plan proved unworkable. The crowd was too big and there were too many exits to carry out the hits.

The Canucks made it to game seven that year, and Shane and Manny paid $15,000 for a pair of seats that put them three rows up behind the Canucks' bench. The night was an event for the Dhak–Duhre gang, with all of Sukh's crew in attendance. For once, Sukh was in what passed for a good mood, and he allowed his guys to bring their girlfriends.

"It's usually just us guys," Shane says. "It was fun. The game was good. There were no issues. It was great. Everybody was having a good time."

Sukh made a point of trying to get along with the wives and girl-friends of his crew, including Shane's partner. "Treated her nice. Bought her things. Polite to her. Gave her money, randomly. A $2,500 Gucci bag, randomly."

After the game, which was won by the Bruins, they all went to a nearby strip club. Despite the loss, everyone seemed in a good enough mood.

The wives and girlfriends didn't have much of a say in the choice of naked female entertainment; Sukh's courtliness only went so far. "The girlfriends always came to the strip clubs," Shane says. "We didn't plan on going to the strip club. We decided on that fifteen minutes before we got there. If they wanted to or not, they weren't saying it. And if they did, it wasn't taken into account."

There were plenty of Hells Angels at the strip club that night, although hit man Jay McBride didn't let the bikers cramp his style. A server with a shot tray walked by and Jay slapped her on the ass. "It was very weird that he did that," Shane says.

The server was outraged. "Did you just touch my fucking ass?" Shane recalls her asking. "She's making this big scene."

In seconds, bouncers were crowding around. Some bikers came over too. The mood had gone from jovial and relaxed to ripe for trouble, and the server wasn't ready to let things cool down. "That girl wouldn't shut the fuck up," Shane says.

Jason McBride's girlfriend came out of the bathroom and walked up to him. The fact that he was a stone-cold hit man didn't do him any good. "She fucking punched Jay in the face," Shane says.

And that was that. Jay erupted and started throwing drinks. A table was flipped over.

"It's really on. Jay's girlfriend jumps on that stripper. Everybody's in."

Jay was indignant, even though he'd started the mess. "You wanna fuck around?" Jay asked.

The lights came on and the music went off as people fled for the doors. McBride was out of control. "He's fucking freaking. He's clocking innocent people. This guy is smashing anybody and everybody."

Shane's old family friend, full-patch Hells Angel Bob Green, got involved too. "This is a guy who used to hold me when I was a baby. Manny clocks him. The bikers are getting beaten up in their own bar."

For about four minutes, it was pure chaos.

Shane noticed that Jay was heading outside, presumably to get a gun from a secret compartment of his vehicle. He followed him to make sure he didn't. *This is not going to happen*, he remembers thinking.

Instead, on the way out, Jay walked up to Shane's longtime girl-friend and knocked her out cold. His reasoning wasn't at all clear, but the punch was for real. "He just laid out the mother of my fucking kid. He really changed the dynamic of things."

Jay was on a rampage as he crossed the parking lot, smashing vehi-cle windows.

"He must have punched out nine car windows" before he acciden-tally slashed his hand on the shattered window of a van, says Shane. "This guy is now squirting blood. People are running for their lives like somebody let a grenade go."

Then the police showed up and began making arrests. Somehow, none of Sukh's guys ended up leaving in handcuffs, though McBride was rushed into surgery and came out of the operating room with a cast the length of his arm.

Shane was understandably upset. His girlfriend had been punched in the face for no apparent reason by a feared killer from his own crew. Sukh tried to downplay things, not wanting a confrontation with McBride. "This guy would have never done that to your girl if he knew that she was your girl," Sukh said. "This guy was blackout drunk. That's got to count for something."

In the aftermath of the fight, McBride seemed to be denying things. "What are you talking about?" he asked. "I hit Buddy's girl?"

He played the bro theme hard as he spoke to Shane. "You know, it's nothing but love," McBride told him. "We're a crew. We're brothers."

Shane's girlfriend certainly wasn't feeling the love. She had a black eye and her face was puffed out from McBride's punch. She wanted to know what Shane was going to do about it.

Normally, Shane would have shot someone for doing such a thing, but this wasn't even close to normal. "Jason McBride, that's a different animal. What do I do? I felt terrible. This is that one time there's nothing I can do about it. This was Gurmit Dhak's right-hand man."

And that was that. The whole incident was basically just dismissed, as if it never happened and the mother of Shane's child didn't really have a black eye from a punch from a hit man.

One thing was for sure, though: McBride's limp apology didn't make things better. Shane's girlfriend was nervous about hanging out with Shane when he was with the guys. If there was an event, she would ask, "'Is Jay going to be there?' She never wanted to be around him after that." And it made Shane feel different too. "I lost respect for him."

And yet he never thought of quitting the gangster life over the punch to his girlfriend's face. "Didn't even cross my mind."

It was a strange and unsettled time in the gangster world. Everyone was on edge, jockeying for position and advantage in this war that was growing ever hotter. No one, it seemed, could be trusted.

On June 23, 2011, a familiar face drifted back into Shane's life. Chris Reddy of the Independent Soldiers had been on the UN's radar since he'd brawled with Khun-Khun at a Canucks game the previous December. Despite the altercation, Reddy was a welcome presence at a dinner with Sukh and Shane one night. He was feeling cheated by his side and seemed ready to turn on his old group. Reddy wasn't a big-time gangster, but he knew useful things, including the addresses of some of the United Nations' enemies, and he was willing to sell that information. Because of the opportunities Reddy presented, Shane's side was prepared to let bygones be bygones—or at least pretend to.

Everyone played along as Reddy appeared to enjoy himself, thinking he was both getting revenge and getting paid. "He's thinking he's the man. We all know—but [Reddy] doesn't know—that he's literally going to be dead tomorrow," Shane says, explaining that although Reddy had the potential to prove useful, no one really liked him and he wasn't going to be tolerated for too long.

At 3:30 p.m. on June 24, 2011—the day after his dinner with Sukh and Shane—Chris Reddy was shot to death in Surrey. At the time, he had been facing charges for possession of a loaded firearm.

Khun-Khun watched the news report about Reddy's death with a knowing smile. "Any time we would do something, we'd always put on the news," Shane says.

That evening, Shane was pulled over by Chris Williams. The gang cop never missed an opportunity to warn him it was high time to get out of the gang life. Oddly, he seemed to care for Shane, in a harsh, tough-uncle way.

"You guys got nothing else to do?" Shane asked.

"Fuck, I don't know how you guys are going to win this war," the cop replied.

"Buddy, why are you so bitter? Why are you so mad?" Then Shane went on the offensive. "I've got more change in my cupholder than you have in your bank account."

The cop was about to leave when Shane added, "Hey, did you hear?"

The cop stopped to listen.

"Right before Chris died, he changed his name," Shane added, referring to Chris Reddy.

"What?"

"He changed his name to Chris-Wasn't-Ready."

That struck a nerve. "You think that's funny?" the cop replied. "He had a family, Shane."

"Yeah, so did Gurm."

"One day you're going to turn around and there's going to be a gun on you," the cop said. "You won't even get a chance to think of all the bad shit you've done to people. You'll get lit up."

Reddy's twenty-four-year-old friend Christopher James Krake also went to Sukh to sell information. Krake had a criminal history that included dealing drugs. He also had at least two aliases, as well as outstanding charges of dangerous operation of a vehicle and flight from a police officer.

Krake gave up valuable intel on his close friends in return for the promise of being paid $25,000, but Sukh never paid. He figured he didn't have to, because Krake had already given up the information.

Once Krake realized he had been stiffed, he went back to his crew to tell them that Dhak's crew wanted information and was willing to pay. That only made things worse. He was questioned on why it had taken so long to disclose this to his friends, who now were starting to put things together.

Krake's body was found on July 6, 2011, on a nature trail near Ranch Park Elementary School in Coquitlam. He had been shot to death.

Shane sometimes thought of Krake and of Reddy—how he and Sukh had dined with Reddy the night before his murder, and how Reddy had seemed like he was on top of the world.

"That's probably happened to me more times than I can count," Shane says. "How many times was I an outsider?"

As tensions between the Wolfpack and the UN continued to escalate, the UN gang planned a show of force in Kelowna. Shane, Fitzy, and Doug Wheeler all lived there now, and on the Canada Day long weekend there were even more guys from their side in town. Sukh, Dip Duhre, Thomas Mantel, and Tucker all drove up for a visit.

They met at a pub in a hotel, where there were fifteen or so of them at a table—"the whole crew." There were cries of "Oh, Rooster" when Shane arrived. The nickname was courtesy of his distinctive hair, which stuck up dramatically at the crown. "They all started busting my balls," the way brothers do. Then it was on to the Grand Hotel and Casino, where Sukh and Dip had rooms for the weekend.

Unbeknownst to any of the UN crew, Larry Amero of the Hells Angels also had a room at the Grand that weekend.

Shane's group started their partying on Friday night at a downtown bar. After a while, they decided to head to another drinking spot, just across a gravel parking lot. Shane and Stevie (Tucker) Leone walked ahead, while Sukh lagged behind to relieve himself against a wall.

Just then, four Hells Angels wearing club vests came into the parking lot from around the corner.

"Hey, you fucking little Hindu," one of them said. "You pissing on my truck?"

The murder of his brother had left Sukh at an unhappy phase in his life. Being called a "fucking little Hindu" certainly didn't improve his mood.

"What the fuck did you say to me?" Sukh replied.

"You heard me, you little Hindu."

Perhaps the bikers were emboldened because they were in a group and wearing their colours, and Sukh was such a small man and appeared to be alone. But Sukh whistled and called out for the others in his own group, who rushed back.

One of Shane's crew whipped off his belt. In a flash, it was around the neck of a biker as he was dragged around the parking lot. The incident was particularly awkward for Shane, who had biker friends in Kelowna. "I'm trying to break it up."

It was a rough night for the bikers. "They got fucking smashed right up."

111

With that bit of business handled, Sukh's group made their way to another bar. They weren't there long when the police gang squad showed up. The guys were about to leave on their own when the cops made it official: "You guys have to leave," one of them said.

Dip stood up to say something to one cop and suddenly there was a scuffle, with a cop headlocking Dip and throwing him to the floor.

"It got real hectic, real quick," Shane says.

While Dip was arrested for assault on a police officer and taken to jail, Shane left the bar with Sukh, who was wearing his gangster best, with a $150,000 white-gold-and-ruby necklace and a $100,000 Rolex. He was an inviting target, for rival gangsters and common thieves alike. "Somebody's always got to be with him," Shane says.

Sukh had to be in his hotel room early. He was under an 11 p.m. curfew as part of his parole conditions after being charged with running an ecstasy ring. Not long after Sukh got to the hotel on Friday, there was a knock on his door. It was the RCMP gang squad, and one of its members informed Sukh that he had to leave immediately because he was a risk to the public.

So Sukh was kicked out of the hotel and subsequently placed under arrest for a parole violation. Along the way, police confiscated his necklace and Rolex.

"It was a deliberate, dirty move to get him out of there. It was after his curfew. They fucked him," Shane says. "He was fucking livid. This cop comes walking out and he's got Sukh's chain in his hand. [Sukh] was wearing Gurmit's chain that night, which was white gold, with diamonds on every link and rubies on every second link. A 150K chain. Plus his watch, beads, and earrings. We're talking 350K here."

The cop ended up giving the jewellery to Shane for safekeeping.

The next day, Shane picked up Dip from the police station, where he had been held on charges of assault and driving under suspension. Sukh stayed in custody a little longer, getting freed by a judge on the Tuesday morning.

Sukh was snippy when he was released and Shane gave him back the jewellery. "I thought he would have been happy with me, because had the cops taken it, I'm not sure he would have ever seen it again," Shane says. "Instead of being grateful and thankful, it was more of a you're-lucky-you-had-my-jewellery-or-else sort of thing."

So much for the show of force.

CHAPTER 11

KILL SITE

"They're staring at me and I'm staring back."
—SHANE DANKOSKI

THOUGHTS OF REVENGE still consumed Sukh Dhak. He ached to do something big—really big—to avenge his big brother's murder. Shane, meanwhile, was battling his own demons. He now needed a gram of heroin first thing in the morning—at a cost of $120—just to get the edge off so he could face the day.

On August 11, 2011, Shane got up, got some heroin into his system, and got ready for work. The day started with a visit, with Manny, to the sports memorabilia man he had dealt with years before. Now they were discussing unpaid debts. "He was starting to pull his bullshit on us," Shane says, noting that it didn't help that the man had recently paid cash for a new Infiniti sedan. "This guy started getting so fucking ballsy."

There were more pressing things to consider as well. The deeper they dug, the more it seemed that Larry Amero of the Hells Angels was behind the hit on Gurmit. An Independent Soldier seemed to have played a role too. Sukh's crew had drafted a list of intended targets, dropping photos into an online Photobucket so that would-be killers could identify them.

"Manny did all that from our laptop that was like a burner laptop. It was bought and used for bad, bad shit . . . and all of our GPS trackers were watched on that. Manny posted the pictures to Photobucket. We would troll [the Postmedia journalist] Kim Bolan's gangster blogs, search bad shit . . . all that."

By mid-August, Sukh had pulled together a hit team for the job. Jason McBride was an obvious choice. McBride was hard-core—a legit, certified gangster. "I can't think of anyone you could be more scared of, honestly. If he wants you dead, you're dead, simple."

McBride's associate Michael Jones was "quiet, really quiet." It seemed that Jones would talk only with McBride. They were a team within a team. "He was probably the guy in the crew that I least knew," Shane says.

McBride and Shane had never really warmed to each other. "I never really cared for him, to be honest . . . He wasn't even someone I liked being around. Granted, Sukh put the team together and we didn't have a say, but still. He had beads too."

Khun-Khun was also part of the team. He had plenty of ideas, lots of energy, and seemed indestructible. He had been on thirty or forty hunting expeditions looking for Amero, mostly in Vancouver and Coquitlam, scoping out nightclubs, bars, and restaurants, and gathering vehicle descriptions and licence plate numbers that might help out.

On Saturday, August 13, Shane had planned a night out in bars in nearby Penticton. He was with his cousin Sheldon and James (Fitzy) Lyle Fitzgerald, in Fitzy's new BMW 750Li full-size sedan. It was a beautiful night, just right for cruising in luxury and hanging out.

At least until Shane's phone buzzed with the message from Sukh.

"Bro, you need to get back to K."

That was that. The BMW was turned around and they headed back Kelowna. The bar-hopping would have to wait.

Sukh had gotten word that "the biker" and "JB"—meaning Larry Amero and Jonathan Bacon—were both in Kelowna. If true, it was showtime.

Time to load up the guns and pull together the team. Time to act out the revenge plan that had been fermenting since Gurmit's death.

Sukh's intel was right. Jonathan Bacon of the Red Scorpions, Larry Amero of the Hells Angels, and James (Looney) Riach of the Independent Soldiers had arrived in Kelowna the night before. With them were Leah Hadden-Watts, the niece of the Haney Hells Angel president, and a friend, Lyndsey Black. Amero had a bright-orange boat called *Steroids & Silicone* docked in the lagoon nearby.

When Shane got back to Kelowna on Saturday night, he switched to his silver Escalade, bringing Sheldon along for the ride. Shane went out on the town to look for his prey.

He knew that Amero was driving his sleek white Porsche Cayenne SUV.

Shane parked his Escalade near the strip club. It wasn't long before he saw Larry Amero leaving the club with Bacon and Riach. Amero looked to his left and then to his right on his way out. Amero and Shane locked eyes for a few seconds. Larry tilted his head as he looked at Shane, as if to ask, *Where do I know this fucking guy from?*

When Shane saw Larry whisper something to Jon, he jumped in his truck and left.

An hour later, he pulled up to the pumps at a Chevron gas station. Sheldon was pumping the gas, with a fifty-dollar bill to cover it, when "all of a sudden out of the blue I see a white Porsche truck coming out of the drive-through," Shane recalls.

Amero was driving and Jon Bacon was in the front passenger seat, focused on his phone. Looney Riach sat in the back. The hoods of the Escalade and the Porsche faced each other, up close.

"Jon turns around and he sees my Escalade. He looks at me and he makes eye contact. He looked right in my eyes. He let me know, *I can see you, motherfucker.*" For his part, Amero looked confused. "I don't think at the time he really put it together," Shane says. "We locked eyes for probably four seconds."

Then Bacon flipped away a cigarette and said something to Amero. "He's staring at me and I'm staring at him."

Amero backed up the Porsche and flashed his high beams three times, as if to say, *Fuck you!* "Then he fucking peels out and he flies out of the gas station."

Shane texted Manny and Sukh to tell them what he had just seen.

"Follow them," Sukh texted back.

Shane wasn't about to overtake Amero's twin-turbo Porsche with his SUV, comfy as it was. He fretted that they had blown their chance of surprising Bacon and his crew. "There goes that. They fucking seen us."

Undeterred, Sukh mustered reinforcements. There would soon be three more vehicles for Shane's side. Tucker was coming into town with Thomas Mantel in an F150 truck with a hidden compartment. Jason McBride and Jones were in a green Explorer. And Khun-Khun and Manny arrived in a rental Jeep Grand Cherokee.

After ten months of mourning, after all the waiting and plotting, it was finally time for blood on the pavement. "We're going to get those guys," Sukh said.

Their first goal was to find out where their enemies were staying.

Shane drove up to the Hells Angels clubhouse on Ellis Street, where Tommy the Prospect was outside. Shane glanced around but saw no trace of Amero's Porsche.

"Are you coming to the party later?" Tommy asked. "Do you know Larry?"

Eureka!

Tommy pulled his arms up to do a muscle pose, and added, "Big Larry. Big, Big Larry. White Rock chapter. Yeah, Larry is up from Vancouver. They're staying at the Grand," Tommy continued, referring to the Delta Grand hotel, half a block from City Hall. "They've got this king suite. We're going over to the Grand. We're going to party it up."

Shane contacted Sukh on his BlackBerry and told him the latest news, straight from the mouth of Tommy the Prospect.

"You've got to be kidding," Sukh said.

"Nope," Shane said.

"Fuck me," Sukh replied.

The team went to check it out—to confirm Tommy's information with their own eyes. They parked away from the Grand, and then walked the grounds of the adjoining casino. It was hard to miss Amero's orange boat, in a slip at the casino dock.

No one was on board, so McBride spit on the boat.

They would deal with its owner later.

There was a sighting of Amero and his group later on Saturday night, at the Gotcha nightclub in Kelowna.

Then Shane's group moved on to the Delta Grand, to get the lay of the land. One of them went right into the hotel and up to Amero's floor. There were eight Hells Angels or prospects in the hotel, along with Looney Riach and Jon Bacon, amping up the danger if the lone member of Shane's group was spotted wandering the hallways alone.

The United Nations crew, including Khun-Khun, McBride, Manny, and Shane, met on the sidewalk across the street from the Delta Grand at about two o'clock on Sunday morning. Most were dressed for murder. McBride and Khun-Khun were wearing their own beads.

McBride made it clear that what was about to happen should never be discussed—but it would still be hours before anything did happen.

Bacon, Amero, Riach, and a female companion had brunch that Sunday. They left their bags with the concierge and went for a cruise on *Steroids & Silicone*, after which they loaded it onto a trailer. Then it was back to the Delta Grand courtyard, where they started boarding Amero's Porsche at 2:37 p.m. Amero settled in behind the wheel, with Bacon beside him. Riach, Black, and Hadden-Watts sat in the back.

The setting couldn't have been more public: the entranceway to a popular resort on a sunny, pleasant afternoon, half a block from City Hall and the Kelowna RCMP detachment. Residents sat on patios nearby. Mothers walked with their children. Some of the Sunday strollers had dogs. Taxis picked up guests as hotel employees loaded luggage into vehicles.

The white Porsche was about to pull away on the circular driveway when the green Ford Explorer pulled up just a little in front of it.

A barrage of AK-47 machine-gun fire from the Explorer tore into the Porsche.

Manny and Jason McBride ran towards the Porsche. McBride fired a semi-automatic rifle as Hairan squeezed out shots from a Glock nine-millimetre handgun. A family was caught in the middle of the chaos. "They literally had shots above their heads," Shane says. "And another man was hiding behind his car."

Amero hit the gas in an attempt to flee. Then Jones, who was driving the Explorer, smashed into the Porsche, pushing it onto grass. It stopped, and Jonathan Bacon rolled out the front door.

Manny was running away as McBride stood over Bacon and fired five more shots, point-blank.

Some forty-five bullets were fired before the shooting stopped, all from the United Nations side. Thirty-four of them tore into the Porsche. One shattered the front window of an art gallery on the other side of the street. And two bullets flew through the outer hotel wall and into a salon inside.

In the aftermath, it was clear that Jonathan Bacon was dead.

Amero convulsed in the front seat of his Porsche, covered in blood.

Looney Riach had rolled out of the car and was nowhere in sight. He had escaped a murder bid yet again.

Hadden-Watts caught a bullet in the back of her neck, which shattered her vertebrae and severed her spinal column. She would never walk again. Black was more fortunate. She took bullets to both of her upper legs, but with therapy she would eventually regain the use of them.

Sukh Dhak was at his home in Surrey when he got word of the shooting. He immediately sent a message to his crew: "Congratulations, LOL, go have a drink."

The plan was to drive away slowly from the kill site and blend into traffic, not outrun it. But as Shane did his best to put the Delta Grand in their rear-view mirror, a police car pulled in behind his Escalade, which had three masks and a Glock .45 pistol on the centre console. Then, suddenly, the officer did a U-turn and drove away. "I literally almost got pulled over leaving a murder—not just any murder, the biggest murder," Shane says.

The other getaway car was the green Explorer hatchback, with Jones, Manny, Khun-Khun, and McBride inside. It was just as well that police didn't attempt to pull it over as it left the murder scene. McBride was inside, in the back, lying on his stomach with a rifle trained on the streets, ready to kill anyone who approached.

Shane drove down Water Street, heading to a mall, figuring it would be as good a place as any to blend in. Cops, fire trucks, and ambulances were everywhere, and helicopters circled overhead. "We couldn't even get to the mall," Shane says. "It was nuts . . . It was just pure chaos."

Shane's cellphone buzzed—a call from an unknown number. Usually, Shane didn't answer unknown numbers, but this time, for some reason, he did.

"Buddy, Shane, what are you doing?"

It was Chris Williams.

"What happened?" the RCMP officer asked.

"With what?" Shane replied.

"You know what. You know exactly what I'm talking about, Shane. Bad, bad mistake. You're going down for this buddy. You're done. You're going down for this."

After they hung up, Shane's mind was spinning. "I was thinking, *Oh my fucking God.* Now I'm thinking about all the mistakes we made, which were a lot."

Eventually, Shane ended up at a food court in a nearby mall. "There were sirens for like two hours straight. You could hear the helicopters hovering overhead."

Shane was on the road with Doug Wheeler the day after the shooting when a white Range Rover pulled up beside them. At the steering wheel was Matt the Rat, with Looney Riach beside him in the front passenger seat. They seemed oblivious to Shane, in his brand new black Cadillac CTS.

Shane was no friend of Matt the Rat, although they had done some business together. "He was such a dick rider. He played both sides. He had no loyalty to anyone."

Doug messaged Sukh to say, "I'm sitting beside Looney right now."

Sukh's text back was blunt: "Kill him."

Shane followed the Range Rover onto the Coquihalla Highway.

Sukh told Shane that he was also sending hitters onto the Coquihalla as backup to make sure Looney was shot. *As if last night wasn't big enough,* Shane recalls thinking.

That fizzled out, though, as Sukh's hit team never managed to cross paths with the Range Rover.

Still, there were some unsettling things to sort out. Matt the Rat was supposed to be on Shane's side, so what was he doing in the Range Rover with Looney? If there was an explanation, they should have been aware of it. "Why hadn't he told us anything?" Shane asked himself.

Later that same day, Shane left Kelowna with his girlfriend and their son Jayden. He hadn't slept because of the stress. They drove the Escalade to the Langley Zoo, with Shane still dressed in the white Armani three-quarter-length capri pants and black V-neck T-shirt from the previous day. He also carried the $1,500 Louis Vuitton man purse Sukh had bought each member of his crew for Christmas.

Shane thought the zoo would be distracting, but it seemed everyone there was talking about the Kelowna casino shooting, which dominated the news.

Shane struggled to act normal. They had a family photo taken. "The stress I was under in this picture, I can't even put it into words. I was trying to hold it together."

So was everyone else, with varying degrees of success. In the immediate aftermath of the murder, Jones had driven the green Ford Explorer to an abandoned residence, followed by McBride and Manny in the Jeep. Weapons used in the attack were hidden in nearby bushes, given that Manny and the others didn't want to drive all the way back to Vancouver with the hot guns stashed in the car. They torched the Explorer on a remote private dirt road between Lake Country and Vernon and then drove back to the Lower Mainland together in the Jeep.

The Explorer was found a couple of hours after the murder, burning. It started a small forest fire. Thanks to a BC licence plate lying on the ground nearby, police were able to trace the burned Explorer to Shane, who had recently hired an honest mechanic to do some work on it. In a stroke of good luck for the police, the Explorer had broken down the day before the shooting, and there were repair records to aid in their trace. "[The mechanic] wrote on the bill after it was repaired—what was fixed, the price, the make, the model, and the plate number, with my fucking name on it," Shane says. "So when they raided my house for evidence, they found that fucking repair bill of the suspect murder vehicles . . . in my fucking house. Imagine."

Shane wasn't mad at the mechanic, despite the headache his honesty had caused. "Well, he was just doing his job. He didn't know what I was about. I always got him to do my repairs . . . He was a great mechanic."

Larry Amero hadn't died in the attack, which meant more worries. The Hells Angel had seen Shane at the Chevron station the night before the murder; they had stared each other down from close range. It would be easy enough to put two and two together. For the time being, Larry was drugged up in the hospital, but he would certainly tell the Hells Angels as soon as he could.

Sukh's group had just murdered the oldest Bacon brother, almost killed a popular full-patch Hells Angel, and paralyzed the niece of the president of a Hells Angel chapter. There would be hell to pay.

Shane was driving back to Kelowna when he got a message from a Hells Angel who owed him $80,000: "Bro, can we meet? I've got the money for you."

The timing couldn't have been more suspect. Everything seemed suspect now. If Shane didn't show up to collect the money, it would be highly suspicious. After all, who didn't have time to pick up $80,000 cash? And if Shane *did* show up, he risked delivering himself to his own execution. He might as well hand the would-be killers a gun and load it for them too.

Shane decided to meet up with the guy in a Home Depot parking lot. To Shane's immense relief, no guns were drawn.

"Bro, we don't know what the fuck's going on," the Hells Angel said. Amero was still in extremely rough shape. "We don't know if he's going to live or die."

Then the Angel ramped up the tension. He told Shane that the Sinaloa Cartel was extremely interested in the shooting. It turned out that Amero owed the cartel for 450 kilos of cocaine, which amounted to hundreds of millions of dollars.

Now Shane didn't just have to worry about the police and the Wolfpack; the world's most powerful drug cartel was involved too. They would demand answers, and their money.

"Anyone who they suspect is involved in this, they're going to kill," Shane says.

As the two men talked, Shane couldn't stop wondering if their meeting was just a setup. Were the Hells Angels simply gathering information? Would the guns come out when the talking stopped?

In the end, Shane was handed the $80,000, and he drove away with the money and unanswered questions.

Shane contacted Doug Wheeler, who had been close to Jonathan Bacon during his childhood. He might be able to make sense of things. They left their phones in their vehicles and went for a walk.

Wheeler was now showing a side of himself that Shane had never seen or even imagined. "He was bawling his eyes out . . . I had never seen him cry before."

He was saying things like "Fuck man, I feel so guilty. I loved Jon."

Perhaps the 'roided-up gangster with the cauliflower ears was thinking of how Bacon's mother used to feed their little gang, back when they were growing up together in Abbotsford.

"Oh fuck bro, this isn't good," Wheeler said.

"He cried over that," Shane says. "That was deep for me. I remember hugging him."

"Fuck man, I'm sorry bro," Shane said at the time.

"He looked hurt. He looked sorry. He looked scared, almost."

"Oh man, Shane," Wheeler said. "We fucked up here. We shouldn't have done this."

"And he was right," Shane says.

Shane thought about his dream of becoming a Hells Angel. If Norman Cocks's jail sentence hadn't put an end to that, this certainly would. He would never get into the Hells Angels now. More importantly, though, Shane thought of how Larry Amero and Jon Bacon each had sons.

Now Jon Bacon's son would be going to a funeral for his dad.

"That still weighs on me," Shane says.

CHAPTER 12

FULL BORE

"We're fucked."
—SHANE DANKOSKI

THE WEEK AFTER the Kelowna hit, Manny and Khun-Khun arrived back in town for a surprise visit with Shane. As they sat together at a booth in a Denny's restaurant, Khun-Khun didn't even want to talk for fear of being monitored by police. He wrote things down on paper instead. "It was the start of him being fucking shady," Shane recalls.

Khun-Khun wanted to take a trip back to the Delta Grand, to survey the scene of the ambush. "I need to check where the cameras are," he said.

The hotel garage was open when they arrived, so Shane, Khun-Khun, and Manny were able to walk in. Khun-Khun looked up, saw a camera, and immediately hid his face, as if that didn't make him look guilty. As they looked around, they saw more cameras, which presumably would have been turned on the day of Jon Bacon's murder.

Looking at all this surveillance, one thought ran through Shane's head: *All right. We're fucked.*

—

It didn't take long for the Dhak crew to find out just how fucked they were.

Shane knew a drug dealer going by the name Dougie Fresh who could be counted on for high-end weed. The stuff was pricey—called "tuna weed" because it arrived sealed in tuna tins—but worth it. "It was the best weed you could possibly get," Shane says. What Shane and his group didn't know was that Dougie Fresh was related to Larry Amero, the man they had almost killed in Kelowna. "We had no clue."

So Shane didn't give it much thought when, after he arrived at Manny's place one night in late August 2011, Manny announced that he was heading out to see Dougie Fresh. It was a regular drug run—nothing unusual. He thought briefly about going with Manny, but instead, he let Manny go off alone to see Dougie Fresh.

When Manny pulled into the parking lot of Dougie Fresh's condo building, he sent a text saying, "Hey bro, I'm outside."

Manny had had the camera in his Acura rewired so that it was always on and he could always see who was directly behind him, even when the car was in drive. Which is how Manny was able to see, on his dashboard screen, two guys creeping up on him as he sat in the condo lot. They were both wearing white balaclavas and carrying AR-15s.

Manny hit the gas as they opened fire.

"They must have put seventy holes in that SUV," Shane says. Bullets destroyed windows and tires and the passenger-side headrest, which was torn down to its metal stems. "This thing looked like it was blown up. If I would have went with Manny, I would have been sitting in that seat."

Although Manny bit his tongue hard in the stress of the moment and bled heavily, he came away relatively unscathed. "He thought he got shot in the face because he was bleeding in the mouth. He's shocked. His whole life flashed before his eyes."

It was a reminder of how their world had changed forever in the wake of the Kelowna murder. There was no going back, and there never would be. The days of heading out alone to buy tuna weed were gone forever. This was the new reality. "This is real. This war is fucking on."

The attempted hit on Manny also meant that Larry Amero and Robby Alkhalil were likely piecing together what had happened in Kelowna. For a time, the events of that day and who was behind them had been a mystery, and there were even theories that it was an inside job or a statement from a cartel about unpaid bills. By now, though—with the dust having settled slightly—it seemed that the puzzle pieces were beginning to click.

"He's a smart, smart man," Shane says, recalling how he sometimes thought about all the Hells Angels from Amero's White Rock charter milling around the parking lot of the hospital where Larry was being treated. Had Larry told them that Shane was buzzing around Kelowna the night before the attack, or about how he'd seen him at the strip club, drive-through, and Chevron station? Had he put two and two together?

"He had to have thought to himself, *That motherfucker*," Shane says. "They knew. They knew I was involved. After Kelowna, it was like hunting season. They put it together. They wanted to get us really good."

Shortly after escaping that night, Manny got a call from Dougie Fresh. "You here?" Dougie asked.

Dougie kept the dumb act going. "So you don't need the weed anymore?"

"Bro, I just fuckin' got shot in front of your building," Manny said.

"Really? It does smell like gunpowder out here," Dougie Fresh replied.

The tuna weed deal didn't go through.

There were thirteen gangsters at the table of a restaurant in White Rock one day in late August 2011, including Manny, Sukh, Dip Duhre, Thomas Mantel, and Stevie (Tucker) Leone. The restaurant was across the street from Gurmit's final resting place.

Sukh rose to speak. "This war just cost all of us our fucking lives," he announced, stabbing a steak knife into the table for emphasis.

"He knew that we were going to lose the war," Shane recalls. "He knew that we weren't big enough to compete with them. He knew we were badly outnumbered, surrounded by killers."

Shane also knew things were about to get far worse for everyone involved. "I knew that everybody here was willing to kill. I knew that we were going to lose the war but that we were going to take some of them with us."

War with Robby Alkhalil alone was suicidal, and he was not the only one interested in battle. Sukh's enemies now included the Hells Angels, Red Scorpions, Wolfpack Alliance, and parts of the old Italian Mafia. There was a who's who of bad guys on the other side, ready to kill anyone in Shane's group.

Sukh had plenty of bad qualities, but he wasn't a coward. "He was literally fearless," Shane says, and for him, winning the war was just one part of the equation. There was a higher goal. "Sukh knew that we were going to lose the war, but he knew that they had killed his brother," says Shane. And so, as the battle lines were drawn, Sukh radiated a certain confidence, as if he was thinking, *If I can kill who killed Gurmit, I can die a happy man.*

At one point during the dinner, Dip Duhre took Shane aside outside the restaurant and drew him close to talk. "Bro, come here, come here," Dip said. "Bro, did we do that Kelowna hit?"

"I kind of smiled at him. I thought, *Did Sukh not tell you what's going on?*" Dip was being blamed for the attack, and yet he was in the dark about what really happened.

Dip pressed on. "Are we responsible for this?" he asked.

For Shane, the question was a minefield. Sukh demanded absolute loyalty, and Shane had always given him that. His girlfriend would cry when he chose working for Sukh over her birthday or Christmas Eve, but it was never really up for debate; when Sukh called, Shane went. And so, when Dip turned to him outside the restaurant, Shane demonstrated that loyalty one more time, almost by reflex.

"You have to take that up with Buddy," Shane said, using the group's nickname for Sukh.

Dip showed Shane his BlackBerry, which was blowing up with messages about the attack. It showed he was talking in private with the Wolfpack side, including with Robby Alkhalil. Now Dip was being asked some very direct questions, and the Alkhalils expected answers as they struggled to figure out who was targeting them.

The truth was that Dip hadn't been told anything about the Kelowna attack, either while it was being planned or in the immediate aftermath, when a bloody blowback could have been expected. Dip had been close to the Dhaks, especially Gurmit. He was smart and extremely well-connected. So when he said he knew nothing, it meant something. Dip's word was a powerful thing in the underworld. He still had the sense of honour that so many others just pretended to have.

"It was years and years and years of him being honest to everybody," Shane says. "It was just a known thing. If you needed something done properly, he would do it. He was so neutral it was weird, and Sukh ruined that for him."

Dip had known the Alkhalils since they were kids. They were always tough, and you definitely didn't toy with them. It had taken years for Dip to build his reputation, and Sukh had blown it up in a flash, leaving Dip exposed and vulnerable.

"He didn't know what the truth was," Shane says. "He was trying to squash the beef. To his knowledge, he was being honest. He was being steady. He was being real. Sukh turned Dip into a sitting duck."

Dip told Shane that he was messaging a private investigator, trying to get answers. The private investigator had told him, "These guys are serious. There's no joke. They're sending hitters from Toronto to clean the streets."

It was just one more thing for Shane to worry about: his life, his friends' lives, his family. It was a weird time—a time of heightened tensions and danger, a time when loyalty was demanded but not, seemingly, always rewarded. There was Dip, left twisting in the wind by Sukh, and then there was Shane himself. He had been connected to the United Nations for about five years before the Kelowna hit, but he had yet to receive his beads—the white-gold bracelet showing he was recognized as an elite member of the gang. Everyone else seemed to be getting theirs, but Sukh was slow to give them to his own guys. "Only select guys had them," says Shane. "You had to put in work to earn those. You may or may not have had to be a killer, with at least one body under your belt.

"Once you get your beads, you're certified," he continues. "I remember going to dinners with Gurmit's entire crew, every single fucking guy had them, except me and Manny Hairan. But I will say, by that time Manny definitely earned them. But Sukh wanted to hold the power and wouldn't give them. I one thousand percent earned my beads . . . But the way Sukh was, it was all about power and what he could hold over your head."

The steak dinner was followed, as usual, by a trip to Gurmit's grave. "There's a sixty-ounce bottle of Crown Royal there," Shane says, "and so Sukh grabbed it, he poured some on Gurm's grave, then took a shot and passed it on. I was last. After that, Sukh pulled out incense. I knew it was happening then. He smiled at me and hugged me. He took out the jewellery box . . . He hugged me. He put the incense all around me. He started burning all this Chinese money, put the beads beside the fire, and then he read some script. He then said a little speech along the lines of, 'We're now brothers at arms, brothers forever. We live together. We die together. These are all your brothers. We come first.' . . . He put the beads on Gurm's tombstone. He bowed his head to pray, and then he put the beads on my wrist. It was one of the best, happiest—if not the best—days of my life at the time."

The investigation into the Kelowna casino attack was dubbed Project E-Nitrogen and the cop in charge of surveillance was Staff Sergeant Sam Gadbahn of the RCMP, a veteran of almost thirty years on the force.

He had started in New Westminster when Shane's dad and uncles were active on the streets there. He also knew plenty about Shane, who respected him even though they were on different sides of the law.

In the months after the murder at the Delta Grand, Gadbahn pulled Shane over plenty of times. He always made a point of having beef jerky and ginger ale with him, as he knew those were Shane's favourite items to buy at convenience stores. He wanted Shane to know they were doing their research.

"We're fucking watching you," Gadbahn would tell Shane.

Shane didn't tell Manny, Khun-Khun, Sukh, or anyone else in his crew about how police were now continually approaching him. He also didn't mention that within days of the Kelowna murder, officers had shown up at his house, saying they knew he was involved and that he'd likely set the whole thing up.

Someone with inside knowledge appeared to be talking. And in the criminal world, you often have the most to fear from those you consider your friends. What friends might be betraying Shane?

Shane knew he wasn't talking, but the situation was dangerous anyway. "I knew in my heart that I was solid," he says, but he was concerned that his crew might not be. What if they were worried about the cops? What if the were thinking, *They're putting pressure on this guy? What if he folds? Let's kill him.*

As it turned out, Gadbahn wasn't the only one watching Shane. One day that fall, a couple of months after the shooting, Sukh messaged Shane to meet him in aisle six of a supermarket in Surrey. Sukh was carrying a couple of green buckets for produce and a jar of peanut butter when he hooked up with Shane, who was pushing a shopping cart.

Sukh reached for Shane and put both of his hands on his ribs, armpits, pecs, stomach, and back—a quick pat-down.

"You're not wearing a wire, are you?" Sukh asked.

What the fuck did he just say to me? Shane asked himself. "I could not believe that this guy said that to me."

A few minutes later, Shane sat alone in his truck in the parking lot and tried to make sense of what had just happened. "I have never been so crushed . . . That hurt so bad. I was willing to lose my life for him . . . It was devastating . . . It was probably the most hurt I have ever been."

It was yet another sign—as if Shane needed one—of Sukh's increasing vigilance and paranoia. He suspected that listening devices were hooked up to grave sites, and forbade members from talking about the Kelowna casino shooting in cemeteries, or anywhere else. "No more talking about Kelowna," he said.

It didn't stop them from going to Gurmit's grave, though. Shane and Sukh and Manny would meet there even before it was completed, when there was just a little card with "G. DHAK" to note the significance of the site. In time, there would be candles and bottles on the site, as well as a proper gravestone. But even before that, it was a special place.

One day, a purple Acura MDX circled around the cemetery while Sukh, Manny, and Shane were there. The Acura stopped about the length of a football field away. It was easy to wonder if they were being watched by police—until they heard the *bang, bang, bang, bang* of gunshots.

It was odd that the men in the Acura hadn't come closer before they opened fire. "I think that they were scared that we had guns too."

Had they advanced, the men could have easily wiped out Shane and his group. They obviously didn't know that Sukh had forbidden his men from bringing firepower to the gravesite, concerned that guns would give police an excuse for arrests.

"They would have killed us. Imagine being killed there. It was crazy."

The call from Sukh's bodyguard came on September 16, 2011, as Shane was visiting the Pacific National Exhibition in Vancouver with his family.

"Bro, where are you? Khun-Khun and Buddy just got hit," said Thomas Mantel. "Sukh's fine but they got Khun-Khun."

Shane later learned that Sukh and Khun-Khun were leaving a dinner in Surrey when they came under fire. Khun-Khun was hit thirteen times as he sat behind the wheel of a rented Nissan Murano. One of the bullets caught him in the chest, but he somehow survived, thanks to a combat-trained surgeon who had just returned from Afghanistan. The surgery wasn't a total success, though. "They shot his dick off," Shane says.

Shane was impressed that the Wolfpack side even knew about the dinner party. The enemy, it seemed, was furious and well-prepared. "Those guys really put work in."

Two weeks later, on October 2, the body of Dhak associate William Lim (Billy) Woo was found dumped near Squamish on a logging road. The fifty-five-year-old ran an autobody shop in Burnaby. His murder was described by police as "targeted."

The war that police had predicted was on, full bore.

Given the rising tensions and the increasing likelihood that Larry Amero was beginning to figure out who was behind the hit at the Delta Grand, Shane knew that his days of hanging around with the bikers were numbered. Those buddies would soon be added to the list of dangerous people who wanted him dead.

That realization hurt on several levels. "They were my friends. I genuinely liked those guys. There was a part of me that wanted to be a Hells Angel. I wasn't just hanging out with them to gain information."

And yet there were constant reminders of how quickly violence could flare up.

Shane was in the Kelowna Hells Angels clubhouse around 2 a.m. one Saturday, a couple of months after the Kelowna shooting. There were about fifty people there. Some weren't bikers, just people who had seemed interesting at bars around last call, including women. Someone pointed out a man in the clubhouse who was from California.

"Bro, that fucking guy right there. That fucking guy, he made me have a fight with another Hells Angel. He made me fight with one of my bros," Shane was told.

In the Angels' world, that was a major misstep. They decided on the spot that something had to be done.

"We've got to do him."

"Yeah," Shane agreed.

"Do him" didn't necessarily mean killing the guy, but it could. At the very least, it meant teaching him a serious lesson.

Shane approached the visitor from California. "Hey, buddy, come with me for a second," Shane said.

"Who the fuck are you?" the visitor replied.

The building at the back of the Hells Angels' Kelowna property was a nice secluded spot to lay a beating on someone. "We're trying to get him in there," Shane says.

Shortly after the California visitor announced he didn't want to join Shane, Tommy the Prospect surprise-punched him, and then continued to beat him up in front of everybody. The beating continued as the man was dragged out to the garage.

"You made me fuck with one of my bros," the man was told.

The California visitor wasn't so cocky now, saying, "I'm sorry. I'm sorry."

His apology wasn't enough to stop the beating.

Then, with the man seeming to sense that he was bartering for his life, the bribery attempts started. "If you guys just leave me alone, I'll give each of you guys one key of coke tomorrow," he said.

Norm Cocks, who was on the scene, sensed an opportunity. "We want more than that," he said.

The man let them know he could up his offer: he had access to fifteen kilos of cocaine.

"We want all of it," Norm said.

A pair of wire cutters were taken out. One of the man's ears was snipped, and one of the Angels appeared on the verge of throwing up.

They made the man clean up his own blood.

"His head was like a marshmallow," Shane says. "Somebody called him a taxi."

Not long after, Shane got a PGP message from a Kelowna Hells Angel who was in Vancouver at the time. The Hells Angel was involved in shipping cocaine with Amero, and knew Shane from a trip to Mexico.

The Hells Angel was livid. "What the fuck are you guys doing?" he asked. "That guy fucking works for me. You guys are trying to tax my fucking guy? This fucking guy—he makes me millions of dollars. You guys are trying to tax my fucking guy?"

Now, the angry Hells Angel was heading up from Vancouver to deal with the problem. Things had the potential to get far more serious within hours. "He was furious."

Shane did what he could to deflect heat from Norm telling him, "'That wasn't them. That was me.' I took the heat for that. It was fucking hot," Shane says. "It was a real thing for the bikers. They had meetings about it. Biker business."

For a while, it felt as if things were going to explode, but instead the tension just fizzled. In the end, the upset Hells Angel decided not to make things worse. "He actually took it really well. A lot better than I thought he would."

By this point, it wasn't comfortable to keep visiting the Hells Angels clubhouse, but Shane knew that if he stopped going, it would look suspicious. Which is how he came to be there on another night in the fall of 2011, when a major party for about two hundred people was underway. One of the Angels passed out a stack of raffle tickets with a picture of Leah Hadden-Watts in a wheelchair, with a brace around her neck.

Tabs were fifty dollars each, and they each held a chance at the first prize of a one-carat diamond ring, with proceeds going to Hadden-Watts. An Angel friend thought it would help Shane's standing with the club if he sold some of them. And so, for the next ninety minutes, Shane walked around the clubhouse selling tickets for the woman he'd helped to paralyze and thinking, *They don't know.*

They raised between $40,000 and $50,000 that night, and about $7,000 of that came from Shane's ticket sales. "Everybody who I went up to pretty much bought them," he recalls. "You know how hard that was for me? That was so fucked up. I'll never forget the way I felt. Talk about salt in the wound."

When the night was over, Shane gave Manny a call. "This fucking chick is in a wheelchair because of us," Shane said.

Manny's reaction was a bit surprising and a lot disappointing. "He kind of laughed about it. He thought it was funny. It wasn't funny. It wasn't funny at all."

CHAPTER 13

CLOSING IN

"They'll fucking cut you in pieces."
—MANNY HAIRAN

MEXICO WAS A BIG PART of Shane's gangster life. "I went to Mexico I think seven times in two years. Me and Manny fucking loved it there. The weather is so nice and I just felt free. No one knew me there. The best part of being there was knowing no one knew me. It was like an escape."

For Shane, there were still plans to accompany a half-dozen BC Hells Angels to Mexico in the fall of 2011 to set up a drug deal with the Sinaloa Cartel. This is something that was happening with more and more frequency during those years as Canadian organized crime groups were choosing to deal directly with Mexican drug cartels, which allowed them to eliminate the middleman and increase their profits.

The RCMP had taken notice of the activity, and the violence associated with it. An internal report, obtained by Daniel Renaud of *La Presse* under the Freedom of Information Act, stated that at least nine Canadians "with extensive criminal associations" were shot or killed in Mexico between 2008 and 2012. "There are regions of lawlessness in Mexico where, despite efforts by authorities to rein in the violence, criminal enterprise has become an almost intractable aspect of Mexican society," the report states.

The RCMP report also suggests that a drug war in Mexico and tight US border surveillance was pushing Mexican drug traffickers to turn to Canada, stating: "An escalation in murders and shootings within the criminal element in British Columbia in 2007–2008 paralleled with reporting of brutal and extreme levels of violence in Mexico [has] raised concern of Mexican criminal influence in Canada."

Manny begged Shane not to go to Mexico. Just suspicion of his involvement in the Kelowna attack would be enough to have him killed by the bikers. "Larry and these guys have friends who are cops who tell them things," Manny warned, adding that his death would be horrific. "If they find out when you're there they'll torture the fuck out of you. They'll torture you for hours. They'll fucking cut you in pieces."

Shane realized Manny had a point. "I could be getting chopped up into one hundred fucking pieces and never see my family again," he says, adding that the risks of heading south were well-known to those in the gangster world. In fact, several BC gangsters hadn't returned from recent trips. That included Elliott (Taco) Castaneda and Ahmet (Lou) Kaawach, both of the United Nations gang and both from Vancouver. They were shot dead as they ate at a Guadalajara restaurant on July 13, 2008.

UN associate Adam Naname (Nam) Kataoka was murdered abroad after suffering some sort of nervous breakdown. Kataoka had thought he was about to begin work as a drug tester when he was dispatched to Argentina in 2009. Kataoka's body was found face down in a Buenos Aires parking lot near a university campus on October 28, 2009, with bullet wounds from two different guns. He was wearing latex gloves at the time of the murder, like a drug tester would wear.

Also unsolved were the September 2009 murders of gangsters Gordon Douglas Kendall and Jeffrey Ronald Ivans, both thirty-seven and from BC. They were each shot repeatedly in the head in a Puerto Vallarta condo complex.

And then there was Jesse (Egon) Adkins, who was believed to have been murdered in Mexico in 2011. There were strong suspicions that Gurmit Dhak had arranged Adkins' murder there, as the UN became more concerned about turncoats in its ranks. Adkins's body was never found, but suspicions festered that he had been killed and disposed of by associates of Gurmit.

Despite the obvious dangers, Sukh Dhak had an entirely different take on Shane's planned trip. He liked the idea. "Sukh goes, 'No, no. Just go. We'll get so much information out of that. It'll be useful,'" Shane recalls. "He was pushing for it."

With eyes wide open, Shane decided to make the trip, heading south with six full-patch Hells Angels and five cartel guys who had been up in Canada.

The Hells Angels had a clubhouse in a high-security gated community by Playa del Carmen—a high-end detached home with plenty of bedrooms. It was clean and beautifully landscaped, a safe and secure place to conduct business or to kill someone, if that's what was required. There was a swimming pool and a built-in barbecue at the back of the property. There was also a backyard table for meetings with cartel members, and golf nearby for those who played.

It was the same place Shane always stayed at when he visited the country, in a bedroom on the top floor. There wasn't as much Hells Angels memorabilia inside as in the Kelowna clubhouse, although there was a Canadian flag, with a Hells Angels winged Death Head replacing the maple leaf in the centre. There was also a large Death Head lamp, with the Death Head's lips sewn shut, reminding bikers and their guests that secrets must be kept.

Hells Angel Joseph Bruce (Skreppy) Skreptak from Kelowna was already there, with his black Silverado truck with expired BC plates and tinted windows. The biker was on Canadian court conditions not to wear Hells Angels gear, but nobody here was checking.

Skreptak was well-known to police in Kelowna. In 2007 he was a founder of the city's Angels chapter. Skreptak was about six foot two and 240 pounds, and reminded Shane of Psycho Sid, the pro wrestler, except that his hair was dark and not blond. His club membership clearly meant a lot to him, and many times Shane heard him say "I'm fucking Hells Angels."

"He was a bad man. A mean motherfucker. Tough as shit too. He talked very matter-of-fact. When he drank he was even worse," Shane says. "He was a kick-boxer. Just a mean dude. I've seen him tax innocent people. Beat up legit guys. He was a fucking bully."

Skreptak seemed happy with his southern living arrangements, and told Shane he'd driven his truck down, not explaining how he'd managed to pass through border stops. "I haven't had to insure it since it's been here," he said.

There were also cartel hanging around. They tended to be smallish compared with the Canadians, and they drove pickup trucks and SUVs, not luxury sedans. They typically wore jeans, stretchy soccer shirts, and running shoes, and most didn't bother with hats.

Unlike the Canadians, they weren't tattooed. "Their arms were completely clean." Also unlike the Canadians, they usually eschewed jewellery, although one of them had a necklace with a cross.

While there, Shane did some touristy things, like checking out the Mayan pyramids and taking a boat ride, but he mostly hung out at the clubhouse. The food was excellent, with plenty of pork and steak, and there was an expensive stereo system in the backyard, with speakers hanging down. As at the clubhouse in Kelowna, Rihanna's song "We Found Love" proved inescapable. Apparently, some of the BC bikers just couldn't live without it.

There was also a maid on duty. She would clean up the pile of cocaine and straws and rolled-up hundred-dollar bills on a table as if it was normal. "She didn't even bat an eye."

The backyard could be an adventure. One day "a fucking snake came zooming through the pool," Shane says. The next day, Shane was hanging around out back when a biker told him, "Bro, don't fucking move."

"What?" Shane replied. "Is there something on me?"

"Do not move," the biker repeated. "Trust me."

Shane jumped up and flung his chair, then swung around and took a look at where he had been sitting. "Right behind my left ear was a fucking tarantula. It was the size of a baseball. I am so scared of spiders it isn't funny."

Someone warned that they shouldn't kill it. "When it's going to die, the first thing it does is release all its babies. There'll be tarantulas everywhere."

A Canadian biker named Scotty captured the giant spider and threw it over the fence.

Spiders and snakes aside, Shane enjoyed the camaraderie, knowing it would soon be over forever. He couldn't escape the feeling of *Fuck, this is what I want, but I can't have it.* "It was a kind of defeated feeling."

It was also easy to worry, if Shane let his mind go there. "I was kind of a little scared," he says. "I always wondered when they would put it all together. Had they known what had just taken place, they would have tortured me and killed me. It was ironic. I had such a good time on that trip. I never had felt more that I wanted to be with them . . . But it's too fucking late."

Shane made another trip in the fall of 2011, to Cancún with a crew from the UN, including Manny and Stevie (Tucker) Leone. Shortly after they returned, they learned that Robby Alkhalil had also been in Mexico with a crew that included heavy hitters like the Cowboys. "We missed them by a fucking day! We were there and they were there." Shane later marvelled at how badly things could have gone, if the timing had been just a little different. "We've got guys in Mexico who are hitters and they do too. It could have been really bad."

—

Back in Kelowna, Shane found himself confronting a challenge of a different kind. On October 22, 2011, he checked into the Crossroads rehab centre. It cost $10,000, and he didn't really want to be there, but his girlfriend had made it clear that it was a huge deal to her. If Shane wouldn't go, she would have to consider leaving him.

"Go to treatment for a week and make her happy," Manny advised.

On Shane's very first day at the centre, a news item flashed on the TV. The words under the pictures said something about a "Surrey shooting." The report didn't identify the latest murder victim, but it did show a black Acura TL with a tan interior. It was Stevie (Tucker) Leone's car. "My heart dropped in my stomach."

Shane needed to know more. Patients weren't allowed to have cellphones, so Shane approached an employee. "I've got to use the phone," Shane told her.

She asked why.

"I think something bad happened to one of my friends."

"Why would you think something bad happened to your friend?"

"Sorry?"

She noted again that it was against the rules to let patients use the centre's phone.

Shane's friend had likely just been murdered—and he wasn't in the mood to argue about the rehab centre's policies. "Fuck you," he said. "I've leaving."

She reminded him that he had put down a $10,000 deposit.

"Keep the ten grand. I don't give a fuck." And with that, Shane was gone from rehab. He hadn't even lasted a day.

Back at home, Shane's girlfriend was understandably unhappy. "She was really upset. She'd tried with everything she had to get me to go there."

For Shane, though, that knowledge was nothing compared with the knowledge that his fears about the shooting had been right. Tucker had been murdered. "He always made everybody smile. He made everybody laugh. It did hurt."

Shane also realized that it could have been much worse: Manny was wounded in the same attack but had been able to flee the scene.

Not long before the shooting, Shane, Tucker, and Sukh had gone out for drinks. There had been talk of meeting up later at Sukh's place. But when Tucker went to the washroom, Sukh had leaned towards Shane. "Don't tell the fucking guy where I live," Sukh ordered.

Shane was taken aback. Tucker had helped with the Kelowna hit that killed Jon Bacon, acting as a spotter. But now there was clearly a problem between Tucker and Sukh. "It really rubbed me the wrong way," says Shane.

Tucker had been loyal. He also followed Jason McBride out of town after the hit, making sure he got away safely. Even with this, Sukh had been treating him like an outsider.

Tucker died without beads, which also struck Shane as unfair. "If everybody had beads but you, it was almost embarrassing. It happened to me. He died over this beef without them, sadly, but he definitely earned them."

Tucker and the crew went way back. He and Manny had been high school buddies and played on the same soccer team, where Manny was a standout player. And there were recent memories too. Shane thought of how he and Tucker had just vacationed together in Mexico, where they'd shared a penthouse suite with a four-inch-high pile of cocaine on the coffee table.

"The next time I saw Tucker, his brains were blown out," Shane says.

The day after Tucker was murdered, Shane had a tattoo artist come to his home and tattoo Tucker's name onto his chest, near his image of the Jesus and the devil arm-wrestling. Shane showed it to Tucker's mom at his funeral.

"She was so grateful."

Shane was driving his new Cadillac CTS from Surrey to Kelowna with his girlfriend and Jayden in late 2011 when he noticed a Nissan Pathfinder behind him outside Abbotsford. Something about it made him suspect it was a police undercover vehicle.

Then a Honda Accord and a Civic went by and Shane got really suspicious. He made sure he was driving within the speed limit and asked his girlfriend to record the speedometer on her cellphone.

Then the Pathfinder pulled him over. The driver knew his name. "How are you doing, Shane? You're driving really fast."

"How fast?"

"Over forty kilometres over the speed limit, which is grounds for impounding your car."

Suddenly, there were ten cops around him.

His Cadillac was impounded.

His family stood by the side of the road as semi-trucks whizzed by, until a cab came to pick them up. He was issued some $1,500 in tickets, enough for his licence to be yanked for seven days. He was also hit with charges for the tow and the storage, which added up to almost $2,000 more in fines. His police file from the time includes this note:

When stopped by police, Mr. DANKOSKI was verbally abusive and threatened officers by saying he was going to get their home addresses and watch their wives. MR. DANKOSKI reportedly told officers that their families were going to personally pay for this out of their own pockets, that he knew where the officers lived and he was going to call and say "hi" that night and that cops are not safe. Mr. DANKOSKI indicates that none of this occurred as reported and that the police fabricated information to be able to impound his car and retrieve their surveillance equipment from it.

He managed to beat all the charges in court, thanks to his hard-ass lawyer Kelly Christiansen. The police couldn't explain why they needed to pull him over in the first place.

Even with the court victory, everything seemed to be closing in. On December 23, 2011, Shane received a registered letter:

From Casino Security and Surveillance department of B.C. Lottery Corporation, responsible to B.C. casinos, community gaming centres and Commercial Bingo Halls

As a patron to our casinos in the province of British Columbia you have engaged in an undesirable activity. As a result of this, you have been prohibited from entering all Casinos, Community Gaming Centres and Commercial Bingo Halls in British Columbia. This prohibition is in effect for five years . . . expiring at midnight on December 22, 2016 . . .

BCLC hereby notifies you that you are not eligible to have a PlayNow.com account during the prohibition period. If you have an existing PlayNow.com account, BCLC has the right to close it. If you gamble on a PlayNow.com after being prohibited, BCLC will retain the bet. If you win, BCLC will not pay the prize in accordance with the rules and regulations.

The pressure wasn't going away after the Jon Bacon murder, and it was getting harder and harder to manage. For Shane, the death of Leone Tucker, coupled with the run-in with the cops and the lottery corporation, marked a turning point. Although it was the last thing he wanted to do, Shane even found himself distancing himself from the Hells Angels as 2011 wound down.

"This Kelowna thing was still the talk of everybody. Everybody. Every gangster, every Hells Angel. You could just feel it," he says. "Shit was just getting too crazy. The gangster world is very small. It just got worse and worse and worse. Nothing good came from that on either side."

CHAPTER 14

BORROWED TIME

"I can do whatever the fuck I want."
—SANDIP (DIP) DUHRE

EVEN THE MOST POWERFUL gangsters are always on borrowed time. Dip Duhre knew it—had known it even before this current war erupted.

"Bro, come here," Dip said to Shane one day during a visit to the cemetery where Gurmit's remains lay. About a hundred feet away was a memorial to Dean Elshamy. Dip told Shane that he had been friends with Dean Mohamed Elshamy, who was a rapper. Elshamy, in turn, had been friends with legendary rapper Tupac Shakur, who was murdered in a drive-by in Las Vegas in 1996, when he was twenty-five. Tupac had written a "Code of Thug Life," which laid out twenty-six street rules for gangsters. They made it clear that causing harm to children was unforgivable, and that gangsters should also "respect our sisters."

Shane was startled to learn that Dip had a Tupac Shakur connection. "The real Tupac?" he asked, as if there were another.

Dip wasn't one to lie, or even embellish. "He wouldn't ever lie to you about anything," says Shane. "He does not lie. He does not talk shit."

Shane learned that Elshamy had been one of the original ecstasy kingpins back in the 1990s, with a press to make pills. Some of those pills were sent to California, which led to the Tupac connection. Tupac would fly Elshamy to California, booking his flights.

One day not long after the Kelowna attack, Shane and Dip pulled into the parking lot of the Mac's Convenience on Scott Road and 72nd Avenue in Surrey. Shane pointed out that chunks of brick were missing from one of the store's exterior walls.

Dip had an Elshamy story to explain the damaged wall. Dip told of how he was with Elshamy around 1 a.m. on May 13, 2005, when the two had driven into this parking lot in Dip's late-model grey Audi. Dip went to the back of the store to get a Coke out of the cooler.

"I heard a *bang, bang, bang, bang,*" Dip told Shane. Dip ran up to the Audi, where he saw that the top of Elshamy's head had been blown off. "It was just like a bowl. The top of his head was on the passenger seat, where I'd been sitting." Dip pulled his gun from the back of his pants and started shooting, with no success.

Two months later, on July 7, 2005, a gunman tried to finish the job. This time, Dip was driving a black BMW with bulletproof windows when he pulled up in front of a small grocery store just east of Glen Drive in Surrey. Four shots tore into his car, but again Dip emerged unscathed.

There would be other attempts.

One day in late 2011, Shane got a call from Dip. "Bro, come pick me up. I've got some running around to do," he said, explaining that he planned to drive to Vancouver to deliver $350,000 in cash in a backpack.

Sukh made it clear to Shane that he didn't think that was a good idea. "Don't drive him to Vancouver with that money, bro," Sukh ordered.

A little while later, though, Dip called again. "Let's go to Vancouver," he said.

This time, Shane agreed. They took the backpack with the $350,000 in it with them.

On the way, Dip wanted to stop at a strip club owned by a Hells Angel. Despite the gang war and Sukh's wishes, Dip seemed determined to go anywhere he chose, whenever he chose. It was no different inside the strip club. There was a velvet rope at the entranceway, and the general public was only allowed to proceed to the left. Dip ignored the rope and went right into the VIP area. It too was cordoned off by a velvet rope, which was supposed to keep everyone out except for Hells Angels and their guests.

"Hey, you can't go in there," a bouncer said.

"I can do whatever the fuck I want," Dip replied, and kept on walking. Shane followed behind, feeling uncomfortable.

Dip sat down and Shane settled in beside him. Then Dip lit up a cigarette, even though there was no smoking allowed in the club. He snapped off the end of the cigarette and tossed the tip onto the floor; it was something Dip always did, though no one seemed to know why.

This time, three bouncers came over. "You can't smoke here. You can't be here."

"Call your boss. Tell your boss that Dip is here and then come back and tell me that I can't smoke."

"They never came back," Shane says. "We sat in that area for three hours. Dip smoked the whole time."

And after that three hours had passed, Dip announced he no longer felt like going into the city. Shane remembers being relieved. Knowing that you're living on borrowed time is one thing; tempting fate is another.

Despite his occasional frustrations with Dip's tendency to do whatever the hell he wanted, Sukh kept trying to pull closer to Dip. Dip still had ties to the other side in their war, and had been extremely close to Jon Bacon before his murder, but that didn't matter. "[Sukh] knew the relationship Dip had with everybody," Shane says. "He was neutral." And on some level, Sukh was aware that Dip's good reputation could be his salvation.

Sukh's reasoning was worthy of Machiavelli. If he had articulated it, it would have gone something like: *I'm going to get Dip on my side. I'm going to freeze him out of valuable information. I'm going to use his relationship with Jon Bacon against him. He will tell Jon Bacon's supporters that he doesn't know what happened in Kelowna, and that will provide cover for me. And, without Dip even knowing, he's going to help me in this war.*

And if Dip got killed in the process, so be it.

Despite Shane's best efforts, it was getting increasingly difficult to live a "normal" life with his girlfriend and Jayden. The Kelowna hit had changed everything, and the watchful eyes of the police were always trained on him, no matter where he was or who he was with.

On January 17, 2012, Shane's lawyer, Kelly Christiansen, fired off a registered letter to Constable Kyle Westerhead of the Kelowna RCMP detachment. She was seeking relief from a troubling incident that had occurred at a Kelowna Rockets Junior A hockey game a few months prior.

This is to confirm I am Counsel for Mr. Dankoski.

My client informs me that on November 4, 2011, he was approached by Police while attending a Kelowna Rockets game. While in the presence of his two year old son . . . he was told that his life was in danger and there was an issue of "Public Safety". . . He was further . . . informed that he was neither arrested, detained, nor a suspect, but he should take the time to listen to the police and accompany them to another location.

Mr. Dankoski followed the Lincoln S.U.V. driven by the police to the Holiday Inn on Leckie Road where he was informed that, in summary, the police knew he was involved in the killing of Mr. Jonathan Bacon and further, it was only a matter of time until he was arrested . . . He was further informed that police believed that there were "credible threats" to Mr. Dankoski's life and police would be stepping up patrols around his home.

Subsequent to this, Mr. Dankoski informs me that the police contacted . . . his wife's place of employment indicating they wished to speak to her. Needless to say this has caused difficulty with his wife's employment status, not to mention considerable embarrassment.

Take this letter as a demand that you provide to my office forthwith full details of the "intelligence" you have indicating the source and nature of any threats of any kind to the wellbeing of Mr. Dankoski. Failure to provide this information forthwith will be dealt with appropriately.

Further, it is my position that contacting Mr. Dankoski in a public setting, in the presence of the public and his child is inappropriate and unprofessional. It is also astounding that the Police would attempt to meddle with his wife's work status by contacting her employer.

Clearly, Mr. Dankoski is erroneously suspected of involvement in the murder of Mr. Jonathan Bacon. As he has told you, this is to reiterate he has no involvement. Given your persistent erroneous beliefs and subsequent actions, THIS LETTER SHOULD ALSO BE TAKEN AS A DEMAND THAY [sic] YOU HAVE NO CONTACT OF ANY KIND WITH MY CLIENT or in any way interfere with his family. The fact that you have told my client he is a will [sic] soon be arrested in reference to the Bacon matter means my client is exercising all his Rights guaranteed by the Canadian Charter of Rights and Freedoms, including but not limited to his Right to Silence and will not answer any of you [sic] questions. I have express and explicit instructions to accept notices of any kind, including but not limited to notices that he was subject to an intercept. As a result, all correspondence can be directed to me.

Govern yourself accordingly.

Yours truly.
Kelly T. Christiansen

—

The walls were closing in—and not only on Shane. The same day that Christiansen sent her sharply worded letter to the police, Dip Duhre was at the bar of the Sheraton Wall Centre, a downtown Vancouver hotel-residential complex. Dip was a regular at the upscale café, just across from the Vancouver Law Courts. Dip had been there the previous day as well—and had asked the pianist in the lounge to play "Speak Softly, Love," the theme song from *The Godfather*.

Dip may have looked relaxed, sitting at the bar, but he was always thinking about his security. "I was one of probably five people that knew where Dip lived with his wife and family," says Shane. "Not only did I know where he lived, I had his garage code. When I would go pick him up, I would circle the block three or four times to check everything out. Then I would back in, open the garage door about a third of the way, just enough so he could duck underneath. And I always had his passenger door open for him. Then I'd shut the garage and we would peel away."

The Sheraton Wall Centre is a prime downtown spot, and it wasn't at all surprising that prestige clients like the American and Cuban women's soccer teams were also in the hotel that day. Dip wasn't there to star-gaze, though; he was expecting to meet the man who he thought was his private investigator. Dip was an alert man, but he had no clue that the private investigator was really working for his enemies.

As Dip sat at the bar, Larry Amero was making plans. Using the alias "Skull Buster," Amero had been texting someone identified as "Dog Whisperer," telling that person that "we need a better team," and then adding, "if I was healed, we would have already drove back and done this proper."

Amero also texted an associate called "Exchange Cowboy" to say that he needed some more surgeries. Amero's spirits seemed to be rising, as he added, "yeah getting shot sucks lol. Yeah, I didn't expect that in front of casino and cop station lol." Exchange Cowboy replied, "for sure," to which Amero replied, "Yeah, I get revenge bro. Gotta be smart, crazy heat."

Amero had urged an associate to "scope" a Surrey pub that Sukh might attend.

Robby Alkhalil was also texting plans that day, using the names "Where's Waldo" and "Side Swiper." CCTV video from the Wall Centre captured Alkhalil in the hotel on the night of January 17, 2012, as Dip sat nearby in the bar.

At around 8:45 p.m., a lanky man walked in. His face and head were partly covered with a scarf and toque. He walked with a notable limp.

Dip was about to get a drink from a waitress, but the lanky man got to him first. He raised an arm and shot Dip repeatedly in the head, then shuffled through the bar area and out the west doors.

Duhre was just thirty-six when he paid the ultimate price for the Kelowna murder, even though he hadn't been part of the crime and didn't even understand what had gone down that day. He died because he trusted Sukh. "Dip went to bat for us," Shane says. "It cost him his life. The man died for no reason. He was a peacekeeper."

Shane was rattled by the senselessness of Dip's murder, and the sense that he himself was living on borrowed time. "They killed Gurmit. In my eyes, Gurmit was untouchable. He was the man. Gurmit and Dip were so smart, and they got it. How could I not?"

Things were heating up for everyone associated with the United Nations, it seemed.

In Mexico, Salih (Sal) Abdulaziz Sahbaz—a right-hand man to Barzan Tilli-Cholli and Clay Roueche—had been shot to death on January 5, 2012, in the Alamo area of Culiacán, Sinaloa. Police recovered more than a half-dozen .45-calibre shells near his body. They also found his identification and money, ruling out robbery as a motive.

Closer to home, Tom Gisby was feeling the pressure too. That had been clear at a Vancouver Canucks hockey game earlier in the season when Sukh, Shane, and their crew dropped in to Gisby's suite between periods, unannounced. There, they saw a Hells Angel and a particularly serious associate.

At first glance, Gisby seemed to be his usual self, with his prescription gold-framed glasses perched above his eyebrows. But then he started to sweat. "We walk in and this guy goes bright red like a fucking tomato," Shane recalls. "You could feel the tension. It was just really, really weird. He fucking knew right then and there it was over."

Gisby's double game had run its course. He could no longer play both sides from the middle. The Dhak side had no patience for someone who was also helping their enemies. The Hells Angel also seemed to sense something was going on with Gisby. "It would have given them a really good look at how shady he was. Sukh fucking loved it."

Sukh shook Gisby's hand that day, a kiss of death of sorts. "The guy's face just dropped. His stomach must have been in his ass."

Gisby moved out of town. A bomb intended for him failed to blow up his luxury motor home in Whistler, BC, on January 16, 2012. A few days later, after Sean Beaver of the Dhak–Duhre group was shot to death in Surrey, Gisby flew south to Mexico. Compared with Surrey, it seemed like a safe haven.

It wasn't.

On April 28, 2012, Tom Gisby's name was added to the grim list of Canadian gangsters and associates who were murdered in Mexico and whose killings were never solved. Gisby was shot in the head at a Starbucks in Nuevo Vallarta, Mexico. Someone had apparently gotten tired of Gisby playing both sides in the gang war. "He wanted to be liked by everybody and that's what got him killed," Shane says.

And then there was Manny. Gunmen came after him again in February 2012, one block from Shane's mom's house. They failed this time as well.

Shane's mother could hear the gunshots from her home. She called Shane to report what she had heard—and to make sure her boy was okay.

"Yeah, Mom," Shane said. "That was one of my bros."

"Oh my God! Oh my God!" she said. "That's what I'm talking about! I don't want to get one of those calls!"

As hunting season between the UN and the Wolfpack Alliance went on unchecked, a different kind of heat was also ramping up: from the Jon Bacon murder investigation. In early 2012, the police message to Shane was simple: "Someone's going to fold. Let it be you. The first guy to talk gets the best deal."

One day, cops approached Shane's girlfriend with a warning. Things were going to get worse soon—way worse—and it was time for her to find a safe landing spot. To prove their point, an officer played a recording of young mother Nicole (Nikki) Marie Alemy from Surrey, who had been shot to death on February 16, 2009, while driving on a quiet street near a park a few blocks from her childhood home.

She had turned twenty-three just two days earlier, on Valentine's Day. Alemy had a four-year-old son and a six-year-old daughter and no criminal record. Her final minutes were captured on the voicemail of a friend, and a police officer played it to the mother of Shane's son. Shane's girlfriend could hear Alemy starting to leave the voice message, and then the *pop, pop, pop, pop* of bullets crashing through the driver's-side window of her Cadillac. Next was a thud as it crashed to a stop.

After that, there was the crying voice of Alemy's son. "Mommy, Mommy, are you okay?" the frantic little boy asked. "Are you okay, Mommy?"

There was no answer.

Shane's girlfriend was also shown photos of Alemy in her white Cadillac, dead.

"Your son's father is a walking time bomb," a police officer told her. "He's a dead man walking. The things he's responsible for, there's no turning back. Do you want this to be you? Do you want your little boy to grow up without you?"

Not long after that, police played the same recording for Shane, and again it had an impact.

Alemy's killer was haunted too, apparently; he died of an overdose.

The war dragged on into the summer of 2012.

Shane had the top down on his Corvette as he drove to a meeting at a restaurant in Guildford, Surrey, with Fitzy. Sukh had summoned a rogues' gallery to the steakhouse that day, including Thomas Mantel, Manny Hairan, Jujhar Khun-Khun, and Doug Wheeler.

"Everyone was showing up," Shane says. "The restaurant is filling up with our guys."

The purpose of the meeting was to introduce them to Donkey, who had just gotten out of custody that day and who was supposed to be a shooter. In those post–Kelowna shooting days, they could use all the clout they could get.

Everyone in Sukh's crew was expected to kick in $2,500 for Donkey's out-of-prison fund, which would give the man $25,000 in seed money to hit the ground running. "We don't even fucking know him," Shane says.

Still, Donkey was a fresh body, and you need plenty of bodies and guns when you're going to war.

Everything was just fine until Sukh saw a man who definitely wasn't part of their group. Shane knew him from back in elementary school, before Shane had dropped out. "We all went back so long," he says.

He now worked primarily for the Wolfpack Alliance, although he'd had enough interactions with Sukh to run up a $150,000 debt. The man's spidey sense told him that something significant was happening that day in the restaurant, and he was soon on his phone, calling for backup.

The UN side had backup of their own, and it was much closer. They were waiting in the parking lot. It had been that way since Dip's day. "Dip always had three Somali guys from Toronto that were ready to kill. He would always call these guys when he needed a shooter. They would immediately show up."

One of Shane's crew walked over to the table where Shane's old schoolmate was sitting. He had his back to the wall—and he knew he was in danger of being trapped there, in a room full of enemies. As soon as he saw Sukh and Shane heading over, he flipped the table to keep from being boxed in.

Any thoughts of a quiet meal were suddenly gone. "Fuck, was it on," Shane recalls.

Chairs were thrown. One of Shane's crew was stabbed in the face. Somehow, Shane pulled a muscle. "There is complete chaos," he says, recalling that, by this point, other diners were stampeding for the door. "Women, kids, men. They're running for their lives."

They would have run even faster had they known the room was full of angry underworld killers. "Can you imagine if they knew who was doing this?"

Shane was in rough shape with his pulled muscle, but he knew he couldn't leave without checking on Sukh. Guards had run in from the parking lot with guns drawn. One had his shirt pulled up over his face with one hand and a gun in the other. It was an interesting plan, but it wasn't working. "He's trying to click it and it won't fire."

Backup arrived in the form of Somalian shooters, summoned on PGP. "They were ready to kill." And yet, Shane's old schoolmate grabbed a gun from one of them. Now, it was him calling the shots, literally, and what followed was forty or fifty seconds of complete chaos.

"Get the fuck back! I'll fucking blast you," he ordered, before he was tackled by Manny Hairan.

The chaos spilled into the parking lot. One of Shane's crew was now behind the wheel of his F-350 truck with its twenty-two-inch rims. Shane, Sukh, and a few others ran to the truck and jumped in, racing off just as police pulled in.

"That was a serious brawl that very easily could have led to a double, triple, or quadruple homicide. No joke," says Shane. "It's a remarkable thing that no one was killed."

Sukh called another meeting the next day, where he announced that he was taxing everyone $20,000 for making him look stupid. Sukh had a point. Perhaps he was even being lenient, by his standards. There were only four or so Wolfpack guys and two dozen on the United Nations side. And somehow, that still wasn't enough.

"They got the better of us. It was a joke. I don't know what happened."

CHAPTER 15

FUNERAL TEARS

"I'm going to lose my fucking life driving these guys around being broke."
—DRIVER/BODYGUARD THOMAS MANTEL

SHANE SOMETIMES VISITED Thomas Mantel at his sixteenth-floor condo in Surrey, with its massive window overlooking the city. Near the window was a prominently displayed card from Gurmit Dhak's funeral, which read, "God has you safely in his keeping, But we have you forever in our hearts."

Mantel was sometimes identified in the press as Sukh's bodyguard, but he had also been pressed into being a driver after Sukh lost his licence for letting a stack of tickets pile up. He was big enough, at six feet, to take on a bodyguard role, but not too physically imposing. He was heavily tattooed with ink on his back, legs, and even his hands. He was tough, but not Doug Wheeler tough. He liked his weed, and he loved his dog.

Mantel shared the condo with his huge Rottweiler named Luda, short for Ludacris.

"He loved that fucking dog," Shane says. "He was a big boy. Nice, big, friendly dog. That dog meant everything to him."

Muscular, loyal Rottweilers were popular in Shane's circle. Fitzy had one named Junior, and another guy had one named Boss. The dogs could be just as tough as their owners.

One day, in the chaos after the murder of Jon Bacon, a man in Shane's circle got a knock on his door around two or three in the morning. Two men were outside, wearing bulletproof vests with "POLICE" on them.

"It's the police! Open up!" one of them ordered.

Boss sprang up from the couch, where he had been sleeping, as the men barged into his home, and bit one of the visitors—hard. "His blood was everywhere," Shane says.

The men managed to pump three shots into Boss, but he kept on biting. They eventually took off, leaving a blood trail.

When Sukh heard of the attack, he quickly concluded that the intruders weren't real cops. "Those guys want us bad," he said.

Danger was certainly close in those days—sometimes literally. Living in the same building as Mantel was Wolfpack rival and hit man Dean Wiwchar. The two men did their best to ignore each other.

One day, when Shane visited Mantel in his apartment, Mantel told him, "I literally got an eviction letter on my door. Sukh has not paid me nothing, bro."

Even though he wasn't being paid regularly, Mantel was still expected to drive Sukh everywhere, and watch his back while Sukh ran errands. This was a time-consuming job, as Sukh was an early riser and worked from 5 a.m. to 10 p.m. or so. Mantel was expected to be on call throughout that time, from the moment he got his first zap ordering him to "Come get me." That left Mantel with no time to branch off and make money on his own or even properly take care of Luda. "He couldn't venture off. Sukh treated Thomas really bad. Really bad."

Not surprisingly, Mantel became increasingly depressed. "I'm going to lose my fucking life driving these guys around being broke," he told Shane.

—

It had never been easy working for Sukh, but it was getting harder by the day—for Mantel and everyone else as well. Sometime after the Kelowna hit, Sukh had concluded that there must be a rat in his group, and his fixation with the idea made him even more edgy than usual. He was paranoid, and that made others more edgy as well. It called to mind the old gangster line, "Help, I'm being chased by paranoids."

By November 2012, Sukh began to take his frustrations out on Fitzy.

Sukh's temper, which always ran hot, became even hotter. He accused Fitzy of lying and owing money—and there was nothing subtle about it. "You fucking goof," Sukh said to him. "Come meet us now."

Fitzy refused to play along. He did, however, accept an invitation to Manny's house one evening, where he found Sukh, angry and drunk, waiting for him. "[Sukh] literally thought he could beat up anybody," says Shane. "Sukh thought he was bigger than he was when he was drunk."

That night, Sukh turned on Fitzy with a baseball bat. He even forced Mantel to join in. Shane could see his group was imploding. "He almost killed him," he says. "But like I say, they had it in their minds that there was a rat. Manny and Khun-Khun literally cried trying to beg Sukh to stop beating him with the bat. It was a savage attack. Broke his ribs, arms, leg. Collapsed lungs. Sukh didn't even spare Fitzy's head. Fuck no, he broke his nose, his teeth. Literally almost killed him."

It was hard to take. Shane loved Fitzy. Shane believed he was a good guy. And yet here he was, on the wrong end of a brutal beat-down.

"Our boss, our leader. Imagine," Shane says. "Now, granted, he had lost his brother. The beef was at an extreme high. The walls were closing in. He was so stressed out. He wasn't sleeping or eating. He was drinking excessively. That obviously doesn't make it okay, but just saying."

In November 2012, Thomas Mantel was there when police officer Doug Spencer went to a house that Sukh was building in Surrey for his parents. The cop managed to walk up on him undetected.

"Are you supposed to be guarding Sukh?" Spencer asked. "I could have killed you."

The cop was right, and Mantel knew it. Sukh had strict rules for his men when they were out in public. One of those rules was that they always had to park with the nose of their vehicle facing outward, so that they could floor it and make a quick escape if necessary. "If you pulled frontward in a parking lot, Sukh lost his mind," says Shane.

Another rule was that Sukh's men were expected to be fully aware of their surroundings at all times. Sukh would continually chide them: "Look at you, on your phones with your heads down," or "Stay off your fucking phone."

On November 26, 2012, Sukh broke his own rule. He was facing conspiracy and drug trafficking charges and had to attend the Vancouver Law Courts that day. During a break in the proceedings, Sukh and Thomas Mantel drove to Burnaby. At 11:30 a.m., Mantel backed a silver Dodge rental truck into a parking spot at the Executive Hotel Burnaby lobby on Lougheed Highway.

As Sukh walked across the parking lot to the hotel for a planned meeting, trailing behind Mantel, he was on his BlackBerry. Staring at his phone screen, he didn't notice as two men in an Audi slowly drove across the parking lot. They got close to Sukh and then cut him off.

Shane later obtained a surveillance video of the incident that showed Sukh's reaction. "He stops. He looks up and into the car, and goes like, 'Who's going to go? You or me?'"

Then Sukh started walking again, into the front lobby, where a Christmas tree was part of an attempt at a cheery holiday mood.

That's when the gunshots started.

Mantel was cut down first, and then Sukh. A gunman ran up to make sure he finished Sukh off. Sukh was wearing Gurmit's white-gold beads on his wrist, which he involuntarily raised in a vain attempt to block the gunfire. At least one bullet hit the string of beads. "They shot him right in the arm and the beads went everywhere."

An ornament from the Christmas tree fell on Sukh. His girlfriend kept it. A grim souvenir.

Sukhveer Singh Dhak was just twenty-eight when he was shot dead in the hotel lobby—four years younger than his big brother Gurmit had been when he was murdered two years earlier.

As for Mantel, he'd died just as he predicted, broke and driving for Sukh.

Not surprisingly, police were out in force for Sukh's funeral in Delta, held in the same room of the same funeral home, the Riverside Crematorium, where Gurmit's service had taken place. Luxury Mercedes, Acura, and BMW vehicles cruised past police vehicles strategically positioned at the entrances and exits. Officers in "Gang Enforcement" jackets questioned many of the attendees. Several of the arrivals were photographed and videotaped.

Sukh's funeral cards read:

He touched everyone that met him with his loving personality. People would naturally gravitate to him and because of this he always brought everyone together. He cared more about his family and friends than words can express.

Sukh, you will hold a special place in our hearts and eternity.

"The Dhak mom was very rich and stuck-up, very short with people, and the dad was very nice, but in the end he was sick," Shane recalls. "I remember at Sukh's funeral his mom hugged me for carrying both her son's caskets, and the dad didn't even know what was going on. Dementia, I believe."

Shane tossed a rose into Sukh's casket before it was closed. He kept one petal for himself, as well as a card from the funeral. Later, he framed these items along with a hundred-dollar bill from his last transaction with Sukh. They were memories of a relationship he cherished—one he never wanted to forget.

Manny Hairan was also a pallbearer, and he was acting strangely. "At Sukh's funeral, Manny would not touch his casket. He walked behind me the whole time, crying so hard, but wouldn't touch it. I thought it was weird." Shane kept saying, "Bro, grab the handle," but Manny kept crying and refusing to touch even a bit of Sukh's casket. "He just would not do it."

After Sukh's cremation, Manny drove Shane to see Shane's cousin Sheldon. It wasn't something he enjoyed doing. "Manny hated Sheldon. He was just jealous of him. Manny wanted my attention. He always wanted to be with me . . . Just like little kids."

Sheldon was sitting on a patio when they drove up. "Look at your fucking cousin," Manny said. "We could hit this guy right now." Then Manny's mood veered off in an odd direction. "Bro, I think I'm going to die," he said, rubbing his head. "Fuck, bro, everything that's going on."

"No man, we're gonna make it out of this war," Shane told him.

"If I can only make it a couple more weeks," Manny replied. "I just need to make it a few more weeks."

Shane had no clue what Manny meant, and so he replied, "Don't say stupid shit."

Shane's gang was being executed and buried, one by one. "They literally killed twenty-five to thirty of our guys. They started at the top and they worked their way down," Shane says, adding that while Sukh's murder may have been a blow to whatever was left of the Dhak–Duhre arm of the UN, it turned out to be a lucky break for at least one person.

Back in October 2010, Shane, Sukh, and Manny had signed a deal with the memorabilia seller that gave them a sliding scale of profits, from 50 percent for monthly profits of $20,000 to $100,000 up to 80 percent for profits of more than $200,000. "Six days after we signed this, Gurmit was killed and our lives changed forever," Shane says.

In time, Sukh circled back to his business dealings with the memorabilia man. He felt he was still owed money, but had given up on collecting the debt and had planned to make an example of him. "Sukh was going to kill him," Shane says.

Instead, with Sukh gone, it was business as usual.

This was not the case for everyone, though. Shane felt an odd rush of emotions after Sukh's death, some of which surprised him. "It was like a sense of relief," he recalls. "As sad as I was and hurt when Sukh got killed, I was relieved, because I could finally live my life. That was the hold he had on me, on us. When [his number] would call . . . I remember it still, I would get near anxiety. Like, 'Oh no, what did I do? What did he find out now?' It was fucked up." Still, the feeling of loss was real. "Sukh was a dick, but at the end of the day, he did have a lot of love for me. It wasn't all bad."

It was hard to shake a sense of unreality after Sukh's murder. Both of the Dhak brothers were now gone, even though they had once seemed so calculating and strong and in control. Sukh had tightened things up even more after Gurmit's murder. "He had everything so calculated. Every time we moved. You get used to it."

And then Sukh had just walked right into his execution, breaking his own rule about staying alert.

There was also a feeling of unfulfillment. Sukh had constantly talked about "the property" and his dream of building his own forever house. Now there was no forever. "Sukh was killed before that property was finished. He never did get to see it finished."

The sudden departure of the Dhak brothers left Shane feeling unmoored. Some of Gurmit's old crew were trying to run things, but it was easy to worry about the future. "Until that point, I almost thought we were untouchable. It took away my sense of safety. If Sukh got it, any of us can get it."

Someone brought Mantel's Rottweiler, Luda, to the funeral home, which seemed fitting. "He loved that dog more than anything."

As if November 2012 wasn't already bad enough, Shane was quietly arrested on drug charges that month. His file with Corrections Canada includes the following note:

In November 2012, Mr. DANKOSKI was arrested for trafficking cocaine and he provided a statement admitting that he associates with gang members (Hell's [sic] Angels) and he discusses a "safe house" where he stored his "stuff." The report indicates that during a search warrant of the location, they recovered drugs, money, a pellet gun and 6 cell phones. The report also indicates that charges were not laid via "departmental discretion."

A bigger plan for Shane would soon be playing out.

CHAPTER 16

MANNY

"The worst part about getting shot or stabbed is not knowing
who it was. Who do you trust? Who can you talk to?"
—SHANE DANKOSKI

ON SUNDAY, JANUARY 13, 2013, Dhak associate Manjot Dhillon was
shot to death in Surrey, not long after posting anti-Wolfpack images on
his Facebook page. It may have been a new year, but the same old war
was still claiming lives.

The next day, Shane, his girlfriend, and his sister visited a psychic in
Vancouver—a spur-of-the-moment outing, which meant the psychic had
had no time to prepare. "She didn't know my name," Shane says. "She
didn't know anything about me. She didn't even know that I was showing up." Shane explains that he's "not, like, a big believer of that shit."
Even so, the visit was an eye-opening experience.

The psychic said Shane's mom was from Montreal, which was correct. She then said that Shane's mother had something to do with flow-
ers, which was correct too—although that could have applied to many
women. Still, Shane's mother had recently kept a flower after attending

the funeral of her niece Nikki, Sheldon's younger sister, who'd died from drug usage.

The psychic got grim as she spoke of Shane's future. "She sees danger around me," Shane recalls her saying. That was obviously correct as well. Maybe she had watched the news. Or maybe his two arms full of tattoos provided a clue. Whatever the case, the psychic wrote on a piece of paper the initials of the person she thought was behind that danger: SD. Shane took it to mean the recently murdered Sukh Dhak.

Then the psychic turned towards Shane. "You just lost a friend from gunpowder. This guy was very powerful," she said. "Dark skin?"

"Yes."

"Small, five-seven? Five-eight?"

"Yes."

The psychic continued. "Is there somebody else, like a brother to him?" This person had a raspy voice, the psychic said, short hair, and a five o'clock shadow. "She describes Manny to a fucking T," Shane says.

"He needs to be very, very careful because danger is coming his way," the psychic continued. "Your friend with the raspy voice. You need to get a hold of him right away. You need to let him know that there's danger."

His girlfriend asked the psychic if she saw death or jail for Shane. She wrote "Jail" on a piece of paper.

After the session ended, Shane got on the phone with Manny. "Bro, you're never going to believe this," he said, outlining how the psychic had just described him so accurately.

In his raspy voice, Manny mocked the suggestion. "So what are you saying, bro? I'm going to die?"

"No, I'm just telling you what she said, bro."

Manny wasn't impressed. "Holy fuck, bro. Don't believe that shit."

Manny put his pregnant girlfriend on the phone, and she ridiculed the call too. "Fuck off, Shane," she told him. "Don't bring that negative shit around here."

Manny then made a comment that has stuck with Shane ever since: "Imagine you didn't tell me this and I died. How would you feel then?"

At 2 a.m. on January 15, 2013, Manny and Khun-Khun were in a North Surrey laneway behind homes near the Patullo Bridge. It was just a few minutes from a strip club where Shane had so often brawled and Manny had recently severely stabbed a man. Manny told Khun-Khun that they were going to meet someone who owed him $20,000.

Later that morning, Shane awoke to a call from Fitzy, who was bawling his eyes out. There'd been an ambush, Fitzy said. Manny was dead.

Everyone in Shane's universe seemed shocked. "I wake up to a whole bunch of PGP messages. A bunch of zaps," he recalls. "I was devastated. I almost fainted. It wasn't real."

A million thoughts raced through Shane's mind. He and Manny had been friends for almost as long as he could remember—from back in the days by the Chevron gas station in Surrey. They'd come up in the life together. They were brothers. And now his brother was gone at twenty-nine. Shane thought of the psychic's warning, which Manny had so casually dismissed. "It was the most eerie thing ever," he says.

While he was still reeling from the news, Shane got a call from Sergeant Dwayne McDonald of the RCMP. The cop was becoming a big—albeit uninvited—presence in Shane's life. He'd shown up for the first time about three months after Jon Bacon's murder, and after that, it seemed like the Mountie was everywhere. He would appear at all times of the day and night, like 2 a.m. when Shane was leaving a bar, or 6 a.m. when he was leaving the Hells Angels clubhouse.

"He was always really nice, really respectful, but to the point. He's a no-bullshit type of guy," Shane says. "He'll sniff you out right away if you try to give him a little BS, and he'll call you out in a couple of seconds."

For months now, McDonald had been putting enormous pressure on Shane. The Jon Bacon murder had been carried out in broad daylight at a highly public location. Someone had been paralyzed and another almost killed. Innocent bystanders had been in the line of fire. This simply couldn't be allowed to go on. The crime had to be solved. And it was McDonald's job to send the criminals that message.

"We know more about you than you think," McDonald would say when Shane brushed him off.

"At this point," Shane says, explaining his attitude towards the cop, "I'm firmly entrenched in the life. Entrenched in the gangster life. I'm selling dope. We're hunting for guys."

No way was he talking to a cop.

But then, just after Manny's murder, McDonald called again. "I'm really sorry for what happened to Manny," he said. "I know who Manny is to you and how close you were. I want you to know Manny really loved you . . . he did."

McDonald had known about Manny's murder within five minutes of the fatal shots and had rushed to the scene. "[McDonald] said the whole drive there he was praying it wasn't true. He said when he got there, Manny had both hands in his pockets. He was laying on his back dead."

McDonald told Shane that Manny looked out for Shane, even while he drew close to police. He didn't offer details, but his tone was definitive. "He protected you a lot throughout this. Seriously, seriously."

Shane tried to brush McDonald off the way he always did but the cop persisted, drilling home the point that Manny had died with his hands in his pockets. "Do you know what that means?" he asked. "He was comfortable. You're probably next. Your time is coming."

Shane knew exactly what McDonald meant when he said Manny had died with his hands in his pockets: Manny had felt safe around his killer or killers, right up to the instant he was shot dead. Whatever setup was playing out that night, it seemed likely that Manny had been part of it—at least until he wasn't.

Khun-Khun, once again, came away with his life intact. He was hit fourteen times but managed to drive himself to the hospital in Manny's SUV. Since this war had started, his penis had been shot off, his left hand had become locked in a permanent lobster-like curl, he'd lost nerve sensation in one foot and movement in his right arm, and he was now attached to a colonoscopy bag. There was a surgical scar from his neck to his groin and literally dozens of bullet entry and exit wounds throughout his body; he'd been struck at least twenty-seven times by gunfire. "He looked like he was put in a blender."

But at least he was alive. Manny wasn't.

This latest funeral was tough, although Shane remembers that he didn't cry. Even though he and Manny had been best friends, something just didn't seem real. "I still remember looking down at his body. I just couldn't cry."

Instead, Shane adjusted the collar on Manny's shirt to cover the triangle-shaped bullet exit wound in his neck. He hugged Manny in his casket and said a few last words to his cold, motionless body. "I promised him that we would get those guys. I promised him as I was hugging his body. I just didn't want to leave him. I just stood there. I just couldn't leave."

Shane thought of the day Manny had told him the news that he was about to become a dad. "He was super happy. He said, 'Bro, you know what? You're the first person I'm telling.' He was really excited." There was a slide show at Manny's funeral, and the last image was an ultrasound of his unborn child. "That caused a lot of people to break down."

No one was more distraught than Manny's mother. "She was trying to pull him out of the casket. She grabbed me by the head. She shouted, 'Wake him up! This can't be real! I want to cook for you! Don't go! Don't go!'" she yelled in Punjabi.

Manny's nephew bawled as Manny's mom fell on the floor, screaming his nickname. "Mindy! Wake up! Mindy! Mindy! Wake up! I'll make you roti!"

The casket was closed, wheeled into a room with a glass window, and loaded into an oven. "We were all standing at the glass window after we put him in the oven, and hugging and holding each other. Many crying . . . And then, after about three minutes, I pressed the button and the fire starts, and then the funeral people close the blinds."

Even though Shane didn't cry, emotions tore through him. "It will fuck with you. He was my brother . . . We beat, shot, stabbed people together and we'd sleep in the same bed together sometimes. We had a bond. We're brothers from a different mother. I miss him every day. I think about him every day. He's my real bro. My real brother. Very crazy to see your brother in a glass jar, after laying in a casket."

Manny's murder was the fourth in two days in Surrey, which brought the gang-war tally to more than twenty shootings in two years. Shane had no doubt what was happening. There was a push underway by the Wolfpack to kill everyone responsible for the Kelowna casino attack, and that meant the killers would soon be coming for him too.

Just after the funeral, Shane and Fitz drove one of Fitzy's workers to Vancouver, popping Percocets and using heroin and fentanyl along the way. In his rear-view mirror Shane spotted a silver van, staying suspiciously close.

"Bro, there's a cop right behind us," he told Fitzy.

He slowed down to let the van pass, but it stayed where it was. Then Shane came to a red light; when the light turned green, he didn't move. The silver van wouldn't go either, hanging back thirty feet or so. Cars honked their horns, but Shane and the silver van stayed put. "This fucking guy, he won't move."

Finally, the silver van started moving. It pulled up beside Shane, and in the driver's seat he could see an associate who reminded him of "Mr. Burns," the twitchy, malevolent figure on the cartoon series, *The Simpsons*. Seeing him reminded Shane that neither Mr. Burns nor the gangster nicknamed "Donkey" had shown up for Manny's funeral. They'd also missed the group's ritual earlier in the day, when the rest of the crew washed Manny's body.

"What's up, boys?" Mr. Burns said, just before he drove off.

Twenty minutes later, Shane pulled into a Robin's Donuts. "We're popping Percocets. I went in to get a bottle of water so we could pop more." When he looked in his rear-view mirror, he could still see the silver van. Then he got a PGP BlackBerry message from one of his crew, letting him know that Mr. Burns had just messaged him, with words to the effect of, "Yo, bro. What the fuck's up with Rooster and Fitzy? They're in Vancouver partying. Buddy could get clipped."

"Bro, we're not in Vancouver partying," Shane messaged back. "We're driving somebody home."

It was clear what was happening. Mr. Burns was creating a smoke-screen. He could then shoot Shane and make it appear that Shane had been reckless that night. The only thing that didn't make sense was why.

Twenty-five kilometres or so from the donut shop, the silver van appeared yet again. This time Mr. Burns was wearing a hat pulled low and a hoodie zipped high. He pulled up alongside Shane again, saying, "Yo, bro, pull over into this parking lot."

Fitzy took a quick look into the car and saw Donkey, lying down— a typical position for a shooter to take right before a hit. He turned to Shane and yelled, "Go, bro. Fucking go!"

As Donkey pulled his seat up and opened fire, Shane raced into oncoming traffic on a bridge. As Mr. Burns chased him, Donkey shot out Shane's driver's-side window and mirror. Shane eventually got enough distance between them and the van to pull into a gas station. He and Fitz looked under the GMC 2500 and found a GPS tracking device. It explained how Donkey and Mr. Burns kept finding them. They had placed it on the truck during the funeral.

This was a whole new wrinkle in the ongoing gang war. Now Shane didn't just have to worry about his enemies, or the near-constant presence of the cops. His own crew had just tried to kill him—and it wouldn't be the last time.

About six months later, Shane was washing his Escalade in Kelowna, wearing a shirt with a big UN logo on the back, when the door to the car wash opened automatically. Between the steam and the darkness, it was impossible to see, but he had no trouble hearing the footsteps behind him. Suddenly someone shouted, "Shoot him! Shoot him!"

Through the steam, Shane saw two men wearing balaclavas. "I was frozen. I just stood there," he says. "I don't know if the gun jammed or he was too scared, but he would not shoot."

Somebody in a vehicle with no licence plate was directing the attackers. He kept telling them to shoot, but there were no bullets.

"They bear-maced me, and stabbed me a bunch of times, and then hacked me in the back of the head with a machete," Shane says. "I was bleeding everywhere, on fire. You can't see anything."

Shane got back in his truck and raced away, with his head out the window. He couldn't really see because of the mace. "I'm driving like Ace Ventura."

Once he was safely out of reach of his attackers, he tried to process what had just happened. "The worst part about getting shot or stabbed is not knowing who it was. Who do you trust? Who can you talk to?"

He couldn't come up with any answers.

A few days after Manny's murder, Shane went to a Kelowna Rockets Junior A hockey game with his sister's boyfriend. As he was walking towards the food concourse, a couple of men walked up behind him. In a low voice, one of them said, "Don't look behind you. Look forward. Don't look sideways. Just keeping walking. Dwayne sent us here."

Dwayne McDonald: the investigator who had told Shane that Manny loved him and that he had died with his hands in his pockets.

There were six thousand people at that game, and the undercover cops managed to blend in perfectly. "The entire time I was at the game I had no clue I was being watched," Shane recalls. "They knew exactly where I was."

The strangers who approached him had five o'clock shadows and Boss jackets. "They looked like gangsters. You couldn't tell the difference."

Which meant that their lives were in danger too, if Shane's enemies moved in for the kill. "They don't know that these four guys standing beside me are undercover cops. They're going to clip them too. Their safety is so on the line it isn't funny," he says. "To a gangster trying to kill you they looked like your friends. It's really dangerous for them." Within minutes, McDonald popped up in person.

"Shane, don't make any sudden movements," he said. "I want you to know that you're safe right now. I want to talk with you for a few minutes."

Shane sloughed him off yet again, and yet again McDonald persisted. "Seriously, just give me five minutes," he said. "It'll change your life forever. You're completely safe right now. We have eyes everywhere."

"I'm literally thinking, *What? I'm at a hockey game. This is fucked up,*" Shane says. "I'm totally mind-blown."

"Give me five minutes," the cop said. "Just five minutes."

Finally, Shane agreed to hear him out.

Shane was directed to drive to a Boston Pizza parking lot about fifteen minutes away, next to a hotel. When he arrived, there were more undercover officers who looked like gangsters in the parking lot. A couple came up to talk with him. One gave him a room number and told him to go look inside a magazine in the lounge, where he'd find a key for the room.

Shane retrieved the key and went to the room. When he let himself in, no one was waiting. Then, a few minutes later, there was a knock on the door. "It's Dwayne," McDonald said. "We can't do this here."

Shane was directed to another room on another floor. This time McDonald was waiting for him, sitting on a couch and holding an iPad. There was equipment nearby to tape the conversation. "This is going to change your life forever," McDonald repeated.

The first image he showed Shane on the iPad was Manny sitting in a hotel room, much like the one they were in. Manny was in his Boss jacket, saying, "Fucking me, Shane, Jay, Khun-Khun . . ."

It was obvious that he was talking about the Kelowna hit. "Now, when I saw this and heard Manny say my name, I literally got light-headed and wanted to faint."

All at once, everything clicked. The lights went on for Shane as to why Manny had cried so hard at Sukh's funeral, and why he'd refused to even touch his casket. No one in the police or on the gangster side told Shane; he sorted it out for himself. He knew Manny's mind better than anyone else. He concluded that it was Manny who had set up the murders of Sukh Dhak and Thomas Mantel, and that he had tried to do the same with Khun-Khun. He was guided to make the moves out of a combination of guilt and self-preservation, and even love. As Shane learned, by the time of Sukh's funeral, Manny had been co-operating with police for almost eight months. Manny had spoken vaguely about having to hang on for just a little longer. Now Shane finally knew what he meant.

It all made sense, if you knew Manny. Manny's love for Sukh was unquestionable. In Manny's twisted logic, it was better to set Sukh up for murder than to have him learn of Manny's betrayal. He would rather have Sukh and Khun-Khun killed than see them lose respect for him. It was twisted love, but it was love. Mantel was just collateral damage. "[Manny] was about to be taken into custody for his role in the Kelowna casino murder. His deal was done. And then everyone was going to be arrested. But Sukh was like a brother to Manny, and Manny would rather have Sukh and Thomas killed and Khun-Khun killed than have them ever know he was the one co-operating. He would not let Sukh and Khun-Khun know he went out as a rat."

As if that weren't enough to take in, McDonald played another clip on the iPad. This time Manny was describing Jon Bacon's murder, saying, "I got out with this gun. I see Larry. I see Jon and then I just fucking let it rip."

McDonald played a series of surveillance clips showing Shane with Manny at the casino hotel that night. As Shane struggled to take it all in, his mind reeling, McDonald reminded him that he wasn't under arrest and had the option of co-operating or leaving. "You're free to go. There's the door."

Shane walked out—but he did so knowing that McDonald had been right when he said that Shane's life would change after their talk. Nothing would ever be the same. "When I left I was broken," Shane says. "I felt defeated, like, *Oh God, I'm done. I'm fucking done. I'm going to jail for the rest of my life. They know everything.* That was like the 'I'm fucked' moment."

Sukh's death, Manny's death, the attempts on his own life, Manny's betrayal: it was all too much. "After that I didn't want to face reality anymore," Shane says, recalling that his already heavy drug use doubled during this time. He would go for three or four days on end, just floating on heroin. "You've never felt more vulnerable. You never felt more defeated. I would do drugs to make me numb out."

Shane knew what he had done, and he knew that the police knew. There was a feeling of inevitability about things. People were coming to get him. *Everyone* was coming to get him. He didn't want to co-operate with the police. He felt cornered and alone. Sudden floods of anxiety rushed over him whenever an unknown number came up on his phone. He could be relaxing on his boat and his phone would ring and suddenly his chill would vanish.

No matter how many drugs he took, Shane couldn't turn off the constant chatter in his brain, couldn't stop trying to piece it all together. At first, police reasoned that Shane had been part of the conspiracy to kill Manny. They accused him of making a warning call to Manny as an attempt to cover his tracks, reasoning that he knew Manny's phone was likely tapped and that Manny wouldn't take a warning from a psychic seriously. "They were trying to say that I was trying to cover my own ass," he says.

Shane knew that wasn't true, though. And eventually, as the rumour mill kept spinning and bits of information became available, he sorted it out. It seemed Manny had made a massive blunder in his final act as a gangster, one that had cost him his life. When it came time to arrange the hit on Khun-Khun—likely, Shane reasons, so Manny wouldn't have to look him in the eye while testifying in court—he'd reached out to Dougie Fresh. "He was our fucking weed dealer," Shane says. "He was with us all the time . . ."

But Dougie was also close to Larry Amero, and Amero knew that Manny had been one of the shooters at Kelowna, where Amero himself had almost died. "[Manny] was expecting they would kill Khun-Khun, and then they killed him," Shane says. "It was supposed to be just Khun-Khun getting hit, but because it was set up by the other side, who knew Manny was a K-Town shooter, there was no fucking way Larry was going to have Manny and Khun-Khun in the same place, same time, and just one killed."

There was talk that Dougie got $500,000 for the double hit attempt on Manny and Khun-Khun, which was enough for him to retire, perhaps in Mexico. So Dougie was off in parts unknown with a boatload of cash for his efforts, Manny was dead, and the police badly wanted Shane to replace Manny as their new star witness. It wasn't such a stretch, given that they already had his house, phones, Escalade, Corvette, and Jeep Cherokee bugged. And it was getting harder and harder to say no. Any talk of loyalty to Sukh and his group just seemed like a bad joke now.

"I was so loyal, I gave up everything. My relationship, my kid, my businesses, and almost my life by death or jail, facing life," he says. "That's what those beads meant. And then they try to kill me? For what? Why? I wasn't co-operating. Sukh knew that. But when he got killed, the rest knew someone was ratting. We know now it was Manny . . . Broke my fucking heart. Broke me to the core."

It was around this time that Manny's girlfriend gave birth. Their baby was a girl.

CHAPTER 17

ALONE

"Walls were closing in."
—SHANE DANKOSKI

DWAYNE MCDONALD WASN'T the only RCMP officer making himself an unwelcome presence in Shane's life during this time. In early 2013, Staff Sergeant Sam Gadbahn also seemed to be everywhere in Shane's world. "Sam fucking knew everything about me," Shane says.

Gadbahn was one of the lead investigators in the Jon Bacon homicide, and he wasn't going away. "Listen, you're going to jail for murder," Gadbahn would say. "No question about it."

"Man, I didn't do it," Shane lied. "You guys think I'm a big fucking player."

"You are."

"I'm a street worker."

"You're going to jail and you're going to jail for murder," Gadbahn replied. "That's inevitable. We know everything and you're going to jail. It's just a matter of time."

Gadbahn kept telling Shane it was in his best interest to talk. "You did do something but you aren't willing to tell us your side of the story," he would say. "You're gambling. You're letting the chips fall where they may."

In an effort to make a personal connection, Gadbahn even gave Shane his personal cell number and told him to call if the cops were ever treating him badly.

One day not long after that conversation, Shane was cruising downtown in his black Cadillac CTS sedan when he was pulled over by the police.

"You down here selling dope again?" the cop said. "Being an asshole? Selling shit?"

Shane immediately called Gadbahn. "Let me talk to him," Gadbahn said.

Gadbahn introduced himself as a staff sergeant, and the patrol officer quickly changed his tone, after turning off the speakerphone.

"Oh, I apologize," the junior officer said, followed quickly by "Yes, sir," and then "Thank you."

After he hung up, the officer turned back to Shane and said, "You fucking rat."

Shane instantly called Gadbahn back and told him what the cop had said. "Sam called that cop back."

The patrol cop listened for a bit and then hung up again. When he turned to Shane again, his tone had dramatically changed. "I shouldn't be treating you like that. It's not professional."

By the second week of February 2013, Shane was in constant contact with police. "They were pressing and pressing and pressing. Turning up the heat."

It was uncomfortable, but it didn't rule out fun entirely. One day Shane and Fitzy were driving around in Shane's brand new high-end GMC 2500 HD, which he had bought with cash. When Fitzy opened the glove compartment in search of napkins, he noticed a tiny red wire. Shane and Fitzy pulled on the wires and found tracking and listening devices.

They decided to make the best of things. While they promptly tossed the GPS onto the highway, they kept the listening device intact.

"We would just say the most fucked-up shit," Shane says, explaining that they were hoping to lead the cops on wild goose chases. "We'd talk about fake shit that never happened. Bodies being in trunks."

The not so carefully hidden wiretap was an indication that the cops were ramping up their efforts. There was nothing subtle about their presence. "They literally just parked a police car in front of my house all day," Shane says.

Sometimes, Gadbahn would compare the police reports to a painting and say it was time for Shane to take the brush in his own hands. And that wasn't his only attempt at metaphor. "The wheel is in motion, Shane, and I can't stop it," he would say. Or, "Here we are. The wheel's getting traction."

In an effort to keep his eyes on anyone who might be creeping around—cops or enemies—Shane had equipped his home with high-end motion-sensor cameras that he could view from a couch in his basement. One night the cameras picked up an SUV making a U-turn in front of his home and then pulling over. Someone got out of the SUV, walked past the house, and then looked back at it. The person looked up at the security cameras before walking away, pulling his hoodie over his face.

Shane recognized him anyway. It was Jujhar Khun-Khun, from Shane's crew. He may have been badly mangled, but he was still capable of pulling a trigger. "He thought I was co-operating. He thought I was the one. They drove up to kill me," Shane says.

Not long after that, police got Shane to step into a van and played him a little clip on an iPad. The voices on the recording included that of Khun-Khun.

"Fucking SD. Fatty and Rooster," one of the voices said.

"Think they're snitching out?"

"We should just fucking clip them. Ha-ha."

Shane wanted to pretend he hadn't heard it, but he couldn't. Members of his own crew were joking about killing him, just in case he was co-operating with authorities. "They [the cops] were not lying. It wasn't fabricated or fake." Shane had received four official duty-to-warn letters in just over a year. They are given when the police have credible information that someone's life is in serious danger.

Also around this time, Shane was pulled over by police as he was driving in his truck with his cousin Sheldon. There were Hells Angels nearby as four police SUVs blocked him in. Shane swore at the officers, loud enough for the Hells Angels to hear. Then a cop spoke to him in a softer voice, one the bikers couldn't hear. "Shane, you need to get out in front of this," he said. "We're making arrests soon."

On another night, Shane was sitting on his couch around 12:30 a.m. when he saw five SUVs pull up on his street. Then, for some reason, they just drove away. Shane called Gadbahn. Why had five SUVs just gone by his place? he asked. Were they cops?

"I think you're being paranoid," Gadbahn said, and then added, "Maybe it's Khun-Khun and those guys coming to kill you again."

"I started seeing the writing on the wall," Shane says. "That my own guys were trying to kill me. It's probably the most stressful thing you can imagine. I started using more dope. It's just really taking its toll on me."

Things got even more stressful on Sunday, February 24. That night, sometime after 10 p.m., Shane was driving home from poker at the Hells Angels clubhouse. He pulled up alongside a four-door Honda Civic parked on the street a couple of houses down. He had never seen the car there before, and there was a stranger inside, just sitting there. "I knew this car was either a cop or a killer," he says.

The man inside the Civic was wearing a hat and glasses. His visor was down and his seat was drawn back. Shane pulled up alongside him. "I had my hidden compartment open. I had my hand on my gun."

"What's up man?" Shane asked.

The man in the Honda tried to ignore him.

"Yeah, man, can I help?" Shane said again.

"Fuck off," the man said.

Shane wouldn't go away, and the man eventually said he was waiting for his daughter, who was babysitting.

"What's your daughter doing there? Is she getting railed?" Shane asked, trying to rile the guy up.

"No, she's babysitting."

Finally the man drove away, and Shane followed him for five minutes, until he was boxed in by several vehicles. The Honda didn't return.

At around 5 p.m. the next afternoon, Shane was counting money in his garage with his money counter. There was a buzzing sound as upwards of $600,000 passed through the machine, but he was still able to hear the loud knock on his door. He went into the foyer, where he saw Sam Gadbahn and a half-dozen or so plainclothes cops. Gadbahn looked calm and collected.

"Shane, we've got a warrant for your DNA and we've also got a warrant for your house."

Shane called his lawyer, Kelly Christiansen, who spoke to police and then told Shane it was legit and to co-operate. They poked Shane's finger for blood, swabbed his mouth, and took a strand of his hair. They told Shane that they believed they'd found his DNA at a murder scene.

Shane was upset. His girlfriend and Jayden were home, and he'd tried as hard as he could to keep his gang life separate from his family life. But that wouldn't be possible on this day. The warrant said investigators were looking for murder-related items, like firearms, gloves, GPS devices, encrypted BlackBerrys, and certain shoes. Drugs weren't on the list.

Shane knew they might not just be blowing smoke. He had been close to the murder site on the day of the attack and had been captured on camera with Manny and with McBride. He was also caught on camera, directly in front of the Grand Hotel and Casino, twelve seconds after the shooting happened.

The police left with every electronic device they could find, including fifteen cellphones, six laptops, and a hard drive for the four cameras on Shane's house. They also left with lots of clothes, including the outfit Shane had been wearing the night before the Kelowna murder, when he and his crew were hunting for the victims. "They left my house in shambles," he recalls.

"So what happens when you guys don't get a match?" Shane asked one of the officers as they were leaving. "You guys going to fuck off finally?"

As soon as the cops were gone, Shane sent roughly $1 million of his own cash to Vancouver for safekeeping with a gang courier. The police hadn't raided the safe houses, which would have been disastrous.

At 8 p.m. that same day, a mini convoy of SUVs pulled up to his house as Shane watched on closed-circuit TV. There were plenty of other cops nearby too, some hiding behind bushes. He watched Gadbahn and five or so other detectives walk up to his door. The doorbell rang, but Shane didn't answer.

"Shane, don't make this harder than it has to be," someone on the other side of the door said politely. "We need you to come outside and put your hands above your head. Don't make us kick your door in."

"Come outside, Shane," an officer said.

"I'm not home," Shane finally replied.

The police didn't believe him. "Shane, we haven't taken our eyes off you for eight days straight. Come out or we're coming in."

Shane scrambled to open his safe and gave his girlfriend $100,000 and jewellery, as well as instructions to call his lawyer in the morning. Then he told her to open the door.

He was upstairs now, and the police were at the bottom of the stairs.

"You're under arrest for the first-degree murder of Jonathan Bacon, attempted murder times four, and conspiracy times five," one of them said.

His girlfriend and Jayden were at the door as he was led away.

"Shane, you might want to give your boy a kiss," a cop said. "You're not going to see him for a long time. You're going to jail for a long time."

He was placed in a marked cruiser for the neighbours to see. The driver was playing "Neon Moon" by the country group Brooks & Dunn. "You want the music turned up a little bit?" the cop asked.

Shane declined.

Shane was taken to the old RCMP station in downtown Kelowna, where he told police not to bother putting an undercover officer in his cell. He also assumed it would be bugged. "You're wasting your time and my time and I'll probably hurt him anyways," Shane said.

Around two in the morning, Shane was woken up when his old friend Fitzy appeared, escorted by Dwayne McDonald. "Shane, we brought somebody here for you," McDonald said.

Fitzy had been driven all the way from Surrey to Kelowna to be housed with Shane.

Once McDonald left, Fitzy described his evening. "Fuck, bro, you're never going to believe this," Fitzy said. He told of seeing a line of heavy-duty black SUVs driving up to his high-rise. He locked the door of his apartment and slid a two-by-four across the door. He looked out a peep-hole to see what appeared to be ten cops standing in the hallway.

Fitzy didn't answer when they pounded on the door.

They pounded some more.

Fitzy still didn't answer.

"James, this is your last warning."

It might have been, but Fitzy still had time to scoop up a bag of her-oin, drop his pants, and lubricate his butt. "I'm trying to shove it all up as they're kicking the door in," Fitzy told Shane.

Fitzy had managed to stash an ounce of heroin by the time a police officer crawled through the lower half of the smashed-in door.

It took police three and a half hours to drive Fitzy up from Surrey to Kelowna. With the handcuffs, the shackles on his feet, and the heroin in his butt, Fitzy wasn't a happy traveller.

In their cell, Fitzy told Shane to cover him with a blanket as he lay on his cot. He didn't want surveillance cameras to pick up what would happen next. After much wiggling and tugging, he extracted a bag of heroin. It was good shit, too. "We literally did line after line after line after line of heroin, all night long."

Shane and Fitzy knew that police had put them in the same cell so that they would talk, allowing the RCMP to capture their conversation on hidden bugs. So they did talk, but they played it stupid, with lines like "These guys are dangerous" and "We're afraid of those guys."

They had been arrested, but they still hadn't been charged, and they knew the police were only allowed to hold them for twenty-four hours before laying charges.

"Do you want to go home to your family?" a cop asked the next morning.

"What the fuck do you think?" Shane replied. "I thought you were hitting me with all of these charges. I thought I was going to jail for murder."

"You are. Just not today."

Sam Gadbahn explained that the Crown attorney had told them they didn't have enough to make the charges stick—yet. But it was just a matter of time.

On that same day—February 25, 2013—a hundred police officers were involved as Jason McBride was scooped up in Toronto and Michael Jones in Victoria. They were both charged with first-degree murder and attempted murder in connection with the Kelowna shooting and the murder of Jonathan Bacon.

Khun-Khun was hit with the same charges, although he was in hospital at the time of the arrests. His health had been declining, and he remained unconscious as he was handcuffed to his bed.

The arrests took place at precisely the same time: 8 p.m. on the west coast. The cops knew that gangsters could easily text warnings to others if given a chance.

Shane's name was kept out of the media after his arrest, and there was no uproar when he was quietly released. It was easy to see why police wanted him on the streets. They had bugged his cars and house and phones and wanted him to circulate, to help them build cases. He wasn't interested, but that didn't stop them from trying.

A couple of weeks later, on March 13, 2013, at 3:13 a.m., Shane's second son was born. Shane was present for the birth, as he had been for Jayden's, and he and his girlfriend named their new family member Jordan. Shane was struck by the number of thirteens in Jordan's time and date of birth, as was the doctor, who said, "I'm going to go buy a lottery ticket."

Shane could have used a little luck at this point in his life. The rest of 2013 passed in a blur. There were sleep-deprived nights with a newborn in the house, or nights spent sitting in the dark basement watching the security camera feed. There were run-ins with the cops, and attempts to avoid his enemies. There was the work of moving product and collecting money. There was also an increasing sense of isolation. Once, not so long ago, he had felt as though he was part of a crew, a brotherhood, a family. That was gone now. His UN sponsor Jason was barely coming around anymore, and other old associates and enemies were dropping fast. With every passing day, the life he'd once led was more and more of a distant memory.

And, of course, there were drugs—always the drugs. But the more he used, the worse things seemed to get with the law. By 2014, Shane says, he "was in and out. Assault, bail, possession, bail, theft, bail, breach.

"It was a very tough year. I was facing life. The heat was coming on hard. They were following me 24-7 'to keep the public safe for when I get killed,' but also all over me because of the Kelowna shit. Walls were closing in. Drug use was at an all-time high. I was spending literally $500 to $700 a day on oxies and heroin."

OxyContin, also known as "Hillbilly Heroin," can be ground into fine powder and snorted. It's highly addictive and numbing, and helpful for countering toxic memories and night terrors—for a little while at least. Eventually, though, the drugs that Shane relied on to get through the day started to take their toll financially and physically. By March 2014 he was stealing, robbing, and jacking for whatever he could get.

Just a few years earlier, he had been a millionaire who owned several businesses, luxury cars, an $80,000 speedboat, and a Sea-Doo, in addition to his executive-level house. Now, he lived like a feral animal. "I was one of the most ruthless pieces of shit on the street."

One day that month, he was scooped up on weapons charges and moved to Surrey's pretrial detention centre. He hadn't done drugs that day and wasn't numb, which made the experience particularly rough. On the Friday of a long weekend, he was moved to a holding cell.

The intake officer asked how much he was using. "About three grams of heroin a day," he replied.

The officer was skeptical that anyone could use that much, despite the fact that Shane was so dope sick he was having trouble walking to his cell, which was the size of a small bedroom, with a toilet, cot, and lights on 24-7. After being strung out on drugs for years, Shane was suddenly cold turkey.

He was woken up around 7 a.m. the next morning by a guard yelling his name. Shane was shaking now, like he was on the verge of a seizure.

"What are you doing?" the guard demanded.

"I feel like I'm dying."

"You're not dying. You're a drug addict. That's what withdrawals are."

Shane had diarrhea as well as vomiting, and the shaking wouldn't stop. There was a disgusting puddle of his own waste next to him as he lay on the floor.

"Dankoski, what are you doing?" the guard asked again. "Quit fucking playing the role."

"I'm not playing the role."

His bones ached. He couldn't have walked if he tried. "I'm shivering, but I'm sweating. I was just lying there, shitting myself."

He hadn't used drugs for forty-five hours when dinner was slid through a slot late Saturday afternoon. He couldn't even think of eating.

A little while later, a Mountie came by with the guard. "I feel like I'm dying," Shane told them.

The cop seemed more sympathetic than the guard. "We should maybe get him checked out," the Mountie said.

The guard wasn't impressed. "You're staying here," he told Shane. "If you're putting on a show and you're fucking this, stop it now. You're not getting out."

The cop called 911 anyway, and a firefighter soon arrived. When the guard told him he thought Shane was faking, the fireman shook his head. "No, he needs to go to the hospital," the firefighter said. "He's borderline cardiac arrest."

Shane was put on a stretcher and rushed to hospital in Surrey, where he was given a needle of morphine. About thirty seconds later, he was levelling out. He felt like a different person.

The doctor gave him a bottle of oxycodone 40s for his withdrawal, and Shane was told to take one every six hours to keep level. He made it to court on Tuesday and again got bail. That night, he snorted the oxycodone.

The downhill slide continued. Shane wasn't being paranoid: plenty of people *really did* want to kill him. Every organized crime group that mattered in the province wanted to put bullets in him. Even his so-called friends yearned for a clear shot. And they would all have to hurry to get the job done before the drugs did.

Worst of all, Shane understood *why* they all wanted him dead. "I knew what I had done," he says. "At that point you can't say, 'I'm sorry, I take it all back.' I hated myself for a long time, for the shit I'd done. People don't realize what kind of toll this life takes on you and everyone around you. It's easy for people to see on the news or read about someone, but to actually live it, every day . . . it's fucked up. Everything you do weighs on you. When I say I was a broken man, that's an understatement."

Long gone were the days when drugs were fun. Now, Shane needed them just to face each day. It wasn't about getting high: it was about getting up to ground zero. "It was just like a numbing agent for me. The moment I started using, I wasn't broken anymore."

From the time he was a little boy, Shane had struggled not to feel broken. He'd heard grim predictions about his future way back then, and now they all seemed to be coming true. "People would always say, 'He's going to be a drug addict like his dad was,' and I was."

Shane seemed to have two life options now: going to prison for murder or getting murdered first.

It was a bleak time. The police were still following him everywhere. They raided his house and condo and impounded his vehicles. When he got his vehicles back, he was sure they were traps wired with listening devices. He was constantly hit with tickets, and soon his driver's licence was suspended. "They would fuck me every which way they could."

Making matters worse, his fourteen-year relationship with his girlfriend was at an all-time low. She'd never been thrilled with the way he prioritized "the life" over their life, but at least there'd been perks. Now it was just stress and more stress, drugs and more drugs. More than once she told Shane she barely recognized him.

Things hit a tipping point on July 29, 2014. Shane had given his girlfriend $10,000 from his tow truck business to put away, which meant shuffling it to her grandmother's house for safekeeping. That night, when his girlfriend was out for dinner to celebrate a girlfriend's birthday, Shane realized he'd forgotten to hold back a few grand in order to pay for his habit. "I called her asking where it was, 'cause I knew she hadn't brought it to her grandma's yet. She lied and said she had, then she said she put it in the bank . . ."

His girlfriend was clearly frustrated about being grilled on the phone during what was supposed to be a rare fun night out. "Can't I ever just go out?" she asked before hanging up.

She had a point, but Shane was livid anyway. "She knew I was spending it on drugs . . . but she didn't realize my addiction was so bad." Shane snapped. "I was raging. I was ransacking the house. I needed money for drugs." He tore into her walk-in closet, desperate for cash. "I ripped every piece of clothing off of every hanger in a freakout."

When he found nothing, he sped down to the restaurant. The host of the party came out to see him. She shook her head in a disappointed way as her parents stood nearby, offering support.

"Fuck you, you fucking cunt," Shane told the birthday girl. Then he turned to the mother of his boys. "Get the fuck in the truck," he ordered.

In an effort to defuse an already tense situation, his girlfriend complied. Shane took her bank card, withdrew $1,000, and drove to see a dealer. Then he smoked heroin in front of her.

"I never saw her look at me like that before."

He also had never hit her before. But this night was different. He looked like a killer and a full-blown heroin junkie as he drove at a hundred kilometres an hour towards the edge of town with a gun on the centre console. "I was so dope sick and fucked up."

"Oh my God," his girlfriend said. "I don't even know you anymore, Shane. You're a monster. What are you doing?"

"You watch the news. You know what's up. You know who I am and what I'm about. Shut up or I'll make you disappear too."

He drove the mother of his two young sons into the bush, "pistol-whipping her and beating her the whole way. Made her get out of the truck. I was going to kill her and then myself, but as she cried and begged, saying the kids needed her and asking if she could call them one last time, I came to and snapped out of it. But she was beat up pretty bad."

His girlfriend's mother was still at their home when they got back, as she had been watching the kids. His girlfriend hid in a closet, but eventually her mother saw her. "Her mom seen her with black eyes, waited till I passed out, and called the cops. She didn't want her mom to see her in the condition she was in. She tried to be solid for me and go in the basement and just try to sleep. But her mom came down and her mom called police."

Even then, he knew his girlfriend's mother was right to call the cops. He knows it still.

The police arrived in the middle of the night, when Shane was asleep.

Shane had known his former girlfriend since she was twelve. "She went through hell with me . . . She had been with me through everything, thick and thin." Now he was being led from their home in handcuffs, charged with assault and uttering threats.

His former girlfriend told the police that she had not suffered physical violence from him before that horrible night. She said that there were no firearms in the house. She also said she believed he had a drug addiction. She told police he was a good father and that she didn't fear him harming their two boys.

Shane arrived home in a cab the next day, with strict bail conditions that included no contact with his former girlfriend and the kids. The Cadillac Escalade she always drove was no longer in the driveway. He walked in the front door and their pug and chihuahua didn't run up to greet him as they always did. His little boys also didn't race to him, shouting "Daddy!"

"There was complete silence. That's when I realized, *Oh my God. She's fucking gone.*

"She packed all her shit and my kids while I was in jail. And she left. That was it. Never looked back after fourteen years with me. And that's when it all hit me. Probably going to jail for life. My friends are trying to kill me. The other side is going to kill me. My family just literally left. And when she left, she took my kids. She also took my Escalade truck, which was fine . . . She took all my hard cash, over 200K, and all my legit money was in bank accounts in her name. That was it. I was fucked."

He felt paralyzed. "I just sat there alone."

CHAPTER 18

ROCK BOTTOM

"Daddy, are you almost done? Are you almost done?"
—SHANE DANKOSKI'S ELDEST SON

REELING FROM THE BREAKUP with his former girlfriend, from being separated from his boys, from the utter chaos that was his life, Shane moved back to his mom's place in Surrey.

"I literally did not come out of my mom's back bedroom for four days straight," he recalls. "I stood there on my feet for four days, wide awake. I had this dresser where I would have all of my little drugs set up and I would just stand there and do drugs for days. My mom would come in there. She would cry. She would go, 'Please go to sleep, lay down.' She went from worrying about me being murdered with my friends on the streets to worrying that she was going to find me in her back room overdosed."

Some of her friends urged Shane's mom to kick him out, but she refused, saying, "At least I know he's here and he's somewhat safe. If I kick him out, he's on the street."

His mother agonized when she saw gang killings on the news, especially when she recognized the names in the stories. She'd never liked the choices Shane had made in his life, and she often begged him to get out. But it didn't change Shane's mind.

While Shane hid out at his mom's, doing drugs to numb the pain, his ex was taking care of selling their old house in Kelowna. Her plan was to move, to start fresh somewhere new. She made it clear she'd be taking Jordan and Jayden with her. But before that happened, Shane's mom convinced her to bring the boys to her house in Surrey one last time, so Shane could properly say goodbye.

On the day this was set to happen, though, Shane couldn't step up. Looking back, he's not sure why, though he expects he was just overwhelmed by the moment. "I went in the bathroom and I smoked heroin all night," he says, still baffled by his own behaviour. "I wanted them there so bad I begged her. And then I went in the bathroom and I did heroin."

Shane bawled his eyes out that night as he thought of how he could instantly end the pain with a pull of the trigger of his Glock .40. He kept playing "Knockin' on Heaven's Door" on a loop. Guns N' Roses had been his father's favourite band, so their version of the Bob Dylan classic seemed to be appropriate exit music.

"I called my sister. I said, 'It's over.' She talked to me. 'Do you want your boys to find you like that? They need you.'"

She stayed on the phone with him all night, trying to talk him out of killing himself.

His son, nearly five, tried to make him feel better too. He kept saying, "Daddy, are you almost done? Are you almost done?" Finally, he fell asleep outside the bathroom door.

Sometime later, Shane decided to come out. "I threw the gun on the floor," he says. "I started crying . . . I literally had to step over my little boy. I never saw him again. That's what drugs do to you. I was a piece of shit. That was my family."

Shane has nothing but respect for how his former girlfriend handled herself that night, for the way she gave him the benefit of the doubt, despite everything that had happened. "She sat on the couch all fucking night," he says. "It's my fault. She gave me every opportunity. She could never blame herself. The life. The life. These are all things that happened because of the life I chose."

Faced with his new reality, Shane grasped for ways to earn money and pay for his drugs. He had no legitimate prospects for making anything significant. His contact in the sports memorabilia business owed him about $150,000, but he had yet to collect it. "I'm robbing people. Driving around with no insurance on my truck, living the life of a drug addict."

Each day at his mom's began with the same goal. "As soon as you open your eyes you literally feel like you're recovering from being hit by a truck. Your bones are sore. As soon as you open your eyes, you need drugs. The first thing on your mind is, *How do I not feel this way?*"

For meals, he would sometimes steal sandwiches from the grocery store. Next, he'd drag himself to a Best Buy electronics store, grab an Xbox, and head for the door. He'd sell it to a dealer for money to buy drugs.

Shane still had the rose petal he'd framed from Sukh's funeral, along with the last $100 he had received from his former boss and friend. "It was the last thing he gave me and I wanted to keep it forever." But forever came early: he smashed the frame and spent the $100 on drugs.

Nothing mattered anymore except for getting drugs. One day Shane went to his sister's home and stole her family's Nintendo Wii from the living room, which was enough for twenty dollars' worth of heroin, or one "point."

"What does one point of heroin do for me? Nothing. And I did that to my sister. You don't give a fuck what you have to do for the money. There's no limits."

Shane's mother now slept with her purse under her pillow. One night he managed to sneak it out anyway, and stole $100. Another time he took his mother's laptop, with thousands of irreplaceable family pictures. "I'm now the customer," he says. "You know what I mean? I sold it to the dealer for a twenty-dollar piece of heroin. This is my mom's photos. Thousands of pictures she'll never get back."

Not so long ago, Shane had bought family members new cars and spent thousands of dollars on family Christmases. Now, he couldn't stop stealing from them.

No one was safe. At some point during these dark days, Shane reconnected with a woman he had first met when she was six. He had helped raise her. Now she was twenty-two years old and still looked up to Shane.

He got her hooked on drugs and turned her out to prostitution, offering her body on Craigslist. At first he charged $120 an hour for her services, but he gradually dropped that to $10 dollars for oral sex. "We did some crazy shit. We were literally living out of my truck at one point."

He also stole and did carjackings. "That was just the cycle for two years. There's me and her at two, three o'clock in the morning, on the streets of Whalley, and I'm waiting on the street. Watch her get into somebody's vehicle, do what she's got to do, get dropped off in fifteen minutes and then give me the money so I can get high, and I would give her a little bit."

He stabbed her in the face once, when she returned from turning a trick drunk and later than she'd been told. "Luckily I didn't get her in the neck or the eye, but I did get her in the cheek and it went right through her teeth and I stabbed her in the tongue. That's horrific. This little girl looked up to me. I turned her to the streets. I turned her into a drug addict, plus I was sleeping with her in the beginning too. Imagine."

There were gang tensions, too, mixed with family tensions. Shane's half-brother on his mother's side lived in the Guilford section of Surrey, near where Robby Alkhalil and the Gianis brothers had grown up. Cousins of Robby Alkhalil still lived there. Shane's half-brother told him that some of the Alkhalil cousins were picking on him and a friend at a recreation centre where they used to hang out. Shane approached the bully and told him to cut it out.

"Fuck you, buddy. Fuck you," he replied. "What the fuck are you going to do?"

Shane had a small blade on him. He grabbed the guy by the scruff of the neck and stabbed him four or so times in the lower back. It wasn't enough to kill him, but it did make a point, literally. Shane ended up charged with assault. The bully was the younger brother of a man Shane called "Iraqi Edward," who was an Alkhalil cousin.

The problems kept piling up. Shane got wind that his United Nations "big brother" and sponsor, Jason, had been texting his former girlfriend. He had sent her a ton of messages on Facebook, asking her to hang out. Separated or not, Shane couldn't let that stand. "I told him he was fucking dead. I said, 'Bro, you're supposed to be my brother. You're trying to fuck my kids' mom? You fucking goof. You better hope I don't see you anywhere. When I do, you're fucking getting it!'"

Shane didn't see him—at least not then—but that didn't stop him from exacting revenge. He went to the place of one of Jason's workers, in Penticton, and robbed him of two kilos of coke and $70,000 in cash. "I told the kid to tell [Jason] it was me, and to call me to get it back. He never even sent me a text message."

By the middle of 2014, Shane was off the rails. His feet were black, the result of wearing no shoes as he smoked crack and heroin in Vancouver alleys. He had dropped from 240 pounds to just over half that. His fentanyl habit was running him $500, $600, or $700 a day.

Shane was having sex with the woman he pimped out, living in his truck part of the time, and feeding himself with food stolen from grocery stores. And he sank to new depths when he sent his former girlfriend a video of him and the woman—who was close to his former girlfriend—having sex. "I regret that to this day . . . I knew that that was wrong."

Still, somehow, he retained shreds of his former reputation on the streets. He convinced old contacts to bring two kilos of cocaine—worth about $130,000 wholesale—to the parking lot of a family gaming centre.

The contacts arrived in a BMW X5 and another vehicle.

Shane got his female partner to walk over to their car and say, "Buddy wants to see the product."

The contacts handed his young sidekick the cocaine. "They're not getting it back," Shane recalls thinking. "I will kill you for way less than this."

He could sense that he was being watched from the BMW. He backed up his truck but the BMW was blocking his exit. Then three men got out and approached him. Shane gripped his Glock .40 as he looked out from the step of his truck's running board, using the vehicle as a shield.

"Buddy, get your fucking car out of the way," he said.

"Bro, what the fuck?" They didn't move.

"Get the fuck out of the way," Shane said. "I'm going to blast you."

One of the three men appeared scared; the other two looked ready for a serious gunfight.

"I fired two shots through my windshield," he says. Then he smashed his truck into the BMW and drove away.

His next stop was to see an old friend in Kelowna with the Throttle Lockers, a support club for the Hells Angels. Shane told him he would sell him "half birds" for $10,000, which was a considerable discount given that full birds, or a kilo, of that quality was worth about $58,500 at the time. The quick deal worked for Shane. It was money now, and the cocaine hadn't cost him anything.

Just a year before, Shane had been to Mexico with this biker. After getting the cash, Shane asked if he could sleep on the biker's property in his truck. It was too risky to be driving the streets like this; not only did he have crack cocaine and heroin in his possession, but he was also high on it. The biker—Shane's one-time best friend in Kelowna—let him stay. They would never see each other again.

Soon after, Shane visited the memorabilia collector and reminded him of his unpaid debts. "You'll pay me every fucking dollar of it," he said. Later, Shane modified this to, "Give me 100G right now and I'll write off every fucking debt."

Back in Surrey, and increasingly desperate, Shane even called up Jason, his old UN mentor who had been trying to sleep with his former girlfriend. Pretending that things weren't so bad between the two of them, he asked Jason for work. Perhaps thinking about their shared past, Jason complied and produced some cocaine.

"I jacked him. I robbed him," Shane says, explaining that he took two birds, worth about $65,000 each. And he felt totally justified in doing so. "I told him, 'Come get your money. Come get your money.' You're my big bro and you're trying to fuck my babies' mom? Not my girlfriend of three months. Not my ex . . . My babies' mom?

"'Come get your money,'" Shane repeated. "'You know where I am. But you won't. You won't come. You know, if you come, you'd better come ready. You're a bitch.'"

No matter how desperate he'd gotten, though, Shane still hadn't been able to bring himself to sell his diamond earrings, which he had gotten from Gurmit, back on the day he got the diamond for his former girl-friend's engagement ring. Now, less than eighteen months later, Gurmit and Sukh and Manny were all murdered and his former girlfriend had fled with their boys. The diamond studs were all he had left from that time, a time when he'd had power and money. A time when he'd been happy. "I just couldn't let them go."

One day, though, as his body screamed for more drugs, Shane went to see the jeweller who used to make gold creations for his group. The earrings were worth $30,000, and he'd hung onto them for as long as he could. It was just a matter of time, he figured, until someone tried to tear them from his head. It took forty or fifty seconds to unscrew and remove them, and he knew a fellow addict wouldn't be so patient, if they caught his eye.

The day he went to sell them, he ran into the owner of the bar where Shane had once beaten up a man for calling Sukh and Gurmit a goof, during a high-stakes poker game, the fall after Gurmit's murder. The club's owner was the same guy whose girlfriend, now wife, had

had Shane's name tattooed on her hip. He was a Hells Angel now, and still bitter about that tattoo.

"So he comes up to me—I'm like a 120-pound crackhead now—and he started getting loud in the mall. The guy wouldn't dare look at me the wrong way two years before this. I had my little shard Kershaw knife, the same one me and Manny always used. And I said, 'Come outside, you goof. I'll fucking stab you in the face.' He let things go. I never saw him again."

The jeweller didn't mention Shane's physical decline, but he must have noticed it.

"I just wonder what was going through his head . . . [He] was always doing jewellery for us. Sukh and Gurmit had a constant bill with this guy. Now I'm standing in front of him looking like this. Everyone's dead, and I'm a full-blown crackhead."

"Would you buy my diamond earrings?" Shane asked. "Would you buy these diamond earrings off me?"

"Yeah, yeah, sure," the jeweller said, taking out a lens to examine them. "What do you want for them?"

"As much as you can. I've got a lot going on."

That was obvious. The jeweller offered him $8,000 for the pair.

"Bro, these are $15,000 each."

"These are hard times."

Shane clearly wasn't in a position to dicker. Just that morning, he'd stolen a sandwich from Safeway. He took the money and left. "I blew through that $8,000 in three days."

There seemed no point in saving for the future anyway. Once the Wolfpack knew he was in town, he'd be "dead within a fucking day," he figured. "The writing was on the wall, right? The walls are closing in. My life's over. It's over. I've got nothing. I have no friends. They're all trying to kill me. What am I living for? Can you get any lower than that? I'm at rock bottom now."

CHAPTER 19

NO TURNING BACK

"This is your life. I know you're a good person."
—RCMP SERGEANT JENNIFER JOHNSTON

AFTER MANNY HAIRAN'S MURDER, Shane had been presented with the option of becoming the new star witness for the Crown. He'd walked out of the hotel room where that offer was made and hadn't looked back. Times had changed, though. Long gone were the days when life had been good—when he'd had a family and friends he could trust, when he'd had $100,000 chains, $30,000 earrings, and stacks of cash. He was a pitiful sight, looking close to death himself. He had dropped so much weight he could no longer wear his old clothes. Shane knew he couldn't go on like this, couldn't slip much further. It was time to consider cutting a deal.

Shane reached out to the RCMP and told them he was ready to take the big step and go over to their side. They gave Shane the option of choosing from a list of five top lawyers to negotiate his witness deal. Shane first called Leonard (Len) T. Doust, QC, of the venerable McCarthy Tétrault firm. Doust was literally a lawyer's lawyer, the one whom members of the legal profession and other high rollers turned to when they got in trouble. He was smart, energetic, and optimistic, and carried his five-foot-six frame with a certain swagger.

In 2004, Doust had represented Vancouver Canucks hockey star Todd Bertuzzi when he was charged with assault causing bodily harm for sucker-punching Steve Moore of the Colorado Avalanche during an NHL game. Bertuzzi didn't get a criminal record for the attack but rather a conditional discharge and an order to do eighty hours of community service.

Shane was impressed with the rest of Doust's client list as well. "He did a lot of big dogs." That included Anton Hooites-Muersing and Dan Russell, both of the Red Scorpions, and Vancouver billionaire David Ho. Doust was also sometimes hired on as a special prosecutor, and had helped out in the Air India bombing trial and shoplifting charges against former NDP MP Svend Robinson.

Clearly, he enjoyed complex, challenging cases. He also loved to soak in the scenery from his eighteenth-floor office at the Cadillac Centre in Vancouver, which gave him a panoramic view of his city.

"Shane, you like that view?" Doust asked during their first visit. He wasn't really looking for an answer. Of course the view was spectacular.

Shane was impressed and decided he didn't need to meet with any of the other four lawyers on the list. "It went really well. As soon as I saw Len, I thought, *Yeah, man.*"

Doust was a polite man who tried not to swear, but he made an exception when discussing Jason McBride of the United Nations. "This Jason McBride guy. Jesus Fucking Christ." He put on his glasses, adding emphasis to his words. "They say he's a hit man. They say he's very dangerous. You know what they did, Shane? They went to my house and put panic buttons in my home. And man, I've got to get a police escort to work every morning. In all of my years of doing this, I've never had to do this."

The elderly advocate also now carried a panic alarm with him. Shane could understand why. McBride was vicious—a "freak, freak, freak killer.

The cops know, like the serious cops and homicide guys. They know. All the big dogs on my case always brought him up to me. They were almost fascinated by him," he says.

When he met Doust, Shane was at a particularly low point in his life, and Doust helped buoy his spirits as he tried to pull him out of drug use and depression. "I had lost all of my friends. They had all been murdered," he says. On top of that, Shane faced an impressive series of charges, including resisting arrest and assaulting a Kelowna peace officer; unauthorized possession of a firearm and knowingly possessing a firearm without a licence; possession of stolen property and theft under $5,000; and breaching bail conditions.

Doust appeared unruffled by the obvious chaos of Shane's life in the summer of 2014 as they got to know each other. Shane had already breached his bail on one of the charges against him, so Doust's first priority was to get Shane out of custody. The Mounties wanted him to stay inside at this point, but Shane needed some sense of freedom, whatever the risk.

"Oh, Shane. All right," Doust said. "I'll get you out of there." And he did.

As Shane sat on his bed in seg, waiting for his release papers to be signed, he recognized the guard who came to free him. It was Ryan—a friend from back in school, when they'd both been in grade four. It had been decades, but Ryan's thin build and mullet hadn't changed.

"Do you recognize me?" Shane asked.

Ryan didn't seem to make the connection.

"Well, I know you," Shane said. Shane explained how he knew him, and Ryan was a good guy about it. He added that his big brother was now a supervisor in the corrections system.

"It's life," Ryan said. "You never know. Everybody's got their own path. No judging."

It's a long, nerve-wracking wait from bail court at 9 a.m. until release time, often around 4 p.m. or so. There was paperwork and doublechecks to make sure they weren't releasing the wrong person. "It's one helluva feeling to get bail and get out onto the street, especially when you need drugs, when you're a drug addict," Shane says. "There's no better feeling."

And yet there were also practical concerns around Shane's release, as he set about totally changing the direction of his life. Instead of being left to his own devices, as he had been in the past, he was now accompanied by a police tactical team, with AR-15 machine guns on their front seat, when he travelled to see Doust. Roads were shut down and sidewalks blocked for when the black SUVs pulled in, two times a week, with Shane's black-clothed handlers.

Through it all, Doust appeared unruffled. He kicked in bail amounts of $5,000 and $15,000 from his own pocket to keep Shane out of custody, infuriating some police in the process. They protested that Shane was still carrying guns and doing drugs—and they weren't wrong. Six months later Shane was up on gun charges again, and Doust handled the $15,000 bail, again. "The cops were fucking pissed."

There was an attempt at rehab, too, during this time, where Shane shared space with a member of the United Nations and an addict with tattoos from the Red Devils, who were supposedly their rivals. Other rehab buddies included the owner of a major auto dealership. That attempt at getting clean ended in an overdose and expulsion.

"I went to a treatment centre for sixty days. That cost $50,000. Got out and used the same day! Now you see why the handlers and the RCMP were so pissed with Len Doust? I was a fucking disaster, and he was paying my bail to get me out. Finally I went and stabbed someone and they denied my bail, and then I had no choice but to stop doing drugs."

As he worked on his plea deal from behind bars, Shane was obligated to tell the Crown his crime history, and that included horrific things, like how he had clipped the ears and fingertips of his enemies. Midway through the fourth day of this process, the Crown effectively threw up their hands. "We've got to cut this down or we'll be here for weeks," someone said. "I think we need to focus on the big stuff." That meant attempted murders, home invasions, and unlawful confinements got priority treatment while frauds and property theft went on the back burner.

Among the stories Shane told them was one about a birthday celebration for Sukh in White Rock. Shane's crew took a party bus there so they wouldn't have to hold back on alcohol or drugs. The evening ended with Shane soccer-kicking a man in the face—a man who had already been cut so badly his intestines were hanging out of his stomach.

There was also a story about a man they had thrown into some bushes after stabbing him in the knee with scissors. It was later decided they should go back and retrieve the scissors, to remove evidence.

As Shane thought back over his time with Sukh, there was no shortage of such incidents. "I've forgotten how many people we've stabbed, hurt," he says, and even with the narrowed focus, the sheer volume of offences had Shane worrying that the Crown might decide to try to classify him as a dangerous offender, with an indefinite sentence. "I was scared."

It was an unsettling time. He felt guilty, ashamed, sad, and worried. People had confided things in him, like the details of murders or drug shipments, never thinking he would flip. He knew that, in talking to the Crown, he had crossed a line. Out on the street, there would be plenty of reasons to kill him.

There was also the realization that this was a forever move. "I'm not ratting out on anyone. I'm not putting everyone in jail," he recalls thinking. "I'm ratting myself out for my part in what I've done, but by doing that, that rats them out too. So now I'm breaking the code, but they fucking broke it first. At this point, everyone's trying to kill me. Even my own crew. For no reason. Who can I turn to for help?"

There was no one he could turn to for help, no one who was offering a fresh start the way the Crown was. "That's the only life I knew," he says.

"I didn't know how to be normal. The only job I ever had was being a full-time gangster. And I had just committed suicide in that life."

There was no turning back now.

Trying to keep Shane afloat during these difficult days was a full team of cops, none of whom were more important than Sergeant Jennifer Johnston and Constable Eric Dykeman of the RCMP. "Jennifer was really good. She knew that I was on drugs and she knew how bad it was," says Shane, adding that his addiction was at its peak during this time. "Eric was very new. He was great. Super-nice guy. Humble. Down-to-earth. Funny. Liked sports. Laughed and joked."

Shane's handlers knew he had been a full-fledged gangster, that he hadn't been dabbling or playing half the role. Mindful of the danger that came with protecting someone like Shane, they travelled covertly, in unmarked cars, with no lights or sirens. They picked Shane up at his mother's house and drove him to Doust's office. Shane always sat in the same spot in the back of their vehicle, beside an officer with an AR-15 assault-style rifle.

Sometimes Shane would point out buildings where he had committed crimes like home invasions, and sometimes he would hear a groan and something like, "Oh, for fuck's sake, Shane. You can't just drop a bomb like that. You've just caused me hours of paperwork."

There was a feeling of constant motion as the protective detail took Shane through the city, ignoring red lights. "We never stopped ever, from the time we left my mom's," Shane recalls.

En route, the cops constantly ran the licence plates of the vehicles they passed, checking for gang links, making sure they weren't being followed. And if their convoy of black Tahoes and a minivan happened to pull up to a restaurant for dinner, police with AR-15s would wait outside to keep guard. Undercover officers would often be inside, looking very uncoplike in tattoos and civilian clothes. Sometimes someone would ask a plainclothes cop what was going on, and the questioner would be told something like, "There's a movie being filmed here. He's one of the guys in the movie."

And, of course, there was a plan in place for what they should do if they were ever attacked in a restaurant. Shane's job was to dive under the table while one cop covered him and another tried to take out the threats.

Little by little, Shane's respect for the people he had once considered mortal enemies grew. Now he made it a point to acknowledge the careful police work that was aimed at keeping him alive long enough to testify. "I made it a thing to always thank them."

Sometimes, though, it all just seemed too much, like the day he woke up at his mom's house and decided he was far too dope sick to work that day, putting in time on the ongoing interviews with the cops. Instead he said, "Fuck off. I'm not going."

He was still using, heavily, and often diverted his $100-a-day food stipend towards drugs, not nutrition. For a time he moved out of his mother's house to a hotel, which he quickly dragged down. "I've got crackheads coming in and out," he says. "Hookers there all fucking hours." Some of Shane's motley visitors slept in the hotel hallways; one stole a big-screen television off a wall.

It soon became clear—to law enforcement if not to Shane himself—that before he could get on with anything else, he had to kick his drug dependency. Jennifer Johnston would try to lecture him, but he wasn't really receptive. He had already lost his long-time partner, his kids, his businesses and friends. "I don't give a fuck about my life, Jen," he would tell her. "I don't care."

Johnston was a strong, disciplined officer, but she was also human. Sometimes she teared up when she told him things like, "You have children. This is your life. I know you're a good person."

At one point, though, his antics and unreliability pushed the cops beyond their limit. They were done with him, they said. Talks for reaching a deal were going off the table. For two weeks, he had no contact with the RCMP officers who had tried so hard to turn his life around. Meetings with Doust also stopped.

"I'd bawl my eyes out," Shane says, remembering how it felt to be so close to screwing up his one last chance at getting out of the life. If the deal was off the table, he'd be going to jail, and God only knew how long he'd last in there.

Faced with no other prospects, Shane finally swallowed his pride and picked up the phone.

"Jen, it's Shane."

"No, I'm done with you," she replied.

He promised to be better—this time.

A nurturing phase followed, with the goal of making Shane happy. Every second day, police would pick Shane up and take him to do anything, within the law, that he wanted to do. That included a hiking trip to Whistler with more than a dozen officers, after a stop for $300 hiking shorts, a $120 hiking shirt, and a $26 water bottle. Pizza and go-karting were also part of the plan. "They rented out the whole track for half a day for me," Shane says. There was also the day they rented out a movie theatre. He chose *San Andreas*, starring Dwayne (The Rock) Johnson. "They did everything for me, and I love them so much."

Then, one day, Johnston called Shane with some news: "I'm not going to be on the file anymore with you." She still cared deeply about his future, she told him, but she had been promoted. Before she left, she made a heartfelt plea: "Please, Shane, don't let me down. I want you to come out on the other side of this."

Two officers were picked to do her job: Sergeant Mike Cheever of the Vancouver police and Corporal Krista Charlwood of the RCMP. "They couldn't have picked better people for me," Shane says. There was something about Krista, who had experience in the Integrated Homicide Investigation Team (IHIT). "I couldn't find it in myself to be rude to her," Shane says. "She was an amazing person who truly helped me so much at such a bad time in my life, while still always being professional. It was really nice to see the human side of these cops. I'm forever grateful for the whole team that helped me, but Mike and Krista have an extra spot in my heart. They're a huge reason I am who I am today."

Sometimes, Shane wanted to tell a rude story, but he wouldn't want her to hear. He would ask her, "Could you cover your ears?"

"Oh, Shane," Charlwood replied. "Stop it. You know I already know everything."

Cheever liked to crack jokes and seemed to understand what Shane was going through. They also shared a love of sports.

Shane still craved drugs, but he was beginning to hate the drug lifestyle. Drug use meant that his bones ached. It meant that he had no energy and didn't want to see anyone. He could be up for five days, feeling like he'd just fallen off a truck. "I don't wish it upon anybody. That's how bad it is. The worst part about it is it just becomes a routine." He wouldn't go to bed at night until he made sure he was ready for the morning, putting his stash somewhere easy to find. And his addiction meant he was constantly looking over his shoulder for cops, robbers, and jealous friends. "It's just a constant battle."

Since his most recent release, Shane had been alternating between his mother's home, hotels, and the streets of Surrey. But now there was a new plan to send Shane off to a drug rehab facility. They were running out of time for Shane to straighten up. "Please," one of the cops pleaded, echoing Jennifer Johnston's words, "don't fuck this up."

He wanted to get it right—he really did—but once again the addiction won out. Put up in a hotel while meeting with Doust on a daily basis, he was soon smoking crack and heroin in the room all day and night, bringing in hookers, robbing people. The same old same old.

And then it got worse. He met two sisters, both of whom were in their twenties. One of them was a mother of two who had moved into the hotel after her boyfriend was murdered. "So she was staying here to get her shit in order. And here I am, a broke junkie."

Shane hooked her up with crack cocaine and heroin while driving her Honda Civic to rob dealers. He sold her fifty-inch television for twenty dollars' worth of heroin, cleaned out her bank account, and stole her car—which he smashed.

This time, police had no choice: they had to kick Shane back into custody. And this time, bail was denied.

CHAPTER 20

THE DEAL

"They were so shocked. So was I."

—SHANE DANKOSKI

SHANE ARRIVED AT the Surrey pretrial correctional centre on November 2, 2014, and was immediately classified as a protective custody inmate. The jail already housed many Red Scorpion gangsters, including Jamie Bacon, the younger brother of Jonathan Bacon. Ongoing efforts on a deal for Shane to become the Crown's star witness in the Kelowna murder trial were hitting snag after snag, but at least both sides were still talking.

Shane's initial evaluation at the centre revealed no mental health issues (although he was under enough stress to drive anyone around the bend), and he was quickly assigned to the third floor. In jails like Surrey pretrial, where you were placed was important, as different floors had very different personalities.

"Tier 1 is all straight johns, legit guys who have jobs but got caught up in shit, and crackheads," Shane explains. The second floor, Tier 2, is a mixed bag of "semi-cool guys," including first-time offenders, some straight johns, tax cheaters, computer scammers, and a few drug offenders. The third floor was hard-core gangster territory, and that was Shane's new home. "The cool guys in the unit are on the third level," he says, "and you go down their tier to Cell 312—the ultimate cell assignment. That's the guy who runs the unit."

Cell 312 went by a few different names: "the Penthouse," "the Handicapped Cell," "the Luxury Condo," and "the Boss Suite." It was bigger than other cells—designed to accommodate disabled inmates, should the need arise, but the rest of the time it was where the most powerful inmate resided.

Shane checked into Cell 312, ahead of another prisoner who was also in for murder. It was always up to the prisoners to decide who got the cell. To avoid trouble and to maintain a certain order on the unit, the guards went along with whatever the inmates decided. There was nothing as formal as a vote about it, either; prisoners tend to know the natural order. "That kind of goes without saying," says Shane. "It's knowing who's who."

The hierarchy thing might sound weird, Shane concedes, but it's a fact of life in certain correctional services centres. The top prisoner got to make the calls. "It's about status," he says. "But if you got two guys who are 'equal,' well, whoever has the bigger charge takes the top spot. So because I was in for the Bacon thing, that immediately gave me, basically, seniority, or status. So it's like, he is in for a murder, sure. But I'm in for a gang murder, and not just a gang murder, like one of the biggest. So again, may sound weird, but that's how it goes."

Shane gained his hold on the unit by assembling a team of five trusted goons to help him run things properly. "They were just a bunch of fucking little shitkickers. Just vicious little guys. I would have to tell them all of the time, 'Relax!'"

On the outside, Shane's shitkickers had been connected to a gangster who now shared Cell 312 with Shane. That gangster had been a friend of Dip Duhre, and had been picked up on first-degree murder charges. "These were like his little goons, and they kind of became mine."

Prisoners would sometimes gather outside Cell 312, where the phone, the toaster, and a table were found. Shane would often have MuchMusic playing in the background, and things would perk up when the guys heard the favourite artists. Shane's cellmate was a music connoisseur of sorts, and he particularly enjoyed West Coast rapper Classified. Others liked Drake, and when certain songs came on, prisoners would rush to crank up their TVs to the same music, creating a stereo effect of sorts.

"'Hotline Bling' was a huge song when I was in jail," Shane recalls. "We would open up our doors and get that stereo going. Open all the doors and play that 'Hotline Bling.'"

Sometimes tunes would arrive on the third floor through far more private channels—like on a USB stick wrapped in a condom, stuffed up the butt of a visitor. Prisoners in Surrey pretrial facing major charges like murder had access to laptops. "It is our right to have access to our disclosure any time we want," Shane explains. "That's why they give it on a laptop. You're in your cell for hours. That way you can go over everything carefully. And if you're friends with those guys who have tunes coming in, you get to borrow their laptop, with the USB full of good-ass music."

And, likely, porn. Those USB sticks also included home-made stuff from girlfriends. Sold on the open market to other prisoners, those sticks could fetch five cigarettes, ten chocolate bars, and three tins of Pepsi.

In the middle of it all, Cell 312 was the unofficial mayor's office, as well as the general store. "Jail is like a city in a city," says Shane. "You can buy drugs, smokes. Anything that goes on in the unit still has to run through me."

Oddly, the top inmate was often also the barber. "Every unit has a barber," says Shane, adding that he was the unit barber during his time in pretrial. "I didn't do it for the money per se, but rather because I enjoyed it and it was something to do."

That said, being the barber came with certain responsibilities. "There is only one set of clippers and scissors per unit, so the main guy on the unit always has them in his possession. You always keep them in clean, oiled condition. And they're never fucked with, because one thing that is very, very important in jail is haircuts. And if the equipment is used for a weapon purpose, they're taken away, so that *never* happens. Now, the main guy on the unit is not always the barber, but he always holds the clippers."

Pricing was about twenty bucks a cut, and it could be paid in phone minutes, canteen, dope, or whatever else might be worth something to those on the tier. Shane hired a kid named Jesse from the second tier to help out. "He would make two dollars per cut he did, and the rest would go to me. So a guy comes to Jesse, brings four pops, three chocolate bars, and five ramen noodles for payment. He keeps a pop and chocolate bar and brings the rest to my cell," he says. "The other guys on the other side of the top tier, say one of them says, 'Shane, can I use the clippers to do three guys' hair?' he had to kick up half to me. No matter what, I get my ten dollars. If he only charges his guy ten dollars 'cause he wants to give him a deal, that's on him, but I'm getting my kick-up no matter what. And guys are honest, like, 'Hey, I cut four guys' hair. Here's a phone card with twenty-five bucks. Here's three cigarettes and five bottles of Pepsi.'"

The guards would watch as guys brought canteen items to Shane's cell all day long. "My entire top bunk is full of shampoo, soap, deodorant, all the expensive shit guys order for me. It's one of the best gigs going inside," he says, adding, "Still cut my own hair today."

The guards seemed to appreciate having a clearly defined top inmate to deal with, and Shane fit that role. When a new prisoner arrived, Shane could expect a guard to say something like, "Dankoski, come down. We need to talk to you." He would be shown the new arrival and asked to find him a cell. An interview would follow, with Shane asking questions like, "Do you smoke dope? Are you a crackhead? We essentially assign cells," he says. "The inmates essentially run the show."

This type of screening arrangement certainly worked for the prisoners—there were no winners if a computer technician with four kids who was charged on some white-collar crime ended up sharing space with a violent, moody meth head—but it had benefits for the staff too. Shane was able to make life a little easier for the guards. He wouldn't, for example, allow fights just before shift change on Friday afternoons. "They might have plans," Shane says. If he felt something was brewing, and it was twenty minutes until the end of a shift, he would get word to the inmates to give it a rest until after the shift change.

It was smart not to stir things up with the guards for no good reason, and that message could be sent in ways subtle and not so subtle. Consider the time a second-tier guy got upset with a female guard and lashed out verbally. "He called her a dumb cunt," Shane recalls. "She walked away and I sent three guys in his cell to smash his head for that. She thanked me for it."

Payback is expected for such acts of jailhouse chivalry. Guards know there's dope, and know that prisoners like to smoke heroin on tinfoil. They can look the other way as things go nice and calm. They could crack down on all the drug use, but who would really benefit? "You take me off the unit, the unit goes to shit," Shane says. "They don't want the main guy gone."

Life on the inside may have followed a hierarchy, but reminders of Shane's life on the streets were never far away. He was down on the health care unit one day when a car thief he had been friendly with in his childhood days showed up. The man's attitude had definitely shifted in the years that had passed since then. "You're a goof, man," he told Shane. "Jamie [Bacon]'s gonna kill you. He wants you fucking bad."

Khun-Khun managed to get in touch too. He and Jason McBride were doing time in a different unit of the same jail, and the letter Khun-Khun got through to Shane sounded an awful lot like a threat, dropping mentions of his former girlfriend, the kids, and even Shane's mother's home.

Hey bro your kids look so cute bro showed me a picture. What a small world. He said he seen you in healthcare. The last time I seen you was on the side of the road. I picked you up + gave you a ride to your moms, you were showing me tattoos of our bros. You weren't looking too healthy then + your head was not in the right place but bro said you were looking good, aside from the beer belly lol. He sends his love and respect to you. I got picked up not too long after that, no one knew how to find you before bro guess everything happens for a reason. I been in for 7 mos now been . . . busy dealing with bs case like everyone else. How about you, hows your time going, When you getting out? One of my boys just got charged recently for something serious but he should not be charged and the cops are like tell us something we'll make it go away etc and hes like so you want me to all out lie + betray my friends for nothing? And there like no, the truth kept pushing him finally he snapped, hes like death before dishonour thats the truth go fuck yourself. Hes charged with BS charges and they are asking him things on someone elses shit, how does that even work? Halarious right? The System? I'm getting a memorial piece done in memory of the bros. Cant wait to wear it with pride.

I was going to say if your going to wear those names then do it with pride or don't do it at all. We can choose our friends but not our bros. Bros are born. Whether you find em or lose em, all depends on ones heart. Shit, heard you telling the guys bro was looking jacked? Hes killing it. Took a few shells point blank and bounced back like he fell down a set of stairs or something. Keep your head up and I mean with one deserving of true love n respect. Shitty what happened to everyone and with every-thing. Better days Soon.

Shane didn't bother to reply. Khun-Khun wasn't telling him anything new. "When I got the letter, it didn't faze me because, ultimately, the plan was already in motion."

The lack of a response didn't seem to cause any trouble with Khun-Khun, either. "I randomly saw him down in health care and he was being buddy-buddy with me."

In Shane's new world, it was just business as usual.

Threats or no threats, life went on. On the night before Christmas 2014, all through the big house of Surrey pretrial, nobody was stirring, not even the always twitchy crackheads on Tier 1. Certainly not the straight johns on the lower tiers. None of them had any drugs. "We had nothing," Shane recalls. "It was dry. It was hurting."

Then, at around 7 p.m., a stranger appeared and asked, "Who runs the unit?"

The new inmate clearly knew the ropes.

"In jail, the Red Scorpions and the bikers, they run the show. It's not even close. There's so many more of them than of us." But in the pretrial centre, Shane guarded his turf jealously. "As soon as one of those Red Scorpion guys would land on our unit, I'd send my little goons and they'd smash him out. I always had the most realest guys."

The newcomer this Christmas Eve knew his jailhouse etiquette. "The very first thing you do is find out whose unit it is." The newcomer passed the initial test.

"Yeah, send him in," Shane said.

"All of a sudden the door swings open," he recalls. The stranger walked into Shane's cell with Shane's five goons standing behind him.

"I brought some shit in, man," the stranger said.

"Really? What did you bring?"

The newcomer reached into his butt and pulled out a condom, with two orange egg-shaped Kinder Surprise toy shells inside. Each was packed full of chunky light-brown heroin.

"Half for you, half for me," the stranger said. "I just wanted to kick up." Once again, this newcomer was demonstrating proper manners. All inmates were expected to share their drugs with the top-level gangsters.

If an inmate was suspected of being high and hadn't kicked up, he could expect a beating.

Shane approved. "Any problems, tell me," he said.

That Christmas Eve gift couldn't have been more appreciated if it had been delivered by Santa himself.

There was nothing weak or degenerate about the gangsters on Tier 3 using heroin. It was just survival, tuning things out for a short time, the same way a mainstream businessman might like a martini or a shot of bourbon. "Anybody you know who has been to jail does dope," Shane says. "They're not crackheads. They're not junkies."

For an instant, though, Shane wondered if his Mountie handlers Mike and Krista had planted someone in his cell to see if he was still using. He shook off that fear quickly enough. "We partied for three days straight," he says.

The stranger was happier too, for what Shane would later call his Christmas miracle. "He had a little pep in his step. His arms swinging around, his head tilted in the air. It was literally like God sent this guy. It was a miracle, a miracle on 34th Street."

Once, a police officer asked Shane why he was still acting like a gangster inside on his unit at the pretrial. Shane didn't even have to think about his answer. "Dude, I still have to play the fucking role. I still have to play the part."

Playing the part was essential to keeping up the ruse that Shane was just another inmate, working with his lawyers and awaiting his day in court. It meant there was no great interest from fellow prisoners when he was routinely taken out of custody by guards to see Doust, or even when he dipped in and out of custody as Doust arranged bail on various charges. That situation never seemed to last, though, as Shane couldn't keep himself out of trouble.

In January 2015, for example, Shane was dressed in nothing more than his underwear when he was picked up on a hotel's video surveillance with a Ruger SR9 nine-millimetre handgun tucked into the waistband, after a guest complained that he'd confronted a group of people with that handgun in the early morning hours of January 24. Shane was arrested for various firearms offences. Once again, he was freed on bail.

Five months later, he was again granted bail after being charged in Kelowna with possession of a non-authorized firearm. He was ordered not to possess weapons. A month later he was charged yet again—this time for assault with a weapon and uttering threats. His police file now contained an entry that read:

Police were called to a Skytrain station with a report of four males fighting. One suspect was observed with a knife and the victim indicated that Mr. DANKOSKI held a knife to his stomach. A knife was not however located on Mr. DANKOSKI at the time of his arrest . . .

For the other inmates in Surrey pretrial, it all just seemed like business as usual for Shane. There would have been plenty more attention— and more danger—had they known that Shane was working on cutting a deal.

Shane, though, knew what was what. And he was certainly feeling the stress. He was facing charges of assault and drug trafficking. There were also two charges concerning possession of an assault rifle, plus more for theft. The mandatory minimum for the whole bunch—all from before the Jon Bacon murder in Kelowna—was twenty-five years. And then there was the Bacon murder and all the related charges, which was easily worth another twenty-five years. If Len Doust could somehow wangle that down to ten or twelve years, Shane reckoned it would be a good deal.

Doust disagreed. "Hold your horses, kid," he said. "I think we can do much better than that."

"Len was always so confident in his dealings," Shane recalls, adding that he appreciated the avuncular reassurance. Still, he knew the outlook was grim.

"Ah kid, keep your head up," Doust would say whenever Shane got down. "In the end of the game, you'll be fine. Remember, when this is all said and done, you'll start your life again."

A huge step towards the "end of the game" that Doust kept talking about came early in 2016. The guards and fellow inmates might have thought Shane was having just another meeting with his lawyer on a Thursday in the first week of January. In reality, though, that was the day things changed forever for Shane—the day he finally signed his deal to co-operate with authorities.

A few days earlier, the police and the courts had quietly indicted Shane on one count of "enhancing the ability of the said criminal organization to facilitate or commit an indictable offence in the murder of Jonathan Bacon and the attempted murder of James Riach, Larry Amero, Leah Hadden-Watts and Lyndsey Black."

The public hadn't been made aware of the charges, and they weren't made aware, either, of the guilty plea Shane and Doust entered on January 7, 2016, in New Westminster Supreme Court. In return for that plea—and a promise to co-operate with authorities in prosecuting the Kelowna casino murder—Shane got a chance at a new life.

Shane certainly hadn't travelled a straight line to get to this day. There had been plenty of hookers and escorts, cocaine, crack, and heroin along the way. "I had almost blown the chance many times," he says. "I was on a bad, bad, bad downward swing."

And yet, for all his crimes and charges, Shane had a remarkably sparse criminal record up to that point. He had committed scores of crimes but had escaped charges and convictions and was freed on bail a half-dozen times. That situation was aided by his work with police. "The reason I kept getting bail was they were building their murder case and they didn't want me in custody. They needed wiretaps and search warrants, et cetera."

Prior to his arrest for helping to organize the Jon Bacon murder in Kelowna, there were only a few very brief periods of jail time on other offences. Although the judge who approved the deal stated that "the culmination of the events to which he contributed represent a wanton, violent and flagrant attack, in circumstances which are deeply disturbing to any civilized community," he then distanced Shane from the actual Jon Bacon murder and attempted murders in Kelowna outside the Grand hotel. He painted Shane as a gangster, but not a killer—this time:

> It is not alleged that the offender, as I understand it, was aware of what specifically was afoot during his participation in the events, nor does it appear that anything that he did was critical to the violent and public attack on the occupants of the target vehicle. Nevertheless, he deliberately participated in an activity which he knew was in furtherance of a criminal enterprise undertaken by a criminal organization, driven by a quest for profit and enforced by violence.

It was a subtle distinction but an important one, the difference between a life term and a couple of years in custody. Shane's prison file expanded on Shane's role on the night of the hit. "Mr. DANKOSKI's role was to confirm Mr. AMERO's location and relay that information to the rest of the group," it reads. "At the time of the offence Mr. DANKOSKI was the 'right hand man' to the leader of the Dhak group, Sukh DHAK . . . He says he was told by DHAK 'There is no leaving.'"

The report also noted Shane's admission to "participating in so many acts of violence that he cannot remember specifics," and to "paying others to do his 'dirty work.'" His record certainly reflected this. Between May 15, 2012, and January 7, 2016, when Shane signed his deal, he had been charged with eighty-one offences, including driving while his licence was suspended; unauthorized possession of a firearm; assault with a weapon; carjacking; theft; trafficking in a controlled substance; and possession of a controlled substance. His record also included charges of resisting and assaulting a peace officer in Kelowna, and unauthorized possession of a firearm and knowingly possessing a firearm, followed by assault and breaching court conditions charges.

Now, with the stroke of a pen, all those charges were wiped clean—or stayed—as Shane pleaded guilty to Participation in Activities of a Criminal Organization. That organization was not named. The files state it was "composed of, among others, Manjinder Hairan, Jujhar Khun-Khun, Jason McBride and Michael Jones."

The deal negotiated by Doust couldn't have been much better. "I heard cops say I got the best deal they had ever seen. I got a sweetheart deal. Deal of a lifetime." With credit for time served, Shane was eligible for full parole on February 6, 2017, and statutory release on May 8, 2017.

By the time he signed his deal, Shane had grown close to his RCMP team of handlers. They were stunned to hear of the legal manoeuvring. "They literally all had their mouths open. They were so shocked. So was I. At the end of the day I literally got three years for my involvement in the Kelowna murder. I was ready to take ten years on the spot."

It was a huge step forward, but there were still obstacles ahead. Shane had literally signed his old life away—an idea that took some getting used to. "When it really comes down to it and you know it's real, that's scary. The only life I had ever known was that life." That life was over now—he knew that—but it wasn't like he could share the news, or his feelings, or talk to anyone outside of his legal team about it. Shane's deal-making was so secret that not even the jail guards knew what was happening. They might let something slip. They might be dirty. Whatever the case, why run the risk? If other prisoners found out about Shane's deal, he was a dead man. Maybe he would soon be a dead man anyway.

Shane wasn't putting innocent people in jail. He wasn't telling the police things about anyone else he ever worked with. In fact, Shane made it absolutely clear to the cops that he wouldn't put anyone from his past in jail. He was willing to admit his involvement in the Kelowna murder and co-operate with the police on the case against the men who'd tried to kill him even though he'd stayed solid the entire time. But he knew the other inmates wouldn't understand this, or how he justified his reasons for co-operating—and they wouldn't care either.

There were other challenges too. He had a major drug problem to beat, for one, and his prison file from the time also suggests that reintegration into society was a concern. His risk of "general and violent re-offending" was assessed as high.

None of this was news to Shane, but there was no going back.

Right: Little Shane and his paternal grandfather nicknamed "Ron the Junkie" because he ran a scrapyard.
(Photo courtesy of Shane Dankoski)

Shane on his fifth birthday in 1990.
(Photo courtesy of Shane Dankoski)

Toddler Shane and his dad. (Photo courtesy of Shane Dankoski)

Certificate of Achievement

This award of distinction is presented

To _Shane Dankoski_

For Superior Achievement & Excellence of
Performance in ___DRAWING SKELETONS___

This _7TH_ day of ___MARCH___, 19_91_

Signed _Dr. Mo._
_Dr. O._

Certificate of Achievement for Excellence in Drawing Skeletons awarded
to Shane Dankoski in 1991. Shane left school at age eleven after
completing grade five. (Photo courtesy of Shane Dankoski)

Shane, Steve (Stevie, Tucker) Leone, and Manny Hairan in a photo booth in Mexico in 2009. (Photo courtesy of Shane Dankoski)

Shane with Doug Wheeler of the United Nations gang.
(Photo courtesy of Shane Dankoski)

Manny Hairan, Shane, and Sukh Dhak at a wedding in 2012.

(Photo courtesy of Shane Dankoski)

A dip in the hot tub on a trip to Mexico with Manny Hairan.
(Photo courtesy of Shane Dankoski)

Shane enjoying the Kelowna waterways.
(Photo courtesy of Shane Dankoski)

Jesus and Satan arm-wrestling (neither good nor evil wins)
in a tattoo on Shane's chest. (Photo courtesy of Shane Dankoski)

Week 1	Monday	tuesday	wedsday	Thursday	Friday	Saturday	Sunday
Breakfast:	Corn Flakes Bran Muffin	Bran Flakes toast	Toast Fruit	Oatmeal French toast	Corn Flakes toast Pineapple		
Lunch:	Hot beef Sandwich wedges	Deli Sub Cookie	* Fish tofu mac. Pears	Grilled Cheese wedges	chicken thigh wedges		
Dinner:	* Fish dinner	sheppards Pie Peachs	teriyaki Chicken w/rice	Spaghetti w/meat balls apple	Curry Chicken Pudding		

Shane's prison meal options at Surrey pretrial centre in 2010.
Asterisks indicate fish meals, which Shane planned to trade.

(Photo courtesy of Shane Dankoski)

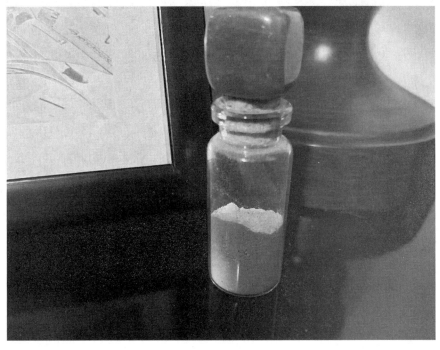

Ashes of Manny Hairan, kept by Shane's bedside.

(Photo courtesy of Shane Dankoski)

Shane flying on a police aircraft in custody with a monitoring device fastened to his ankle. (Photo courtesy of Shane Dankoski)

Police surveillance photo of hit man Dean Wiwchar dressed as a construction worker before murdering John Raposo on a crowded Toronto patio on June 18, 2012. Toronto police photo provided to media.

Police surveillance photo of Robby Alkhalil (left) walking towards the Sheraton Wall Centre in Vancouver shortly before murdering Sandip (Dip) Duhre on January 17, 2012.

Police photo of Robby Alkhalil
escaping jail in disguise.

The Most Wanted poster for Robby
Alkhalil advertising a $250,000
reward. The numeral "1" means he
is Canada's most wanted fugitive.

(Photo courtesy of BOLO program)

Police surveillance photo of Larry Amero.

CHAPTER 21

COLLABORATORS OF JUSTICE

"We used to watch The Voice, *and then baseball, Raptors games, and NHL. And we would all bet on the games—noodles, chocolate bars."*

—SHANE DANKOSKI

SHANE WAS EAGER to get on with his life. It wasn't going to be easy—there were obstacles like jail time and a drug addiction to manage—but at least his path was clear now, and he had some ability to help himself. A case management document in Shane's prison record lays it all out:

[I]t is feasible that some of Mr. DANKOSKI's decisions may have led to the death of some of his victims. However, that is not known as a fact according to the currently available information.

Mr. DANKOSKI says he is unsure what led him to the lifestyle or what kept him in it when he saw his friends being murdered. He says it was "all he knew" and he admits he witnessed his father, a drug user, assault his mother. When he was 7 years old his father was murdered. He was subsequently raised in poverty. He only has a grade 6 level of education and he has no history of legitimate employment. He has been trafficking in drugs since the age of 14 . . .

In essence, Mr. DANKOSKI has lived a life of crime and violence, and now he has an opiates addiction to manage. There is much to his credit, however; first, he is no longer identified as an active gang member. He is enrolled in school and he is motivated to attend programs and learn viable employment skills.

As the case management report indicated, one of Shane's goals while serving his sentence was to get credit for school equivalency. He may have been lacking a diploma, but he knew he had a brain. "I'm street-smart. Give me a kilo of cocaine, I'll turn it into $180,000 no problem," he says.

But it wasn't easy to get any traction. The teachers showed up only once or twice a week, and just for an hour. And other beneficial programs were just as spotty. "Animal therapy" saw dogs brought in once a week to interact with prisoners; the dogs got training, and the prisoners got unconditional love. Shane enjoyed it, but it was cancelled not long after he arrived. The vague explanation was that the program had put people at risk.

With nothing better to do, Shane came up with his own animal therapy. He would feed the raccoons outside his cell. His furry visitors would reach his window by going through two fences, each of which had double barbed wire. "I would just feed the little guys cheeses," Shane says. "They'd come with their little buddies."

Even with the challenges around accessing programs, Shane was doing okay. During his long and difficult plea deal negotiations, he had been accepted into a special unit at a secret location within the corrections system. Living Unit Five (LU5)—also called the "Collaborators of Justice" unit—was unlike any jail Shane had seen the inside of before.

He arrived at night, wearing shackles. At first he was placed in his own cell, outside the unit. A meeting needed to take place before he could be integrated with the other inmates, so authorities could make sure he wasn't bringing any grudges with him. With that bit of business out of the way—and with the new prisoner officially classified as medium security, with a moderate escape risk and a high public safety risk—Shane was introduced to the other inmates.

"As soon as a new guy comes, the first thing the unit director does is [he] brings the whole unit into a room," he explains. They sat around a table, where Shane was introduced. "Then it goes around the table, [with things like], 'Hey, I'm Shane, former UN member. I'm in for blah blah blah, in this case for killing one of your brothers lol' . . . After that, they give everyone a chance to sit and talk one-on-one with the new guy."

Inmates are reminded that it's best to leave their past behind. "The director says, 'Guys, all the beefs and all that shit is done. We're all here together. You guys have a gym, a fucking movie theatre room. You're unlocked from 7 a.m. until 10 p.m. daily. You have a kitchen. You have everything here. Let's all get along. The past is the past. If there's any issues, hash it out now. Whoever starts an issue will be immediately kicked off the unit.' We had access to three phones all day, all night."

And so Shane settled into the custody version of a high-end gated community, complete with a handbook to help him adjust to LU5. It began with a pep-talk welcome message from the warden. "Managing your sentence requires courage and dedication on your part and commitment on the part of staff at all levels to role model pro-social behaviors," it read. "Together we can create a positive environment in which you can work towards a return to the community while ensuring public safety."

Inmates were informed that they had the right to go to the correctional investigator if they felt they were being mistreated. And they were also given a list of "don'ts." Shane was made aware that "the sale, loan or gift of personal property between inmates is prohibited," and that, "prior to use, all electronic equipment must be inspected to ensure that no contraband or unauthorized items are contained within the unit and the unit must be sealed with tamper proof seals. USB ports will be secured with USB port blockers. Tampering with the security seals or USB port blockers will result in the seizure of the equipment and disciplinary action."

The "Boundaries and Out of Bounds Areas" section of the handbook made it clear that LU5 was very distinct from other parts of the institution:

> LU5 is a self-contained unit with a separate population from the rest of [the prison]. In order to maintain your safety, it is imperative that you remain within the boundaries of your unit unless under escort by a Correctional Officer. The boundaries of LU5 consist of the yard fence, the range barriers when closed, and the door at the end of the yard hallway. When the dome area is open, the barriers around the dome are considered boundaries. The area beyond these boundaries is considered "out of bounds."

In the yard and gym and everywhere else, the LU5 inmates were to remain separate from the rest of the prison population. "You are not to communicate with inmates of any other populations," the handbook stated. "The yard and gym may be closed at any time at a moment's notice. If this should happen, you are to comply with the security staff's direction immediately."

There were some jobs available, like "a range cleaner, shower/laundry room cleaner, yard/gym cleaner, garbage removal, barber, food service, and orientation/program clerk," among others. Inmates would be paid $5.25 a day when working, attending school (teachers only showed up on Mondays here), or participating in a program. If they weren't working or were certified sick, at outside court, or segregated, they would get $2.50 a day. If they refused to participate in programs, they would still get $1 a day. They could also get cash transfers from the outside, with a maximum of four per fiscal year, and none more than $750.

Inmates were told there would be zero tolerance for drugs and alcohol, and that the facility was also entirely smoke-free. That led to a section in the handbook called "You've Been Caught—Now What?" Any inmate caught with drugs or alcohol faced the prospect of serious discipline, including a review of their security classification and institutional placement; a review of their accounts (savings, canteen, etc.); the denial of visits; and/or suspension from their job or work program.

For prisoners getting methadone for drug treatment, precautions were in place so that the inmates didn't smuggle it out and sell it. "You are NOT allowed to bring any items (jacket, cup, etc.) with you when you go to receive your methadone. After receiving your methadone dose, you are required to wait 20 minutes (supervised) in the designated area in LU5. You cannot return to your cell after receiving your methadone until you have been observed for 20 minutes, you are not allowed to associate with other inmates during this time . . ."

They were also advised that all their telephone calls might be monitored.

Shane's personal correctional plan noted that he was thirty years old and that "he has no history of legitimate employment." His plan indicated a high need for improvement in management of his emotions, choice of associates, eliminating substance abuse, and improving his education with an eye towards employment. Under "Expected Objective and Gains," it stated: "Mr. DANKOSKI is currently on the Opiate Substitution Therapy Program. He will meet his objectives by taking his methadone as prescribed and receiving ongoing counselling and interventions through the Methadone Intervention Treatment Team."

It was a very different life from the one Shane had known on the outside just a few short months ago, but not everything was new and strange. Not long after his arrival at LU5, Shane was greeted by the familiar face of Daniel Ronald Russell, who had been a high-ranking member of the United Nations gang. With his prescription glasses and smallish stature, Russell didn't seem threatening at first glance. He stood five-eight or five-nine on a stocky frame. He had been skinny on the streets, but had beefed up behind bars. Perhaps he could now pass for a fitness trainer, but nothing more imposing than that. "He didn't look like a gangster," Shane says.

And yet Russell's non-threatening appearance belied the fact that he had been an aggressive predator on the outside. "His sole purpose in life was, 'How can we kill the Bacons?' This guy was just ruthless. He wanted to kill the Bacons more than anything."

Russell had been sentenced in April 2013 to twelve years in custody after pleading guilty to manslaughter for taking part in the 2008 murder of stereo installer Jonathan Barber and for plotting to kill the Bacon brothers. It turned out that Barber was an innocent man, mistaken for the gang's real target. Barber's girlfriend was also injured in the attack.

Now, as Shane met him on the special unit, Russell was a changed man who seemed ready to let bygones be bygones. He hung out with a new buddy from the Red Scorpions, the old Bacon allies. In this new underworld order, it wasn't unusual for the former arch-enemies to bake cookies and make popcorn together before settling in on the couch for an evening of television. On the streets, they would have been expected to kill each other without a second thought; now they politely shared a channel switcher.

"I didn't know you were coming here," Russell said to Shane. "I didn't know you co-operated."

Shane wasn't about to ruin things by bragging about the sweet deal he had gotten and how he was due to be back on the streets in a couple of years. Nobody talked much about their sentences anyway. "You don't talk about your release dates with guys," Shane says.

Russell's laid-back approach to old rivalries fit in with a general attitude on the unit—the sense that "we're not gangsters anymore. We're past that part," says Shane. And the approach appeared to be working for Russell. "Dan was laid-back in jail, talked a bit about God," Shane said.

"He took a turn for sure."

The God stuff wasn't uncommon on the unit—though not always because guys had truly found religion. Shane noted that some of the less devout inmates also strongly identified as Christian, which meant they got out of their cells for Bible class. Others attended Indigenous programs, including non-Natives who claimed First Nations ancestry. Shane suspected they did this more for the access to tobacco pipes than any culture.

Identifying as Muslim had its benefits too: halal chicken breasts and a prayer rug, which was also useful as an exercise mat. "They can't deny you and tell you you're not a Muslim." If an inmate was given a quiz on the religion as a kind of test, there was always a friendly Somali a few cells over who was happy to do it for a price.

LU5 wasn't summer camp, but it was far better than provincial jail, where inmates were locked up for most of the day, with breaks for lunch and dinner and an hour in the yard. It was, recalls Shane, an entirely different world.

For us, they cracked our cells at 7 a.m., and they stayed open until 10 p.m., unheard of. We literally had a full-out, brand new gym. State-of-the-art equipment and machines, which was paid for from the RCMP. It was 80K. Any gyms in prisons I've seen literally have equipment from the eighties, with steel free weights. We had one wall that was an entire mirror. Rubber floor, with brand new free weight dumbbells. And then, beside that, we had a movie room, with an eighty-inch plasma with leather sofas. And the director would bring in . . . *all* the newest movies.

They slept on real mattresses, not the grey, stretchy mats you find in most prisons, and they had real pillows, not the hardened little units other prisoners used. They even got to wear their own clothes.

And the lounge couches in the co-operators' unit were bro-friendly leather, facing the wall-mounted, big-screen plasma TV. "So we used to watch *The Voice*, and then baseball, Raptors games, and NHL. And we would all bet on the games—noodles, chocolate bars. If you didn't know better, you wouldn't know you were in jail."

Despite all this, and the glimpse the specialized unit offered of a different kind of life on the outside—one that didn't include old grudges and violence—Shane was harbouring a secret. He didn't feel the same way as the others in the specialized unit. He was still thinking about prison as a time out and not a fresh start.

"I was pretty fresh off the streets, and I was stuck on those ways, thinking, *I am still a gangster*," he says. "The reality hadn't set in that it doesn't work that way. You don't get out and go back to where you left off. I thought I was still probably going to get out of there and be a gangster again."

He kept those thoughts to himself.

One of Shane's new prison buddies was Quang Vinh Thang (Michael) Le.

"Mike Le was no joke, back in the day," Shane says. "Gurmit called him a money-maker, smart. Mike Le was a serious guy. He really was."

On the outside, Le was a founder of the Red Scorpions and a mortal enemy of Shane and his United Nations group. Now they were friends, and Shane appreciated his chill, largely positive personality. He liked to work out and was proud that he'd pulled himself up from 130 pounds.

"Hey, bro, I'm fucking up to 134 now," he told Shane.

"No way man," replied Shane, who weighed about twice as much.

Le had pleaded guilty to conspiracy to commit murder for plotting the Surrey Six slaughter in a Surrey high-rise on October 19, 2007. Six people had died that day, including two innocent bystanders. The jury heard that the slaughter was ordered because victim Corey Lal had refused to pay a $100,000 tax to the Red Scorpions. Then Le had gone on to testify against old gang mates.

Shortly after Shane arrived in the co-operators' unit, Shane and Le were told they had to meet. "If you guys start problems on the unit, you guys are both gone," they were told. The meeting went well, and soon the former mortal enemies were poker buddies.

"He ended up becoming my best friend," Shane says. "He ended up becoming a good, good buddy. People couldn't believe we bro-ed up in there. Every single day we played poker, watched movies together."

The Triad triangle tattoo on Le's hand and RS (Red Scorpion) on his wrist—clearly visible as they played poker—did bother Shane a bit. Shane had a UN tattoo on his ankle, but that was more discreet. "I'd be staring at his wrist," Shane recalls. "It just always brought back memories."

Le kept Triad secrets even after he cut his deal with authorities. Just as Shane had done, he'd refused to talk about anyone or any crimes not related to their deal. The Triads allowed members to join other groups as well, as long as the Triad remained their primary allegiance. Le would boast to Shane, "I will never give up any of my Triad guys—never."

Shane knew Triad members were the real deal, even if they didn't always look the part. They could be very average, even forgettable, with no flashy earrings or chains. "They're low-key. They don't have a look to them," he recalls. But, as Gurmit had said, they knew how to earn. "They're smart as fuck. They're rich."

On the outside, at least. Now, Shane and Le would play poker for canteen goods. "He ended up owing me a fuck ton of canteen," Shane says, and always urged Shane to forgive the debts and let him off. Shane replied that he wouldn't leave Le with no canteen money, but he wasn't about to totally erase the debt either. "He got caught up on this [saying], 'I shouldn't pay a thing.'"

A wedge was forming between the buddies. Things came to a head one day when Le set out to wax his floors. The floor wax was in the possession of Jack Woodruff, who had grown up around the Hansen brothers and was now in prison for double homicide. He stood about five foot six and weighed about 250 pounds. "He's a little sausage," says

Shane. He was also dangerous. "Jack had a lot of bodies under his belt. He was a hit man." That said, he wasn't imposing. Woodruff now had a stent in his heart and was somewhere around sixty years old.

There was a dispute over who got to hold the floor wax, and Le went to Woodruff's room seeking possession of it. Soon they were swearing at each other.

Inmate Kyle Darren Halbauer didn't appreciate the commotion. And he was a guy worth listening to—a convicted killer and a member of the white supremacist White Boy Posse.

Shane suggested Halbauer butt out. Not long after that, Le had Woodruff in a sleeper hold. "Jack's going purple. He's tapping out," says Shane. Shane broke the fight up, but Woodruff's face remained purple.

"He's lucky I didn't fucking kill him," Le told Shane, then added, "You need to mind your own fucking business."

"Try me," Shane replied.

"Come in my cell," Le said.

Shane felt he had to take him up on the offer. "Either you go or you're a bitch . . ."

But when Shane walked into his cell, Le jumped back as if to say, *Oh fuck!* Shane pushed him against a wall and hit him three times. Le dropped and turtled on the floor. "I punched Mike in the head for Jack."

With that, Shane left the cell. The point had been made. There was no need to overdo it.

In the aftermath, Jack left the unit on a stretcher, with a purple face and a broken rib, and Le and Shane were both sent to seg for a short stay, after a review of security cameras.

Mike Le was up for parole in a few weeks, and beating up a sixty-year-old man with a bad heart in a dispute over floor wax wasn't likely to help his case. Even so, Le never snitched that Shane hit him. Instead, he lied, saying he got the welt on his face after being hit by Woodruff, whom he'd then fought off in self-defence. It didn't work. He lost his parole bid, was moved off the unit, and was transferred to a similar unit in Quebec to serve out the remaining two years on his sentence.

On the day he was to leave, the door to the unit swung open and Mike Le appeared, flanked by four guards. He was gathering up his belongings and saying goodbye to the LU5 residents. "I wish you best in life," he told his fellow inmates.

He shook the hand of everyone except Shane.

Episodes like the one with Le served as a reminder that life on the collaborators' unit wasn't all posh workouts and cushy couches. There were other reminders too—some of Shane's own making, and others over which he had no control.

In the former category are the events of May 5, 2015, the twenty-second anniversary of his father's murder. At 9:05 on that grim day— in the middle of the difficult year in which Shane and Doust were still working on the deal that would change Shane's life—Shane was escorted from LU5 to the segregation unit. A correction report explained:

> After all inmates were secured in their cells Inmate Dankoski was handcuffed, the handcuffs were double locked, he was then patted down and escorted to yard #3 for SCU [Solitary Confinement Unit] for assessment . . . Upon conducting a search on Inmate Dankoski's cell the following items were seized; 1 pair of grey sweatpants, 1 Proscan flat screen TV and plug (neither are on his cell effects sheet), various paperwork containing canteen information for other inmates, debt sheets, gambling information and an inmate statement of finance . . . 1 expired blister pack of Clindamycin which according to HCU is no longer on his file as being prescribed to him was also seized and he had loose pills of various size and color in an empty urine container and lastly 1 green lighter was seized as well.

—

In summary, Shane was caught moving drugs and running a gambling ring. An internal report continued: "while Mr. DANKOSKI admitted he would have considered himself a gangster at the time of the index offence, he asserted he is not a violent person."

A follow-up report dug Shane in deeper: "The information stated that he has been posturing, muscling, selling medication, and threatening towards other inmates in the unit. Follow up interviews have confirmed this information which has been considered Believed Reliable (BR). In conclusion it is the belief that his behaviour cannot be managed within the unit at this time."

It was a damning assessment, to be sure, but Shane would be given a second chance—for now. He was released from segregation after five days, with some conditions. He was moved to the cell closest to the Control Post, was not allowed to engage in inter-cell visiting, and was to report hourly to the Control Post during all inmate movement times. As well, he wasn't allowed to enter the gym when another specified inmate was present.

It wasn't an easy adjustment, after the relative freedom of the last few months, but Shane knew he was lucky to still be on the unit. Even so, May and June were tough months. Thinking about his own dad led naturally to thoughts about his own boys and how much he missed them. Family was never far from Shane's thoughts—a fact that is reflected in his prison record. "He accepts that his current situation is the result of his decisions and crimes. He appears willing to self-disclose about his personal history," the report notes. "He voices remorse for the harm the index offences caused to the victim, although there is a sense his remorse is more related to the impact his incarceration is having on his family. He is having a difficult time being separate from his children."

And now here he was, a month before Father's Day—which was always a depressing time for inmates. "It's a pretty sombre day in there," he says. "Everybody's walking around like, *Oh, fuck!*" Shane's police handlers had brought him a package that included a small rock his son Jayden had painted for him. It was red and green, with sticky eyes, and it instantly became one of Shane's most cherished possessions.

Shane hadn't talked with his former girlfriend in nearly a year. So he was caught off guard when he was told she might pay him a Father's Day visit. She also was amenable to bringing the boys, whom he had also not seen for nearly a year. Then the day came, and she and the boys didn't show up. There was no explanation. "She just ghosted me," Shane says. "She backed out and didn't do it. I was so fucking broken."

Shane was still in the collaborators' unit on August 1, 2015, when a check of CCTV footage showed him receiving a package that was thrown down from the segregation yard directly above LU5. The footage caught Shane and another inmate searching a small area where the package landed. The other inmate picked up the package and they went together into the computer room. (The package was later confirmed to contain fentanyl and tobacco.) Shane was later shown throwing something back up to the segregation yard from the LU5 yard.

Guards had interrupted a fairly simple transaction that involved just a little arm strength and a contact on the other side of the wall. "We had tobacco and they had weed," Shane says. "We were doing a trade." Shane got a young inmate to throw his package of tobacco over the wall as their part of the deal. "It snagged the fence. It hit the top of the fence."

As a result of the footage, Shane was placed back in segregation. The subsequent search of his cell turned up burnt tin foil, a cigarette, and a pen barrel with residue. And that was just the beginning. The note that a guard included in Shane's prison file that day goes into greater detail:

During a search of inmate SD's cell, I located a piece of aluminum foil with brown burn marks inside an envelope on top of

SD's desk . . . also located a "joint" with an unknown substance by the desk area hidden under a towel by SD's shampoo bottles. The remainder of the cell was searched, with nil results . . . The contraband was seized and placed in the evidence room . . . Inmate D was charged, and was escorted to Segregation without incident.

More information floated to the surface as the guards continued to investigate. Shane had been prescribed Suboxone, a medication for treating opioid addiction. When taken orally, Suboxone stops heroin and other opiates from having an effect. However, when crushed into a powder and put in lines, it is a powerful drug on its own, which prisoners love.

The hard part is keeping your prescribed Suboxone from going down your throat or dissolving—not easy when the medication is given under supervision. But inmates are nothing if not inventive. Popping a bit of paper towel into your mouth before pretending to take the tablet is key. The paper towel stops the tablet from dissolving, which means it can be retrieved back in your cell, then buffed with sweetener and sold. "It ended up being like a goldmine," Shane says.

It also ended up being a lot of trouble.

Shane's fellow inmates were interviewed following the initial drug charges—the ones related to the tossed package—and many spoke of Shane trying to trade his Suboxone for fentanyl. And on August 3, prison staff found evidence of this activity. A report written at 2:45 p.m. stated that a K9 dog named Brody had been led into Shane's cell for a search. Brody's handler wrote:

I opened the bottom drawer of his desk for K9 Brody to search. Inside the drawer was a blue pen barrel sitting in the drawer, after further inspection of the pen barrel I observed a white residue inside the pen. The pen barrel was seized and placed in an evidence bag. The white residue in the pen barrel was NIK Tested and tested POSITIVE for SUBOXONE. Inmate was charged and the pen barrel was placed in a contraband locker.

Shane was removed from the Collaborators of Justice unit and transferred to the facility's maximum-security ward. The hole Shane was digging for himself just kept getting deeper. A few days after his transfer out of LU5, guards in the seg unit noted that he was in a surly mood at dinnertime. He complained about finding a hair and a string in his food. According to a report, after the meal and now back in his cell, Shane covered his cell window and began calling one of the officers a "fucking goof." The incident continued for some time, the officer wrote, "as I/M DANKOSKI continued to call me a 'fucking goof' and accused me of placing the string in his meal tray. I told I/M DANKOSKI that I did no such thing . . ."

Although Shane didn't think of himself as a violent person, and told prison officials who interviewed him that he had left the gang life behind, his actions seemed to be at odds with that assertion. His former neighbours in LU5 appeared to agree. A mid-August report that identified LU5 inmates only by number was particularly damning.

Inmate 4 indicated Mr. DANKOSKI attempted to encourage violence between two other inmates, that he is muscling and intimidating and verbally threatening another inmate constantly and that his attitude is affecting the entire range.

Inmate 5 indicated that Mr. DANKOSKI was calling names, threatening, and inviting him to fight, that he is selling his Suboxone and that he has threatened several inmates on the range . . .

Inmate 6 indicates Mr. DANKOSKI is blatantly disrespectful . . .

Inmate 8 indicated that Mr. DANKOSKI has called out another inmate to fight and that he is selling his medication and collects canteen.

Inmate 9 indicated that Mr. DANKOSKI is a bully, has threatened inmates, has a gangster attitude and brags about selling his
Suboxone. This inmate also indicated that he has observed other
inmates in a condition other than normal.

. . . Inmate 9 indicated that Mr. DANKOSKI continues to
divert his Suboxone and sells it to other inmates. He described
Mr. DANKOSKI folding a small piece of paper like an envelope
in his mouth and pouring the Suboxone into it and then manoeu-
vres the paper into his cheek. Inmate 9 indicates Mr. DANKOSKI
only attempts this when certain nurses are on shift. He also noted
Mr. DANKOSKI has instigated conflict between other inmates
on the range.

By this time, the Security Intelligence Department had gotten
involved and were questioning whether Shane had passed the breaking
point. The department made note of Shane's intent to purchase and
import drugs into LU5, and referred as well to his "willingness to en-
danger the safety of inmates in LU5 by disclosing the sensitive nature of
their cases and breaching related security protocols." They concluded
that he was "no longer manageable in LU5."

On September 1, a top-level meeting was convened at the facility
to discuss Shane's future. "He admitted what he did was stupid and
regrets that now," a prison report states. Later that day, however, the
warden approved Shane's involuntary transfer to maximum-security
Kent Institution. The language in the report in his prison record is cut
and dried:

As a result of his behaviour, Mr. DANKOSKI was transferred
to maximum security and removed from the Collaborators of
Justice Unit.

In sum, Mr. DANKOSKI has demonstrated a lengthy history
of using threats, intimidation and violence to meet his needs.

This behaviour was evident, and is inherent, within the drug and gang subculture and has continued despite his incarceration and an agreement as a Collaborator of Justice.

"Unfortunately, I fucked it up," Shane says. "If you made it to that unit you were extremely lucky. We really had it made. [But] I was just still too caught up in the gangster mentality. That was the stupidest thing."

The days of popcorn and movies in LU5 were over.

CHAPTER 22

STRIKE THREE CREW

"I was crying because I was such a broken man . . . It was like
everything just coming out of me. I was trying to connect
the dots. I had never done that before."
—SHANE DANKOSKI

SHANE LEFT THE TOP-SECRET FACILITY that houses the Collaborators
of Justice unit in shackles in a van with a half-dozen other prisoners.
It was pitch-black and around two in the morning.

Normally, prisoners progress from maximum to medium to minimum security and then parole and freedom. The prisoners travelling
with Shane in the van were heading in the opposite direction: all had
been nabbed behind bars for things like selling drugs and fighting. These
men were down to their third strike, and they weren't a happy group.
One guy called Shane a "fucking rat," and Shane replied with a comment
about how hilarious that was, pointing out that it was easy for the inmate
to be brave when they were both shackled and separated by Plexiglas.

Their destination was Kent Institution in the upper Fraser Valley
of British Columbia. The place looked like a real prison, with tow-
ers and three fences topped by barbed wire. "It wasn't like the little

pampered-ass place I was just at," Shane recalls. "This was the real deal."

Following the van's arrival at the facility, three guards walked Shane down a darkened basement hallway. "All you could hear was the shackles and the keys, as we're walking down this echoing hallway," he says. "They put me on the old health care unit. A haunted-ass old, dark, abandoned building."

The sound of keys jingling on the guards' belts was a new one for Shane. Soon, he would learn to listen for that jingling sound.

The guards had to keep turning on lights as they walked down the hall, though half of them didn't seem to work and the other half just flickered. And to Shane, it felt as if it was getting colder and colder the farther they went. "It smelled mouldy, musky, fucking dirty. Terrible."

"Where the fuck are we going?" Shane asked.

"Just keep walking."

"You gotta be kidding me."

The cells he passed were empty, with their doors open. "It was like a fucking unit that they didn't use anymore. There's just nobody."

Shane asked how much farther they would be walking.

"You're going down this to the end," a guard said.

"Why?"

"I don't know. That's where the warden wants you."

They stopped in front of the last cell on the left side. Someone radioed out to an unseen person. "Open Cell 26 for Dankoski."

There was a sound of metal scraping as the door slid open to his new home.

"Step in, and when you get in, lay down on your stomach."

Shane's leg irons were removed and the door closed. Then he was ordered to drop to his knees and slide his arms through the cell bars so that his handcuffs could be safely removed. As the jingling of the guards' keys marked their progress back down the hallway, Shane found himself alone in the semi-darkness.

Now what? he thought.

Overhead, lights flickered, revealing graffiti on the walls with the names of gangsters and gang symbols. There was also what appeared to be smeared feces, cum, dried toilet paper, and blood. "It was freezing, freezing cold, ice-cold and dark as fuck."

I can't do this, Shane thought. That thought was immediately followed by another: *Oh my God. How the fuck did I end up here?*

"I couldn't see an end in sight. I couldn't see a way out. I sat in the bunk bed and I bawled my eyes out for two hours like a fucking little bitch." It was the first time in recent memory that he had cried. "I felt like nobody deserved to be in that position. I was literally begging God to help me. I'm screaming, 'Hello! Hello!' and there's nobody."

Shane's new surroundings didn't improve with the morning light. "It was the most rancid cell I'd ever seen in my life."

Not for the first time, Shane considered the contrast between where he'd once been and where he now was. It seemed like just yesterday that he'd had a well-used money-counting machine, stacks of cash, Cadillacs, Sea-Doos, trips to Mexico, a loving family, dozens of friends, executive houses, no-show businesses, an endless supply of drugs, and beautiful, unquestioning women. Was it only three years ago that he'd been out on Okanagan Lake with a half-dozen buddies and an equal number of topless girls? He'd worn diamond chains and diamond earrings, and held a bottle. Now, he had only his police handlers and his mother and sister to talk to. As the lights in his cell continued to flicker, he lay on his hard, filthy mattress and thought over and over, *How the fuck did I go from that to this?*

"I'd had so much money. I'd had so many friends. And now I had nothing. I had nobody. I burned every bridge that I had. I was crying because I was such a broken man, really heartbroken, a broken soul. It was like everything just coming out of me. I was trying to connect the dots. I had never done that before."

As Shane tried to adjust to his new home, his new home tried to adjust to him. On arrival, he was classified as an "Inmate in Danger." He would be kept away from the general population, at least until the Security Intelligence Department had time to review his circumstances and formulate a plan. A report noted that he was trying to get himself off drugs, and was taking part in the Opiate Substitution Therapy Program, which provided methadone, to take as prescribed, as well as ongoing counselling and interventions through the Methadone Intervention Treatment Team.

Not long after arriving, Shane was seen by Mental Health Services after his mother warned that he was a suicide risk. Shane tried to downplay things, and his prison report notes that he was assessed as "not being suicidal and or posing a threat for self-injurious behaviours. Furthermore," it continued,

Mr. DANKOSKI confirmed that he was not having any current suicidal ideations. Neither did he have any thoughts to self-harm at that time. Although in the same interview, he acknowledged feelings of hopelessness, because he had lost connection with his daughters [sic] and spouse. He admitted there was no future for him and nothing to live for without them. He hurriedly clarified that currently he was not feeling suicidal; neither did he have thoughts or intentions to commit self-harm. Mr. DANKOSKI admitted that one year ago, while living in the community, he had struggled with thoughts of suicide. Again, he countered, he never reached the planning stage nor would he commit to any plan to act out suicidal ideations, although suicide thoughts kept ruminating in his head, and this is more so especially when his mood fluctuated.

Krista and Mike, Shane's police handlers, told him that threatening suicide would only make his situation worse. He wouldn't even have cloth sheets to sleep on if he carried on with this. "That fucks you," they said. "What are you doing?"

And so Shane shut up about that and settled into a numbing routine. Prisoners in segregation are locked in by themselves for twenty-three and a half hours a day. In the remaining half-hour, they can use a microwave, phone, or shower. Shane would call his mother during this time, and every other day he would shower—though the showers in Kent were not for the faint of heart. There were no shower curtains on the side, only black prison bars. The water would start off ice cold, and it would take about five presses of a button to generate real warmth. Shane would arrive in shackles from his feet to his waist and hands, and would keep his sandals on. It was best not to think of the previous occupants, some of whom had left Band-Aids and toothpaste behind on the floor.

The shower shut off automatically after ten minutes. A prisoner was given a razor when he was almost dried off. The razor had to be returned intact before the prisoner was let out of the shower area and back onto his unit.

Shane had one small window looking out onto a white hall. Days passed where Shane did nothing but lie in his green jumpsuit on his hard cot with its two-inch mat and single blanket. There was nothing to read and no television. And for days on end, only the occasional jangling of keys let him know there were other humans nearby. His cell was about ten feet by ten feet, meaning he could almost touch both walls at the same time just by holding out his arms. "It's horrific. It's literally horrific," he says. "It gives me a weird feeling in my stomach just to look back on. It was the worst time of my life." Despite what he'd said in his entry interview, he contemplated suicide.

Looking to blame someone other than himself for his troubles, he decided Mike and Krista were at fault. Why weren't they looking after him? Couldn't they at least get him a television and a pen and paper? When they visited him, they said they couldn't do this. Shane thought it was more like they wouldn't do it.

Soon enough, he caught on that they were upset with him too. Not so long ago they'd overseen his placement in the cushy confines of LU5. Shane had blown that, and now here he was in maximum security, upset with them? "They were mad at me, and understandably so. You're sup-posed to be going forward, and here I was going backward," he says.

The cops still held out hope that he would somehow become a better inmate by the time he hit the witness stand. They would make the two-and-a-half-hour drive to see him and he would refuse to even say hello. It was a tough stretch for all concerned.

Eventually, though, something odd happened to Shane in his cramped, musty cell. "In seg I found myself. I found who I was," he says. "I had so much time to reflect. It breaks you down as a man. You have nothing. There's no end in sight. There's nothing to look forward to." Shane reflected on how he couldn't blame others, no matter how tough his childhood had been. "Every single thing that I thought about was my own fault," he says. He sometimes recalled the visit to the psychic he, his sister, and his former girlfriend had made the day before Manny's death, and how the woman had told him he was in danger from some-one with the initials SD. "That was Sukh Dhak. That's where I always went with that," Shane says. Sukh had been both a protector and a threat, and Shane had always assumed that the psychic was referring to the deadly connections they'd shared. Now, behind bars, Shane saw that he himself—initials SD, just like Sukh—posed the biggest threat to his own well-being. "It was only there that I really truly found who I was, and started to really think: *How did I get here? Why did I get here? How can I be a better person?*"

Day after day, his mind would race from memory to memory, from thought to thought. He remembered the last time he saw his sons and how he'd stepped over his sleeping five-year-old boy as he lay outside the bathroom where Shane was bunkered, considering ending his life. Would he ever see his sons again? How would they react if he did? How do you say "I'm sorry" after that?

He thought about the murder of Jon Bacon, the near murder of Larry Amero, and the paralyzing of Leah Hadden-Watts. The events of that day marked a dividing line. Before the Kelowna attack, Shane and his crew had been living the life. Now, things could never truly be made right.

There was also the guilt. "It's not lost upon me what I've done," he says. "Yes, I got away with a lot, and some would even say with murder. My life sentence is that I have to carry around every fucking day what I've done. There's not a day that goes by that I don't think about that girl in the wheelchair. I got a good deal, but it didn't include wiping my memory clean."

He thought about what others thought of him ("This fucking guy. Fucking piece of shit. He's a rat.") and about loyalty, and how hollow the word sounded now. And he thought about drugs, about using again, about how they'd be able to numb the pain, at least for a while.

And at the end of it all, he blamed himself, thinking, *It's all my fault. Nobody pushed me. I just followed the path. It was all my own decisions . . . It was just all dumb, poor, stupid, selfish decisions.*

He had taxed people when he had no right. He had sold drugs when he knew they were poisoning people in his community, including himself. He had stolen, even from his own family. And now here he was, locked in a tiny cell at the end of a dark hallway. Shane's only company now was sad noises—cries, screams, yells—from distant prisoners who could be heard but not seen.

He knew he could shower every other day, but why bother? He stopped eating too. "I didn't even get up. No desire. No will to do anything."

Then, one day, a guard walked by and stopped to talk. He was a four-bar—the four stripes on his sleeve indicating that he was a case manager. The four-bar opened his window.

"How are you doing? You doing all right, buddy?"

It was an odd question to ask. Still, Shane appreciated the connection with another being with a beating heart. And the four-bar actually seemed to care. He came by on another day and opened the window again.

"Hey," he said.

This time, Shane made a plea to the stranger. "Is it possible to get a TV? I'm dying down here."

The four-bar told Shane he wasn't sure if his stuff had been transferred yet, but twenty minutes later he was back at the cell with Shane's TV. Soon, Shane had cable and fifty channels and a connection to the outside world.

Mornings now began at 5 a.m. with MuchMusic and videos for songs like "Hotline Bling" by Drake, "White Iverson" by Post Malone, "Hello" by Adele, "Thinking Out Loud" by Ed Sheeran, "Lips Are Movin" by Meghan Trainor, "Animals" by Maroon 5, "CoCo" by O.T. Genasis, and "Stay with Me" by Sam Smith.

It made a huge difference to his mood, and that in turn made a difference to his attitude. He stopped refusing to see Mike and Krista. He knew now that none of this was their fault. They'd been with him almost every day for a year and half. "It wasn't their fault," he says. "It was my fucking fault."

During Shane's entry interview at Kent, he'd expressed gratitude for the deal he'd gotten. His prison report indicates that he knew how "lucky" he was for receiving only two years, and that he was aware it could have been much worse. "Although he didn't demonstrate remorse for the victims per se," the report reads,

> he did demonstrate remorse for his involvement in the "gang" lifestyle. He commented that everything happened so fast and he was earning a ridiculous amount of money that it was hard to stop . . .
>
> Mr. DANKOSKI reported that this is his first period of incarceration and that it has been a huge wake-up call for him. He stated that he doesn't want to spend the rest of his life in jail or end up dead as those are pretty much the only two options when you're involved with a gang. He stated that he wants to be a good father and work a "normal" job with a "normal" income.

. . . Mr. DANKOSKI was polite and well spoken during the interview. He appeared quite open in regard to his criminal history and gang connections.

As Shane sat alone in his cell contemplating his past, present, and future, he realized that somewhere between LU5 and these early days in Kent, the BS he'd told the prison authorities had become the truth; it wasn't just an act anymore. He no longer thought about going back to the life he'd once led. He had decided to transform himself into someone with real pride. As he sat with this knowledge, Shane felt an odd emotion. It was a new feeling, something like gratitude. "I wouldn't change it for anything. I found out who I was in that cell."

There were sad stories all around him, and Shane had plenty of problems of his own, but it was time to work on pulling himself up. Not that it would be easy. "There were days I was so lost and depressed I physically couldn't get up to my feet," he says.

I didn't know how I could live to endure one more day of it. It broke me down. I cried. I genuinely wanted to kill myself. It was in that cell that I found myself. A lot of reflecting, thinking, crying. And in the end, I wouldn't change it for a thing. It made me want to be better. Do better.

Never had, never will play the victim, or poor me, this is all self-done. But, when I was in treatment the doctors said I had PTSD from my dad and whatever. Well, they didn't know even 10 percent of what I've been through, when you've buried your best friends with half their faces missing, riddled with bullets, that's not to touch on the losing my family, and seeing my dad black and blue on life support. I've learned a lot about addiction. And mental health. The point to everything I've just said is: Drugs are a numbing agent. To cope with and numb exactly what I was going through. If you look at my life, when I started using drugs, the worse shit would get, the more drugs I would do, and when I was so fucked up and couldn't even stand up, eyes rolling in the back of my head, overdosing basically, that was exactly where I wanted to be. So I didn't have to face reality, face life, face what I've lost.

In Kent, though, something miraculous was happening. Since Shane had checked into pretrial custody, he had repeatedly failed to kick drugs, despite numerous costly rehab stints, including one in which he left in an ambulance after overdosing. But now, as he sat behind bars, Shane was reborn. He was clean. "I always knew if I could get over the initial phase, I could do it, but it's so hard to get to that point," he says. "But I knew once I passed the craves, and the terrible withdrawal, that I could. And I never looked back."

Without the drugs clouding his mind, his vision for his future started to get clearer too—and for the first time, he found himself wanting things he'd never wanted before. "I knew who I wanted to be when I got out. I wanted to be a normal member of society who paid taxes. I wanted to be a normal person with a job." He knew it would be work. *It's not going to come soon and it's not going to come easy,* he remembers thinking. But that was okay. It was something to work for. He imagined being out, and interacting with normal people like the one he now so desperately wanted to be. He tried to imagine what they might talk about, and how those people—who wouldn't know anything about his past—would see him. And he set himself a goal: he wanted a normal person to treat him like anyone else, to maybe say "good morning" or thank him for holding open a door. *When a normal person says a nice thing to me,* he thought, *that will mean I've made it.*

CHAPTER 23

KILLING TIME

"If you've got a minute, can I speak with you for a second?"
—MASS MURDERER ROBERT (WILLIE) PICKTON

IN THE SUMMER OF 2016, Shane learned he would finally have a neighbour. They would be allowed to visit and talk face to face, just like other humans. After months of being alone, with no one but guards and his police handlers to talk to, it sounded like great news. But there was a catch. Before he was even allowed to meet his new neighbour, Shane had to sign paperwork saying he would not harm him.

"They said, 'We're going to put you with someone, and if you hurt him, we'll charge you,'" he says, recalling that, at the time, he wondered if he would be sharing a living space with one of the gangster killers from the Surrey Six massacre. He honestly didn't care who it was. "I just wanted to get out of seg."

Shane signed the paperwork. And not long after, his new neighbour came by to introduce himself. "Hello, hello. Hey, I'm Rob," he said.

"How you doing, buddy?"

"Good, good. Great. Nice to meet you."

The soft, polite voice belonged to Robert (Willie) Pickton, the pig farmer who'd been convicted of murdering six Vancouver-area women and who was strongly suspected of killing forty-three others. "I was just happy to finally have company, and it ends up being Willie Pickton," Shane says.

Shane was startled by the smallish man at his door, though he recognized him right away. "When I was younger, Pickton was in the news every day in BC. I didn't picture him to look like that or to talk like that or to sound like that." From the news broadcasts, Shane had somehow pictured the serial killer as rugged and dangerous-looking, but Pickton was balding and oddly careful about his appearance, with the nervous habit of continually combing the narrow strips of hair that fell over his ears. And yet this shy, socially awkward mass murderer was personally responsible for two government commissions: the Missing Women Commission of Inquiry, which ended its probe in 2013, and the National Inquiry into Missing and Murdered Indigenous Women, which published its final report in June 2019.

Pickton was a far different type of killer from those Shane had known. Gangsters in Shane's world often killed loudly and publicly; Pickton was quiet and deadly. In the late 1990s and early 2000s, Pickton would quietly drive alone in his red pickup truck from his seventeen-acre pig farm in the Greater Vancouver suburb of Port Coquitlam to Vancouver's Downtown Eastside, where he would hire down-on-their-luck women in the sex trade. More than half of these victims were Indigenous, and initially there was no great uproar when they vanished into the dark, one by one by one.

For Shane, Pickton's voice took some getting used to. "He was very quiet. He was very soft-spoken. He was very polite." Pickton was also particularly clean, and always seemed to be either going into the shower or coming out of the shower. "His hair was always wet," Shane says. "He always had a towel around his neck."

To comb his skullet, he would stand at an odd angle to catch his reflection off the Plexiglas bubble that housed the guards. Other times he could be found sitting on the floor, clipping his nails and humming to himself.

Not long after they met, Shane and Pickton told each other how they'd wound up in prison. Pickton said he had been framed and that he would soon be freed. When Shane talked of the gang wars and the Bacon brothers, Pickton looked stunned. He had no inkling there had been such an underworld war, even though it had been almost nightly news and was waged close to his home. "He looked at me like I had three heads. He didn't have a clue what I was talking about. It was almost like he was under a rock for the last fifteen years."

"What do you mean, you were shooting bacon?" Pickton asked at one point.

"I said, 'The Bacon brothers.' He hadn't a clue who I was talking about. Maybe he thought we were both pig farmers."

Pickton certainly had a deep and troubling interest in pigs. Investigators found that body parts of some of Pickton's victims were delivered to a rendering plant in Vancouver where he dropped off the waste from butchered pigs. And expert evidence at Pickton's murder trial indicated that he'd likely used power saws for both butchering pigs and dismembering female human bodies.

"'I think we're talking about two different types of bacon, Willie,'" Shane said to him. "He didn't really get the joke."

When Pickton finally realized that Shane had been joking, he let forth with a fake-sounding laugh.

Pickton told Shane of the volumes of mail from strangers that he received while in prison. "He got so much mail it wasn't funny. A lot was from faraway places like Brazil. He only opened the ones that caught his eye. Like people colour the envelope or use thick markers—shit like that. Out of ten letters, he'd open one. The others went right into the garbage. One day, he brought the stack over to my cell. I said, 'I'll read them.' So I read about twenty of them, and the majority were from men. And they all gave their return address. Some had pictures."

"Even women write me," Pickton told Shane.

"Willie, you should marry one."

"When I get out of here, I'll be way too busy."

He wasn't joking. He spoke of how he had drawn up blueprints for a rendering plant he planned to build. He also noted that he had just written a book, which authorities didn't want published. He said he got it published anyway by mailing it in five- or six-page blocks to a man from California who had written to him. When Shane asked why the California man would do this, Pickton said that didn't matter. "As long as I get my book out there."

In his life before prison, Pickton had run a topsoil and landfill business, which seemed to explain the large mounds of dirt on his property. A police search of that property yielded bones and body parts, like hair and human tissue, as well as victims' personal items and clothing.

Despite his horrific actions, Pickton didn't appear immediately frightening—and he never spoke to Shane directly about his crimes. He would just walk up to Shane's cell and summon him in a quiet, soft voice. "I'm really sorry to bother you. Are you busy?" Pickton would say, and Shane would wonder, *How busy can I be?*

Then Pickton would say something like, "If you've got a minute, can I speak with you for a second?"

Sometimes Pickton would start talking about horses. "He had a weird fascination with horses," Shane says. "Whenever that guy would see horses on TV, he'd come to my cell and talk about it."

Pickton and Shane fell into a certain routine. "He was always very polite to me. He was never disrespectful. He would do my laundry. He'd warm up my food. He cleaned the shelves. He'd fold my laundry. In the beginning, he didn't know if he should touch my clothes."

Although he was polite and respectful, Pickton couldn't get Shane's name right, and kept calling him Shawn. "I'd correct him and he'd call me Shawn three minutes later."

Shane quickly learned that Pickton was a man of definite habits and tastes. He never had chips or chocolate or any snacks except for unsalted peanuts, and he would trade mustard for Shane's ketchup. "He ate ketchup on everything, and I am not a big ketchup guy."

Pickton didn't lose his temper as he spoke of conspiracy upon conspiracy, and how he had been framed through one of them. At one point he told Shane that the dead women at his farm were killed by his brother. Another time he blamed it on bikers. He also said a woman went to the farm and asked to be tied up. In all the stories, he was an innocent man, destined to be set free someday.

The stories Pickton told Shane didn't jibe with what he'd told an undercover cop, who was once placed in his jail cell. Pickton told the cop he had almost fifty victims, and that he knew he was in deep trouble:

PICKTON: I buried myself.

OFFICER: How?

PICKTON: Got me. They got me on this one.

OFFICER: No, no shit, give me a break, fuck what have they got?

PICKTON: I don't know, there's old carcasses.

OFFICER: So what have you got? You know what I'm saying.

PICKTON: DNA.

OFFICER: Fuck . . .

PICKTON: Oh, only ah, I was kinda sloppy at the end, too, getting too sloppy.

Shane noted that Pickton seemed to need constant stimulation. "He would sit on his cell floor with his back against the bunk bed, with his TV on, always on mute. He would literally be surrounded by stacks of papers, writing. He would just write and write and write."

Pickton liked to stay busy, and gladly handled prison chores like weed-whacking, changing light bulbs, and cleaning up segregation cells once prisoners left. Once Shane asked him to take some sheets out of the dryer.

"I already did," Pickton said. "They're already folded."

Shane eventually decided that Pickton believed his own lies. "I don't think he genuinely tried to trick me. I think it's just what he really thought."

He also didn't come across to Shane as a particularly intelligent man, which was a fair assessment. Dr. Larry Krywaniuk, an expert on IQ tests, pegged Pickton's verbal IQ at 80 and his performance IQ at 95. That averaged out to 86, placing him in the eighteenth percentile for global IQ. A score of 100 is average, so Pickton fell into the low-average category.

For all his murders, Pickton presented himself to Shane as a defender of vulnerable animals. He also saw himself as a victim of sorts and gave Shane some paperwork in an attempt to explain his work and life. One paper was entitled: "THIS NIGHT MARE CAN HAPPEN TO YOU"—as if the average person was also a mass murderer. It includes the sentence:

NOW FOR THIS BAZAAR EVENT OF WHICH ACTUALLY TAKEN PLACE OVER A NUMBER OF DAYS AS THESE LARGE GROUP OF IGNORANT POLICE OFFICER'S ALL STOOD BY AND WATCHED WHILE MY POOR GROUP OF LIVE STOCK FARM ANIMALS ALL SUFFERED TO THE MOST EXTREME AS THEY LEFT DEFENDING FOR THEM-SELVES WHILE BEING ALL LOCKED BEHIND POLICE BARRICADES.

Pickton told Shane that Christmas was his favourite time of the year. Prison Christmas meant apple pie and ice cream, which Pickton enjoyed. As the only prisoners in H unit, the two men ate together from a special canteen order. "He ate his whole dinner, potatoes, stuffing, turkey and gravy. We traded meat. He eats dark meat and I hate dark meat. He likes dark meat," Shane says. "He passed on the ham."

Pickton was particularly excited when he saw peanuts in the canteen. "You know, Shawn," he said, "I think I'm just going to grab these salted peanuts they have."

"You can order that any day," Shane replied.

"Not in the big bottles."

There was also Christmas music on TV, on a channel with a video of a log burning.

Conversations wound back to his plans to get into the recycling business, big time. "I'm going to have to hire about sixty or seventy people. I'm working on buying the property right now."

He sounded so definite that Shane found it easy to accept that he might actually be innocent. He certainly said it enough times.

"Is he getting out?" Shane once asked one of his cop visitors.

"Are you fucking nuts?" the cop replied.

While Shane shared space with Pickton, Wolfpack hit man Dean Wiwchar was also a neighbour of sorts. Wiwchar was locked up on G unit, which was right beside the unit where Shane and Pickton were housed.

Shane and Wiwchar could see each other, if they stood at the guards' bubble in between units and craned their necks in just the right way. There was also a janitors' door in the middle of the hallway, and they would stand, each on their own side, exchanging insults. "We would beef literally every day," Shane says.

Shane would point out all the mistakes Wiwchar had made in his hits, while Wiwchar would come back with the usual "You're a rat" line. Shane would often end with, "Well, you should probably rat too and come on this side, because those guys used you and you're doing life anyways."

Wiwchar clearly wasn't one for shame or introspection. He would strut around Kent, his hair gelled and his shirt off. "He thought he was a model. He was always loud. Yelling, swearing."

Wiwchar was skinny, at six foot three and 175 pounds, and had a distinctive walk, in which he dragged a leg. Behind bars, though, he was mostly just a voice to Shane. At night, Shane would hear Wiwchar yelling across the space between the units: "Dankoski, where are you . . . ?" he'd say, or maybe, "It's the UN rat."

It was pretty much what Shane expected from Wiwchar—who'd seemed well-suited for his job as Robby Alkhalil's main killer but not much else. "He's a street guy who has balls, who's down to kill, but he's not smart enough to be a drug dealer," Shane says.

"Are you fucking Pickton?" the captured hit man would shout.

"Hey goof, what's up?" Shane would yell back.

"Not much, you rat . . . Are you getting Pickton to suck you off yet?" Back and forth it would go.

Wiwchar wasn't big on boundaries and would sometimes shout things like: "So does your mom still live in the same house in Surrey, Dankoski? 'Cause you know when I get out, I'm gonna kill that fat bitch."

"Good thing you're never getting out, then," Shane would reply. "Hey, you're doing life for guys that used you . . . How does that feel? Everyone knows you were just the bitch . . . And look where you are . . . They never liked you. They just needed someone stupid and broke who would do their bitch work. Imagine, you have thirty more years here."

Shane's favourite insults were the ones that took aim at Wiwchar's professionalism. "Bro, you fucked up that [John] Raposo hit so bad," Shane would shout. "Are you that stupid, Mean Dean? Really, a hit in front of cops? And throwing your wig and gloves in garbage cans as they watched? Fuck, you're stupid. No wonder you're sitting here for the next thirty fucking years, you goof!"

Shane was referring to how Wiwchar was captured on surveillance cameras running down an alley off College Street in Toronto, leaving a trail of evidence as he fled the murder scene.

"Jay McBride, you'd never catch him doing that," Shane would continue, noting how the UN killer would float away after his murders in his disguise, blending into foot traffic. "Come on, man, amateur hour. You call yourself a hitter?"

Such comments seemed to strike a nerve with Wiwchar. "Shut up, you rat," he'd shout back. "You think your buddy Dip had a hole in his head? It was bigger than an orange. Yours is gonna be bigger than that."

Whenever Shane had had enough, he'd fall back on reminding Wiwchar that he might as well be a rat, given that he was sitting in jail for guys who hadn't cared enough to protect him. "Between me and you, do you really think that Larry [Amero] and Robby [Alkhalil] give a fuck about you? They paid you to do a hit because you're a bitch."

For Shane, it was a point of honour to remind Wiwchar that the United Nations didn't need to hire hit men to do its murders; they were done by members. "We never collected a dollar," Shane would tell him. "Not one. It was pure heart and it was pure love. You fuck with us and we'll show you. You got paid to do a hit and you got caught."

Wiwchar had been promised $100,000 for the hit on John Raposo—an associate of the Wolfpack Alliance—but that wasn't doing him much good now.

When he ran out of other things to say, Wiwchar would go back to dragging Shane's new acquaintance with lines like, "Hey, Dankoski, who fucks who? Did they plant you there to get a case on Pickton, you fucking rat?!"

"Are you thinking of how you're never getting out because you're a shitty hit man?" Shane would shout back.

Guards listened to the entire thing, recording and writing it all down.

Pickton listened intently too. "He would sit there, legs crossed like a woman, drinking his coffee with a smile on his face, and then he would say, 'Jeez, Shawn, those guys are quite violent. Seems they don't like you much.' He never got involved, never said much," Shane says. "One time he asked me, 'Why are those guys always yelling at you?' I said, 'Fuck them guys, Willy. They're goofs.'"

Still, Wiwchar seemed happy enough with himself as he interacted with other prisoners. "I would hear them through the doors all day, joking and laughing. Seemed like he was always right in the mix. He used to walk around Kent like he owned the place, telling guys, 'I'm Wolfpack, and I'm with Larry and Rabih [Robby Alkhalil] and blah blah blah.' Finally guys got sick of it and jumped him, like four guys, and stabbed him up really good."

Once he was fit to travel, Wiwchar was shipped to a Special Handling Unit in Quebec. The attack on him wasn't just physically painful for the murderer; it was a statement that he wasn't as well-connected as he liked to boast. "Dean doesn't get stabbed up if he's one of Robby and Larry's tight guys," Shane says. "Larry and those guys, they run the jails. Nobody's going to do that to one of their tight guys."

Even on the inside, the gang life could take its toll.

CHAPTER 24

THE TRIAL

"Wow, I'm free."
—SHANE DANKOSKI

ON FRIDAY, MAY 5, 2017, three days ahead of his mandated release date, and on the twenty-fourth anniversary of his father's murder, Shane Dankoski was released from prison. With three months to go until the murder trial in which he would be testifying, he left Kent in a caravan of five black SUVs, a helicopter circling overhead. All his earthly goods were carried in his Michael Jordan backpack.

Leaving brought a rush of emotions. He was thirty-one years old, but it felt like being reborn. "It was one of the best feelings I ever experienced," he says. "It was probably the most natural high you can ever feel." He looked at the mountains, smelled the fresh air, and thought, *Wow, I'm free.*

It was tempting to look back at the prison, but other inmates had warned him against it. If you look back, the superstition goes, you're going to come back. Still, it felt odd not to have a picture to carry in his mind of the building that had been his home for the past few years. "It's really weird to be locked in a place where you don't know what it looks like from the outside. It took everything I had in my power not to look back. I wanted to so bad."

His police handlers, Mike and Krista, gave him a new set of clothing, which included Michael Jordan running shoes and Under Armour sweatpants. They also accompanied him to his first meal post-release. They stayed with him in the restaurant while other police circled the lot. In custody, Shane had sometimes daydreamed about this meal. When the time finally arrived, he went to an A&W on a back road near Agassiz and ordered a teen burger combo with cheese and no tomato, and washed it down with a Coke.

Not long after that, Shane found himself alone in a hotel room, arranged and paid for by the police. He opened the door and peeked out. He looked left. He looked right. He did it again. He just stood there for a while, opening and closing the door and trying to come to grips with what he was feeling. "It was freedom," he says, adding that he eventually worked his way up from opening and closing the door to walking through it. He went to the hotel lobby. "I went and got a bottle of water, just because I could."

The hotel where he was staying had a hot tub, and one night Shane joined a guy and a girl there. They were clearly friends, not partners. As they made small talk, Shane noticed them staring at his tattoos and the black monitoring bracelet on his ankle. He told them that he was there for work and that his name was Ryan. Seemingly unbothered by the monitor, they asked "Ryan" if he wanted to go for a drive. He didn't hesitate to say yes. "I've had no human interaction other than Pickton for the past year. Anything is good," Shane recalls.

It would be three months before Shane told the woman his real name and opened up about his past as a gangster. When she told her family, they encouraged her to get away from him. But by then they were already in love.

"I understand where your family is coming from," Shane told her. "One hundred percent."

Shane spoke to them directly. "I told them, 'This is my past . . . I can't prove anything beyond words. I can just show you.'"

The feeling of shedding the mask he'd worn ever since he stepped out of Kent was indescribable. Leaving prison was one thing, but now he was truly free. And most surprising of all was the girl.

"She ends up liking me for me."

In early August 2017, Shane flew to Kelowna in an RCMP aircraft as the murder and attempted murder trials began for Michael Jones, Jason McBride, and Jujhar Singh Khun-Khun. It felt odd to be back in the city. When Shane was last there, he'd been severely addicted to drugs. "I hadn't been back since getting out of jail, and prior to that I was running amok on the streets. I last used in Surrey pretrial. Never again."

This time, things were going to be different. If there was any doubt about that, it was dispelled the moment the aircraft landed. Waiting on the tarmac was a convoy of black Ford Tahoe SUVs, with police standing guard with AR-15 assault rifles.

"It this for me?" Shane asked his police handler, Krista Charlwood.

"Yeah."

"Don't you think it's a little dramatic?"

Krista shook her head. "No, this is what we have to do. These guys are dangerous and they want you."

The RCMP wasn't leaving anything to chance. For the past three months, tactical officers had done mock training scenarios to prepare for this moment. Their team included a heavy hitter from the Canadian Security Intelligence Service who was said to hold a law enforcement record for the longest recorded sniper head shot. This superstar also had an uncanny ability to blend in and hide. Everyone hoped his deadly skills wouldn't be necessary during Shane's visit.

Shane was handed a bulletproof vest and a beeper before he stepped off the plane. He was also given strict instructions—and a warning:

"If you beep this beeper, the response is going to be something you've never seen before. So don't beep unless you need to."

Shane was quickly ushered into a Tahoe, between two police officers, and was given an explanation of who would move where if they happened to be attacked by occupants of another vehicle. There was also a scenario for what they should do if they were attacked by occupants from more than one vehicle.

Roads were blocked as they moved into the city, and as the familiar streets and buildings flashed by, Shane wrestled with some uncomfortable feelings. He'd spent so much time here, and had so many memories. Maybe it wasn't entirely surprising that he found himself "holding onto the last little bit of gangster, the last little bit of pride."

For an instant, he considered backing out, thinking, *No, this isn't me. I can't do this.* He thought back to the day Sukh had presented him with his white-gold bead bracelet. That had been one of the happiest days of his life. UN members had said words like "Death before dishonour" like they really meant them. They had called each other bro as if they were truly brothers from different mothers. It had all felt so real, like family—until it didn't.

Shane gave himself a reality check. His "bros" had been ready to kill him. They'd even joked about it. He had heard the tape. And his old "big brother" in the UN had been eager to sleep with the mother of his children.

It was a time for reflection, a time to remember everything that had happened and how it had all led him here. *There's me, living by the code,* he remembers thinking. *Fucking threw my family away for this life, and then guys trying to kill me? Trying to fuck my kids' mom? Where's their fucking code? But then we go down for murder—oh, okay, now the code matters again? Fuck that. Fake fucks. Fake life. It's all about who can make the most money. It's nothing to do with brotherhood and all that.*

Shane had no trouble admitting to himself that he'd broken the code when he agreed to co-operate with the police, but he kept coming back to the fact that they broke it first. "Had they not broke it first, on every level possible, I would have been sitting in that box with them that day, and who knows where I'd be now? Jail most likely. But those were choices *we* made together, and you don't sell out when it goes south. You all go down together, which I would have. I was a firm believer that if you do shit, and you get caught, that's on you. You can't go snitch your way out. I wholeheartedly believe that had Sukh not been killed . . . he would have protected me against them, and said, 'No, we can't assume he ratted out, we need to know for a fact.'" Shane hadn't ratted. He stayed solid and loyal right up until his own side tried killing him.

But Sukh had been killed, and things had played out differently—and now here Shane was, about to testify on behalf of the Crown.

As Shane arrived at the old Kelowna RCMP detachment building on Doyle Avenue, he tried to prepare himself mentally for what was ahead. The trial was expected to last for months, and he obviously couldn't be wandering about in public during that time. With this in mind, an apartment-sized suite had been constructed for Shane in the former police station, which had been built in 1962. There were also living quarters for his team of bodyguards, all of whom carried military-style machine guns in addition to their pistols. Security cameras were everywhere. Doors could be opened only with facial recognition or fingerprint-identifying technology. Inside the living quarters, the new fridge was fully stocked. A games room was installed. So was a TV room with a seventy-inch television and a smoking area. Windows were tinted so that no one could peek in. Shane's bed had a Tempur-Pedic mattress to promote maximum rest and cut stress. The new leather recliners also couldn't have been better.

"They went all fucking out," Shane says of his accommodations during the trial. "It literally was like you were staying in a five-star resort. I'd never seen anything like it."

And if Shane needed any further evidence of the fact that things had changed in Kelowna since his last visit, it came in the form of Dwayne

McDonald, who was now well on his way to becoming deputy commissioner of the RCMP. Back in the day, the then sergeant had given Shane some advice: "Dwayne McDonald once told me it's not hard to tell the truth. Just tell the truth," Shane recalls.

That's exactly what he planned on doing.

The trial began on Monday, August 14, 2017, six years to the day from the attack at the Delta Grand hotel that had ended the life of Jonathan Bacon, paralyzed twenty-one-year-old Leah Hadden-Watts, and almost killed Larry Amero. The accused all faced charges of first-degree murder, four counts of attempted murder, and an assortment of firearms offences. They also all faced the threat of life prison terms, with no eligibility for parole for twenty-five years.

Although a publication ban was in place during the trial—and its terms are still in effect today—it can be reported that the trial lasted eight and a half months, and on May 1, 2018, McBride, Jones, and Khun-Khun all pleaded guilty. McBride pleaded guilty to second-degree murder and attempted murder and was sentenced to life imprisonment without parole eligibility for eighteen years. Jones and Khun-Khun each pleaded guilty to conspiracy to commit murder and were sentenced to ten years, two months, and fifteen days in prison, after they were given credit for pretrial custody. At the time of his sentencing Khun-Khun was already under a ten-year prohibition from possessing a firearm after pleading guilty to an earlier kidnapping charge.

Shane recalled being "completely devastated" when Crown attorney David Rouse called to tell him of the plea deal. The lesser charges meant they could be back on the streets on parole relatively soon.

"Really?" Shane said. "Wow."

For nine months, he'd watched the trial play out, and he'd done his part to support the Crown's case. It hadn't always been easy—there were sleepless nights and plenty of self-doubt; there were times when he felt good about what he was doing, and times when he hated it—but through it all, he'd stuck to his end of the deal. And now, in the end, they had gotten off easier than they deserved.

Rouse praised Shane for his efforts and said that McBride's lawyer, Alan Gold, wouldn't let go of the issue of witness credibility. He also stressed that the deal guaranteed convictions. If they had gone to a jury trial, they could possibly have been acquitted.

There were a few other positives as far as Shane was concerned. *Jay McBride is going to have a life tag,* Shane recalls thinking at the time. *He's going to have to check in* [with parole officials] *for the rest of his life.*

But even with McBride and the others tucked away for the foreseeable future, Shane still had to look out for his own safety. On August 21, 2019—more than a year after the trial wrapped up—Shane got a Facebook message from Doug Wheeler, who had gone back to working for the Bacons. The message said, "What's up you rat You still alive hahha."

Shane didn't reply.

CHAPTER 25

REMINDERS

"Now it's your turn."
—JON BACON IN A DREAM

WITH JAIL AND THE TRIAL in his rear-view mirror, Shane set about trying to get on with this life—or rather, building a new one. It wasn't always easy, especially because his old life never seemed very far away.

Around suppertime on Thursday, July 21, 2022, two men walked into the North Fraser Pretrial Centre in Port Coquitlam, BC. Overhead video cameras recorded that they wore high-visibility vests and dark clothing and presented ID cards at the front desk.

Robby Alkhalil was an inmate at the centre at the time, awaiting trial for ordering Dean Wiwchar to murder Sandip Duhre in Vancouver. The charge against him was first-degree murder. He was already a convicted murderer and drug trafficker.

The pretrial centre was a high-security facility for men. Built in 2001, it combined old-school steel and concrete with state-of-the art technology. Prisoners had to stand before a locked door and press a red button to be buzzed through different segments of the hallways. The wait at different stops was about thirty seconds, all of it under cameras.

"You don't just walk around freely," says Shane, who served time there. "The cameras above you are following you."

That said, Alkhalil likely enjoyed preferential treatment from guards while inside, just as Shane had during his jailhouse days. "Whatever unit he was on there, he was the man . . . They would kiss his ass."

At 6:48 p.m., *three* men in contractors' uniforms walked out of the detention centre and into a waiting white Econoline van, which headed west on Kingsway Avenue. The third man was Robby Alkhalil, who was discovered missing shortly afterwards, during a prisoners' headcount.

The Port Coquitlam RCMP were called at about 7:30 p.m. By this time, Alkhalil had already been off the grounds for forty-two minutes. The pretrial centre was less than a forty-five-minute drive from the American border.

A day later, the RCMP issued a statement that laid out what was already painfully obvious for anyone who knew Alkhalil: "Investigators are dealing with the possibility that Alkhalil is trying to flee by using his connections across Canada, the United States, Europe and Asia. A Canada-wide arrest warrant and an Interpol Red Notice are being prepared."

The notice came as the RCMP released photos of the two men they believed helped Alkhalil escape. They were bald Caucasians in their thirties. "All the suspects were wearing high-visibility vests, but the public can expect that they have changed their clothes . . . We are also hoping someone will recognize the photographs of two suspects who helped Alkhalil escape from jail."

The case took a stunning turn on Saturday—two days after the escape—when police admitted that they had mistakenly released bogus images of Alkhalil's accomplices. "[I]nvestigators can now confirm that previously-released images of ALKHALIL's suspect/associates are stock images that do not represent the suspects themselves," the RCMP stated. Exactly who the images represented was not explained. How they came to be published by authorities also remained a mystery.

On Monday, July 25, the RCMP dropped another bombshell. Authorities somehow had no images of the real men who helped Alkhalil escape from custody, even though they walked under a string of security cameras. "After reviewing CCTV footage no useful images have been identified for release to the public to further the investigation," the force stated.

As authorities bumbled, Robby Alkhalil had time to put continents between himself and Canadian law. "My theory is that he left the country shortly thereafter," former BC solicitor general Kash Heed said in an interview. "He could be anywhere at this particular time."

Shane agrees. "He could have been in a whole other country before they knew he was gone."

The breakout left Shane wondering how much help Alkhalil had inside the jail. In particular, how did he make his way to a supposedly secure area to meet the bogus contractors? "How did they time it properly for him to know to be there at that time?" Shane wonders. "Somebody that was working there had something to do with this."

A month after he walked to freedom, Alkhalil was convicted *in absentia* of first-degree murder for planning and supervising the attack on Dip. He was sentenced to life behind bars with no hope of parole for twenty-five years. He was also sentenced to twenty years for conspiracy to commit murder for the murder of Sukh Dhak. At the time of his escape, he had already been serving a life term with no chance of parole for twenty-five years for the John Raposo murder in Toronto.

Shane wasn't shocked by Robby Alkhalil's well-orchestrated escape, which seemed like something out of a *Mission: Impossible* movie. "He knew he wasn't staying in jail forever," he says. Shane speculates that Robby was far, far away from the North Surrey jail shortly after his escape. He likely bolted by taking Highway 1 to Zero Avenue, and then crossing the border into the United States. "He was literally out of the country before they knew he was out of the jail," Shane speculates. "You could be at Zero Avenue within twenty minutes."

Shane's guess is that Robby eventually fled to some village in Iran, where he is probably still living under a new identity. He already had a string of aliases, including "Rabi," "Robby," "Philip Betencourt Furtado," and "Philip Bettencourt Furtado," and he most likely has more now. Shane figures he "just mixed in with the locals that live there."

And he'll likely stay there. "He knows what's at stake this time," Shane says. If Alkhalil was somehow caught and returned to Canada, he would face a grim future. "For him now, it's straight to Quebec, right to the Special Handling Unit, and he will most likely do out literally his first fifteen years there—which is twenty-four-hour segregation. You don't leave your cell. Your cell has a shower. They wheel the payphone into your cell once a week for fifteen minutes. And you have two French channels on a thirteen-inch black-and-white TV." Even so, Shane figures that Robby is still in the gang business. "The life, it just doesn't stop," he says, adding that Alkhalil probably now conducts business through encrypted messaging services like PGP.

Shane doesn't allow himself to forget that Alkhalil is lethal, and responsible for more killings than his two first-degree murder convictions would suggest. "No way he's done just two first-degree murders and got caught for both," he says. He also knows that Robby is an expert at changing his look with wigs and hats; he did it in the past whenever he felt the urge to alter his appearance. Shane saw him on a daily basis when they were kids, but thinks even he could still be fooled. "It's crazy, man. You would never know it would be him approaching you."

When it comes right down to it, Shane doesn't think Robby will be found, and he wonders, sometimes, whether they will meet one last time. "He's so smart and lethal," he says. "One day I'll turn around and it will be him. I always thought he would be the one who would get me."

Robby Alkhalil wasn't the only old acquaintance in the news in the years after the trial wrapped up, forcing Shane to think back on days that he would just as soon have forgotten. On May 20, 2024, media outlets reported that Robert William Pickton had been speared with a jagged piece of wood by another inmate in the maximum-security Port-Cartier prison in Quebec. The attack left Pickton, who was seventy-four years old, in a medically induced coma. Ten days later, he was declared dead.

When Shane heard of the attack, he thought back to the ten months he'd spent with Pickton on the ultra-high-security range in Kent. He pictured the odd, quiet, extremely polite senior citizen who crossed his legs when he read. "Ninety-nine percent of the population would be happy that happened and would think I'm a goof for saying this, but part of me feels bad for him," Shane said after Pickton's murder. "And I know that's wrong and fucked up, but I'm being honest . . ."

Shane figures it all comes down to the fact that it's harder to objectify someone when you've actually met them, even when they've done unthinkably horrible things. They become human. "Don't get it mixed up," he continues. "He's a piece of shit for everything he's done to women. That don't give him a pass. I'm just saying it's different, how I see him. I spent a long time living with the guy. Make no mistake about it—I would have smashed him for what he did to those women the first chance I got in any other setting, but it wasn't any other setting. I had to sign papers that I wouldn't hurt him and all that shit."

Barely a month after Pickton's death, Shane saw some other familiar faces in the news, this time from back in his Whalley days. On June 30, 2024, there was a violent altercation between American rapper Rick (Rozay) Ross and his crew and some hard-core Canadian audience members. The Canadians confronted the visitors at the Plaza of Nations across the street from BC Place Stadium following the concert, a response to the anti-Drake diss song "Not Like Us" by Kendrick Lamar being boomed through the downtown Vancouver venue at the end of Ross's set. Videos showed Ross struck in the face and one of his group knocked to his knees, where he was hit with a volley of Canadian fists and feet before being carried away.

A day later, Ross tried to make light of the incident, posting a photograph of himself in front of his private aircraft with the caption, "Vancouver it was fun, till next time."

Shane noted that at least three of those Canadians in the audience were full-patch Hells Angels aligned with the Wolfpack Alliance. "Rick Ross truly has no idea who he was dealing with that day," Shane says. "He's lucky he left Canada on his feet and not in a body bag."

Robby Alkhalil, Robert Pickton, the guys from back in Whalley—all were reminders of a past Shane was trying to put behind him. But none had quite the same impact as a leaked audio recording of the voice of Jamie Bacon, Jon's brother. Recorded in the prison where Jamie was serving a murder term, and made without Jamie's knowledge, the audio was released to the public by Kim Bolan of Postmedia. In it, Jamie laments gangster life and talks of co-operating with police.

"I've learned through this that the game is fake, bro. It's all a lie," he says, making no romantic allusions to any gangster code. "These guys are all goofs. They all play all sides of the game. Almost every biker is working with the police. Okay. I've seen it, bro . . . They think that they're gods, and they are little goofs that need to be locked up in the [Secure Housing Unit] and die with their teeth and hair falling out."

Shane couldn't get the recording out of his mind. He knew it meant that Jamie Bacon was now in considerable danger. "In jail, that's *a huge deal*," he says. "It can't and wouldn't just be forgotten about. It would require a response." He goes on to explain:

Let's say Jamie is on my unit. We're very close, same crew, we're both running the unit together. Third-tier back-table guys together for five years, and that call gets out, I've got absolutely *no* choice. I have to send five of my goons to his cell to smash him the fuck out badly! And/or stab him . . . and then from there he's gone off the unit right to protective custody . . . and if I don't do that, the other top guys on the other units send five guys to stab me and him. It's jail politics, no ifs, ands, or buts.

It's incredibly dangerous in prison. People don't understand. One day you're literally the top guy, like Jamie. He fucking was in Surrey pretrial and called the shots all over BC; with one phone call he would have guys beat badly, and in the blink of an eye it can change for you. I've seen it.

CSC [Correctional Service Canada] has an obligation to keep inmates safe, and that got out, the cops instantly would have called the jail and said this is out there, get him off the unit now. And into seg.

Jamie spent 2.5 years straight in seg while he was in Kent Max because of his safety, and he started to get crazy. He was smashing his head on the walls. He was smearing and writing on the walls with his own shit. This was done by design. The homicide investigators had put him there "for his own safety" but it was a tactic to have him break and co-operate, and he stayed solid! And then he watched it all play out—his brother get killed, his fellow Red Scorpions guys rob him blind, people are ratting him out . . . his girlfriend overdoses and dies . . . and finally, after doing a real fourteen years straight of complete hell, unimaginable hell behind those walls, he finally said what I say all the time: it's all fucking fake, no loyalty to anyone. No brotherhood. No honour. Pure backstabbing goofs.

No matter how hard Shane tries to forget about that recording, it stays with him. Sometimes he dreams that Jamie's brother Jon is still alive. He's wearing a black shirt with bullet holes and he's approaching Shane. "All of a sudden Jon Bacon comes walking upstairs. He has bullet holes in his face."

In those dreams, Jon tells Shane, "Now it's your turn."

In the dream, Shane tries to explain that he wishes things had gone differently, and that the attack in Kelowna should never have happened. "No, I'm sorry. I'm sorry," Shane says.

"We have to kill you," Jon replies. "You're going to burn now. Now it's your turn. Now it's your turn."

In those nightmares, there are hot pokers in a fire, ready to burn Shane's flesh. "He has these things on the burner, waiting for me."

The Kelowna attack is never far from Shane's mind, both in his dreams and in his waking hours. He has had contacts reach out to Leah Hadden-Watts, who was paralyzed as a result of the gunfire that day. She spent seven months in the hospital, and when she got out, she had to cope with the realization that she would never regain the function in her legs and would have only limited use of her upper body. She also developed severe osteoporosis, meaning she could suffer spontaneous fractures of her spine. Her life expectancy had been cut by about 70 percent.

Reaching her wasn't easy, as her uncle was the president of the Hells Angels chapter in Haney, BC, but Shane's guilt spurred him on to figure out a way. Even in his most ruthless days he'd had a rule about never hurting women and children, and the Kelowna attack broke that rule. "I would have never ever set that up if I knew that she was there," he says.

She wouldn't meet with him, and he understands why. Even so, and even though he knows it's unlikely, he holds out hope that someday she will accept his apology.

And then there's Larry Amero. Shane thinks often about Amero— about how his crew tried to end the biker's life, and how Amero tried to end his in turn. "I feel bad for him," Shane says. "For some reason, I feel for the guy. We both played the game and we both lived the life. I wanted him dead and he wanted me dead. I understand where he was coming from in trying to kill us—me."

Shane realizes now that so much of what's happened in his life is the result of decisions made by himself and Amero. "We're all in a sense the same type of people," Shane says. "Have the goal of making the most money."

In September 2023, after Amero was convicted in the murder plots that ended the lives of Sandip Duhre and Sukh Dhak, a letter he'd written was read out at his sentencing hearing. In it, the biker expressed some regrets. "I've made mistakes in my life, but I've learned from them and promise to do better," he wrote. "As a parent, I can't imagine the pain. I've learned the hard way how precious life and time are, losing both friends and most of my son's childhood, and even hurt the people I care about most in the world—family." He wrote of missing eleven years of his son's life while he was in custody on murder conspiracy and drug importation charges.

Shane has often thought of reaching out to Amero, but decided instead to include his words here, in an open letter:

Dear Larry

I'm sure this book will answer a lot of questions you have, or maybe didn't even know you had.

Since August 14, 2011, I've often thought about what it would be like to talk to one of the victims from that day. What would I say to them? The lives of everyone in that vehicle and their loved ones changed that day forever, no question about that. But so did the lives of everyone involved on "our side."

As you've read, I lost my relationship of fourteen years, both of my sons, my house, vehicles, businesses, jewellery, $1 million in cash, all of my "friends," and almost my life on many occasions from being shot by your side and mine to overdosing.

I'm a big boy, I made my own decisions. For the most part, the ones I didn't make, Sukh made for me.

I also often wonder what my life would have been had I made the decision to become a Hells Angel; by the end, that is truly where my heart was. My loyalty was to Sukh and my crew, but I was spending almost every day with the Kelowna guys. Things changed when Norm [Cocks] went to jail and we know how the rest went. Not sticking with it is one of my biggest regrets still till this day. Would the Kelowna shooting have happened? Would Sukh have killed me for switching? Would everyone still be alive?

Our sides have tried so hard to kill to each other, I wanted to give the view from the other side of our war.

When you and Robby Alkhalil sent Dean Wiwchar to kill Sandip Duhre, you killed an innocent man.

You made a bad decision, but you acted on the information that you had. Sukh started a lie that was lethal; he knew what he was doing. Dip was Gurmit's friend. When you guys whacked Gurm, Sukh relentlessly pursued Dip's friendship, and he did it mainly because he knew the respect everyone had for Dip, and that would be an advantage in this "war."

Dip wasn't behind the attack at Kelowna that almost killed you. Not only was he not behind it, but as you've now read, he didn't even know "Sukh's guys" were behind it. That's a 100 percent. He suspected something, but Sukh Dhak couldn't be honest with him.

I don't have any skin in the game anymore, Larry.

I've been honest throughout this entire book. I've done my time, I've lost everything this life could've taken from me already—I've got nothing left to gain or to lose.

Sukh Dhak set up Dip. Sukh sent Dip to the slaughter.

Dip himself didn't know the truth about a lot of shit because of Sukh's lies and stories.

We all suffered because of Dip's death. You. Me. Everybody. Dip acted like a peacemaker for so long in our old world.

Dip could go to bikers and settle things down because they respected him.

Dip could break down a situation. He was capable of violence, but that was a last resort.

By not telling him the truth, Sukh turned him into a sitting duck. You're in prison because of that lie.

Dip's four kids don't have a father because of Sukh's lie.

That's why his wife is a widow and Balraj lost a brother.

Dip was a peacekeeper.

Dip died for no reason.

Dip always looked at the big picture.

Dip would sit and listen to what everybody had to say and then speak at the end. He gathered information and then put it to good use. He tried to be fair and think long-term.

Dip always wanted to talk first, and then, only if that didn't work, he would resort to violence.

Sukh's way was the opposite. He would react with violence first. Then maybe he would talk later.

Dip was set up, hunted down, and killed, all because of false information put out there by Sukh.

Dip played no part in the attack in Kelowna that almost killed you.

If Dip was still alive, a lot of other murders wouldn't have been carried out. I'd guess 50 to 70 percent of the gang killings in our world wouldn't have happened.

That's how much respect Dip had.

Bystanders would have been safer too. Whenever hits happened, Dip was adamant that it didn't happen in a public place where women and children might get hurt.

Dean Wiwchar killed a good guy and for no reason. And we are all still suffering.

Believe it or not, I truly wish you the best, and I know the feeling of lost time with our kids because of our selfish decisions. I hope you can make it up to your son one day.

Shane

—

Shane has no idea if Larry will ever read his words. He hopes he does, and that they explain some things about the circumstances that led them both to where they are today. But even if Larry never sees the letter, Shane will never regret writing it. It was one more step in moving on.

CHAPTER 26

ANOTHER CHANCE

"I don't deserve to have another chance—but I do have one."

SHANE DANKOSKI

YEARS HAVE PASSED since the day Shane learned that Manny Hairan was co-operating with the police. Years that included jail time and his own co-operation with the authorities; years that have seen him trade one type of life for an entirely different one. And yet he still mourns the death of his friend. Shane often thinks of how Manny protected him, even after Manny turned on the group. That detail that Dwayne McDonald shared isn't lost on Shane, even as he sheds the once-comforting myths of a gangster code.

"I really miss him. It fucking breaks my heart," he says. "I have a picture of him beside my bed."

Shane knows there are people from his old life who are angry that he's getting a second chance when so many of his so-called brothers are dead or in custody. He knows some survivors of his old life are thinking *You got away with murder. You committed murder and you're not in jail.* "And some of that may be true," Shane says. "I don't forget that.

I guess in a sense I did. A lot of people will say I got away with murder. I know that every single day. I don't deserve to have another chance—but I do have one."

Shane plans to build something positive with his second chance.

Since leaving the life, Shane has had plenty of time to reflect on his complicated relationship with drugs. They made him rich, for a while; then they took almost everything from him, including his family.

Shane thought hard about drugs after an incident in December 2023 when he pulled up to a Tim Hortons to get a coffee. There was a guy in a grey sweatsuit and black running shoes who appeared to be in his early twenties, standing close to the nearby gas station. He was with a girl who walked away. As she left, the man collapsed to the pavement.

"I got out of my truck, ran up to him, stood over him, and started shaking him," Shane says. "I was first to him. People at first thought I hit him. I could tell just by looking at him he was a drug addict. That's from all my years in the life. So when he dropped, I instantly knew."

Shane immediately started doing chest compressions. "He went blue. He stopped breathing. I used my knuckle and, as hard as possible, I rubbed it back and forth on his sternum. That usually will get someone to snap out." But instead, the man's chest stopped moving.

Shane's place was just half a kilometre away, and his wife, Alesia, rushed to get some Narcan—naloxone, a medication that quickly reverses an overdose of an opioid like heroin, fentanyl, or oxycodone. They gave it to him as Shane continued with the chest compressions. Shane kept saying, "'Hang in there, buddy. I know you're strong. You can do it, bud.' I held his arm and said, 'You got this, bro. Don't let go. Stay with me, buddy.' I was the only one there who knew it was an overdose. So I just did what anybody would do."

The man was breathing again when an ambulance crew arrived to take him to a hospital. "It felt surreal to be on the other side, because I never thought that would be possible. I'm the junkie. I'm the one who uses fentanyl. That would be me."

Or, that *was* him. Shane has been clean for eight years and plans to stay that way. He got himself clean at Surrey pretrial and hasn't touched drugs since. Now, he thinks often of how maybe he can stop others from falling into the trap he fell into. "That's the best rehab you can get. It's something I'm very proud of. If you want to, you can. Every day is a battle, but here I am. It would be easier to do dope and numb the pain, but that's not me. That's not who I am anymore."

These days, Shane finds himself drawn to people who are far from his old life, like Alesia, the woman he met as his parole ran out, who is now his wife. "She's into books. She's not into partying. She doesn't know anything about the corrupt life. She's a nerd in that aspect. For me it was perfect. It was music to my ears. I thought, *Wow, I like this.* She didn't have fake tits and veneer teeth."

They married and now have two beautiful daughters, Jaida and Jayla. It took some time, but her family came to accept Shane into their homes and their lives, and Shane says Alesia's mom has even come to be one of his closest supporters. Shane knew the person he wanted to be in the future. He also knew that if they saw him change, things would work themselves out.

And they are working out. Shane found a full-time job making more than $100,000 a year—legally. "The first time I ever did my taxes, I wanted to frame my T4. I never thought I could get past it—the sickness. I don't do anything. I don't even drink. It's such a good feeling.

"My new life hobbies are spending every minute I'm not working with my wife, Alesia, and two beautiful daughters, Jaida and Jayla," he continues. "That may sound cheesy or clichéd, but it's true. I lost that before and I feel so lucky to have it again. Now I make the most of it. My daughters are in dance, gymnastics, and swimming, and that fills my days."

It's not easy, though. Every day is a struggle, he says. "It's always a work in progress. When you're an addict you're always an addict. The first thing I say every time someone asks me how I got off drugs is, 'It's not what got you past them or off them, it's what *keeps* you off them.'

I've been doubted my entire life. When I was a little boy, people would say, 'He's going to grow up and be a drug addict like his dad, a junkie.' And then, when I was a drug addict like my dad, it was, 'He's gonna end up murdered like his dad.' And I see the pattern . . ."

There are plenty of full-circle moments for Shane to contemplate when he's thinking about his life then and his life now. Sometimes he remembers the shock of being handed his dad's ashes in a box, thinking he was getting a cake for his seventh birthday. Sometimes he calls up happier memories, of time spent with his former girlfriend and his two sons. But even those can leave him feeling worn out and tested.

Shane still has no contact with his sons. Mornings are particularly tough, and often he wakes up shouting their names. "There's not a day I don't wake up thinking of them. I've shed more tears [in the] last year than in the last twelve before that. I have bad days. I miss my sons more than you know."

Sometimes he thinks it would be easier to go back to dope and numb himself. But he knows he can't go backward. "It's not one foot in, one foot out. It's about being fully committed to being out."

One thing that keeps him fully committed is the image he carries in his head of his sleeping five-year-old son Jayden on the last day Shane saw him, when Shane was too dope sick and suicidal to say goodbye. Shane replays the memory of stepping over him and walking away. Back then, his former girlfriend would tell the boys, "Daddy's sick. Daddy's sick"—code for "Your father is a drug addict."

"This is a child that I loved more than anything," Shane says. "Why would I do that? It's one of the toughest things for me to talk about, to think about. There's nothing worse."

Shane looks ahead now too. On every single sober day, he thinks about the day he will see his sons again. About the day he can finally tell them, "Daddy isn't sick anymore."

CHAPTER NOTES

CHAPTER 1: HOME FRONT

Bob Green—the man who drove Shane to the hospital to see his father for the last time—lived the life of a genuine hard-core biker. He died a hard-core death too. On October 16, 2018, he was shot to death at age fifty-six in Langley, BC, during a night of booze and drugs at a party of the 856 gang, a Hells Angels–associated biker club that got its name from a telephone prefix of Aldergrove, BC.

Green's death was a reminder of how brotherhood can go horribly wrong in an instant. His killer was fellow biker Jason Wallace, who had been a buddy right up to the point when he shot Green dead. Wallace's friend Shaun Clary helped him flee after the shooting. Clary's dismembered body was found a couple days after the escape, while Wallace paid for the crime with a seven-year prison sentence for manslaughter and drug trafficking.

"Ron the Junkie" spent his final years as a widower. He enjoyed gambling, including on horses, and his friends included Oddy Hansen. The Hells Angels appeared to enjoy Ron's presence. When he died, Bob Green spent two hours at the funeral.

CHAPTER 3: YOUNG THUGS

It was senior Hells Angel Dave (Gyrator) Giles who pointed out to Shane the lips of the winged skull on the club's logo. They are sewn shut.

That part of the crest is red, for blood. The image underlined the strict no-talking rule inside the club.

CHAPTER 4: GANGCOUVER

Rental cars were particularly popular with hitmen. For example, someone heading to Toronto could go a roundabout route, heading west when the ultimate destination was east. That could mean flying to Winnipeg and then doubling back to Edmonton. There they would get behind the wheel of a car rented by a woman who knows someone connected to the club. "It was all just to distance yourself," Shane explains.

To make things even more difficult to trace, the rental car would be outfitted with stolen plates. And before it was returned, the odometer would be rolled back at a friendly garage. Shane also continually had the odometer rolled back on his Corvette, just to keep the value high. "My kilometres were never going over 20K," he says.

"In 2009, the world media's attention was drawn to the gang violence in BC," writes Vancouver cop-turned-academic Keiron McConnell in his paper *Vancouver Gang Violence: A Historical Analysis.* "The BBC, *Los Angeles Times, Chicago Tribune,* CNN, *The Economist,* and even *Maxim* magazine either featured or requested a story on the situation."

Some of the coverage was over the top. A headline in *The Economist* asked "British Columbia or Colombia?" "I do not intend to minimise the impact of gangs in 2009, as it was significant," McConnell writes. "However, comparing a country whose homicide rate is 30.8 per 100,000 to BC, whose homicide rate was 0.97 per 100,000, even in this atypical year, is sensationalistic journalism."

CHAPTER 7: STRANGER AND STRANGER

Dave (Gyrator) Giles died in the summer of 2017 after thirty-five years in the outlaw biker club, and months after being sentenced for taking part in a massive international cocaine smuggling conspiracy. He was sixty-seven. He had been hit with an eighteen-year term for his role in plotting to smuggle half a tonne of cocaine. His sentence worked out to a bit more than eleven years, after credit for time served.

There's material on bikers working on the docks in Kim Bolan, "Drug pipeline: How crime groups infiltrate and exploit our docks" (*Vancouver Sun*, May 9, 2015). This excellent report documents how "Hells Angels bikers, other gangsters and convicted international smugglers work as longshoremen handling the 1.5 million containers that flow annually through Port Metro Vancouver.

"More than two dozen of the longshoremen unloading container ships on the docks of Metro Vancouver are Hells Angels, their associates, other gangsters or people with serious criminal records, a *Vancouver Sun* investigation has found."

There is also Freedom of Information search A022-00549/JI. That includes Intelligence Bulletin: "Longshoreman trainee shot at BCMEA training facility," produced by Transport Canada (2019-03-14 Serial: MSOC/W 013.0), and "Smugglers embedded in ports of B.C.: Mass corruption allows organized crime groups to thrive, report says" (Peter Edwards, *Toronto Star*, February 28, 2018).

CHAPTER 10: REAL HECTIC, REAL QUICK

As a bizarre side note, it was later reported that Boston gangster James (Whitey) Bulger was also at the hockey finals, attending while on the run and under an alias (see "Whitey Bulger witnessed Bruins Cup win in Vancouver: report," CTV News, n.d., https://bc.ctvnews.ca/whitey-bulger-witnessed-bruins-cup-win-in-vancouver-report-1.1365912/).

CHAPTER 13: CLOSING IN

The RCMP continued to keeps tabs on the dangers of travel to Mexico. A follow-up Freedom of Information search of RCMP records showed that things hadn't improved by 2016. A study published that year (2016) by the Center for Studies on Impunity and Justice (CESIJ) at

Universidad de las Américas assessed that Mexico had a 99 percent impunity rate; with approximately 7 percent of crimes being reported and fewer than 5 percent of recorded crimes ending in convictions—meaning that over 99 percent of crimes committed in Mexico were going unpunished by the justice system. Several years later, Mexico's impunity rate remains extremely high. According to a 2019 study published by the non-governmental organization Impunidad Cero, there is an estimated 1.3 percent probability that a crime may be reported, investigated, and solved in Mexico.

CHAPTER 16: MANNY

Nicknames like "Mr. Burns" had a random quality in Sukh's group. Sukh would write down several PGP handles on paper and members would get whatever handle they pulled out. "Sukh would put them in a box and we would grab them out at random."

Shane never saw Mr. Burns after the attack on him. He later heard that the shooter, Donkey, had overdosed and is now dead.

CHAPTER 20: THE DEAL

Not surprisingly, Adam Lam built up a criminal record in the years that followed, with convictions for assault with a weapon; hostage taking and break-and-entering during a 3 a.m. attack during an intended drug rip-off; driving with more than 80 milligrams alcohol in his system and break-and-enter with intent. The final straw came when he was seen shooting a gun at a firing range while under a firearms prohibition.

He didn't have legitimate work, besides his supposed duties as a part-time volunteer at his brother-in-law's nail salon.

Lam was ordered deported on November 19, 2014, from the North Fraser pretrial centre and his appeals were finally exhausted by April 4, 2016. As a last-gasp effort, he claimed he had become a better man since meeting a woman named Tiffany, but authorities weren't moved, and the deportation went ahead.

CHAPTER 25: REMINDERS

Prison escapes are extremely rare, and when they do happen, fugitives are usually recaptured within days, notes Kevin Antonucci, a senior communications adviser for Correctional Service Canada. "The annual number of escapes have been declining in recent years, with the number of those who escaped federal institutions across the country representing about 0.1 percent of the total inmate population," Antonucci says. "Escapes from maximum and medium-security institutions are very rare as the vast majority of escapes, when they do happen, are from minimum-security institutions." And some of those escapes from minimum-security institutions are simply cases of offenders being late reporting back to their institution. Almost all actual escapees are caught within a day or two.

Since Alkhalil's escape, authorities have offered hefty rewards for information leading to his arrest—$250,000 in October 2022, which was lowered to $100,000 in May 2023. He was named Canada's most wanted fugitive by the Be On the Look Out (BOLO) initiative in October 2022.

BIBLIOGRAPHY

COURT CASES

Interveners Factum of the Respondent Matthew James Johnston (Pursuant to Rule 42 of the Rules of the Supreme Court of Canada), Court File No. 39635 in the Supreme Court of Canada (On Appeal from the Court of Appeal of British Columbia) between Her Majesty the Queen Appellant (Respondent) – and – Matthew James Johnston and Cody Rae Haevischer respondents (Appellants) – and Anil Kapoor and Sarah H. Weinberger Amici Curiae – and Director of Public Prosecutions, Attorney General of Ontario, Criminal Lawyers' Association (Ontario), Independent Criminal Defence Advocacy Society, Criminal Trial Lawyers Association (Alberta), Trial Lawyers Association of British Columbia and Canadian Civil Liberties Association.

R. v. Vallee, 2018 BCSC 892 (CanLII), 2018-06-01, File number: 25023

R. v. Iser, 2012 BCPC 70 (CanLII), The Honourable Judge H.K. Dhillon, Provincial Court of British Columbia, 2012-03-09, File number: 215491-2-C

R. v. Pickton, 2005 BCSC 1498 (CanLII), 2005-10-24, File number: X065319

R. v. Pickton, 2005 BCSC 1258 (CanLII), 2005-09-06, File number: X065319

R. v. Pickton, 2005 BCSC 1463 (CanLII), 2005-10-19, File number: X065319

HMTQ v. Pickton, 2005 BCSC 836 (CanLII), 2005-06-08,
File number: 65319-2

R. v. Pickton, 2006 BCSC 1448 (CanLII), 2006-09-29,
File number: X065319

R. v. Pickton, 2006 BCSC 434 (CanLII), 2006-03-15,
File number: X065319

R. v. Pickton, 2006 BCSC 341 (CanLII), 2006-03-01,
File number: X065319

R. v. Pickton, 2006 BCSC 1881 (CanLII), 2006-12-18,
File number: X065319-46

R. v. Pickton, 2006 BCSC 392 (CanLII), 2006-03-09,
File number: X065319

R. v. Pickton, 2006 BCSC 1063 (CanLII), 2006-07-06,
File number: X065319

R. v. Pickton, 2006 BCSC 383 (CanLII), 2006-03-08,
File number: X065319

R. v. Pickton, 2006 BCSC 995 (CanLII), 2006-06-27,
File number: X065319

R. v. Pickton, 2007 BCSC 1033 (CanLII), 2007-07-11,
File number: X065319-76

R. v. Pickton, 2007 BCSC 1293 (CanLII), 2007-08-27,
File number: X065319

R. v. Pickton, 2007 BCSC 42 (CanLII), 2007-01-10,
File number: X065319-54

R. v. Pickton, 2007 BCSC 61 (CanLII), 2007-01-12,
File number: X065319-59

R. v. Pickton, 2007 BCSC 1033 (CanLII), 2007-07-11,
File number: X065319-76

R. v. Pickton, 2009 BCCA 300 (CanLII), 2009-06-25,
File number: CA035704

R. v. Pickton, 2009 BCCA 299 (CanLII), 2009-06-25,
File number: CA035704; CA035709

R. v. Pickton, 2020 BCSC 1200 (CanLII), 2020-08-13,
File number: X065319

Sandhu v. Canada (Public Safety and Emergency Preparedness), 2016
CanLII 22119 (CA IRB), January 28, 2016, File number:
VB3-03224; 3050-2618.

R. v. Khun-Khun, 2019 BCCA 305 (CanLII), 2019-08-23, File number:
CA45319, Court of Appeal for British Columbia.

BOOKS

Edwards, Peter and Luis Horacio Nájera. *The Wolfpack: The Millennial
Mobsters Who Brought Chaos and the Cartels to the Canadian
Underworld*. Toronto: Random House Canada, 2021.

Hall, Neal. *Hell to Pay: Hells Angels vs The Million Dollar Rat*. Toronto:
HarperCollins, 2014.

Langton, Jerry. *The Notorious Bacon Brothers: Inside Gang Warfare on
Vancouver Streets*. Mississauga: John Wiley & Sons, 2013.

ARTICLES

Albaladejoen, Angelika. "Canada's laws leave door open for
money laundering by LatAm groups." *InSight Crime*,
February 15, 2018.

Austin, Ian. "Gang leader Sukh Dhak laid to rest: Gang squad officers
were 'monitoring and keeping the peace' at Delta service."
The Province (Vancouver), December 10, 2012.

Badelt, Brad and Kim Bolan, "Man escapes second attempt to kill him:
Four shots fired into car of Indo-Canadian with links to gangs."
Vancouver Sun, July 7, 2005, B1.

Bailey, Ian and Sunny Dhillon. "Police draw lines to quell gangs; As the Lower Mainland struggles with another public wave of violence, the police alliance tasked with containing gangsters is employing an unusual strategy to keep the bloodshed in check." *Globe and Mail*, May 12, 2012, S1.

Bains, Camille. "Two B.C. men killed in Mexico were involved in drug trade, says RCMP." Canadian Press, September 28, 2009.

Baron, Ethan. "Gangster's parents still proud: Crime groups may be violent, but they don't shoot 'everyday people'." *The Province* (Vancouver), December 18, 2009, A3.

Barrera, Jorge. "B.C. man killed in Argentina on run from U.S. drug probe, investigators reveal." *Ottawa Citizen*, November 14, 2009, A5.

Barrett, Jessica. "Five UN gangsters sentenced to prison for 'wicked, evil' plot: Crime; Jail terms up to 14 years for gang members who planned to kill Red Scorpions." *The Province* (Vancouver), July 16, 2013, A9.

Bolan, Kim. "South Asian man shot dead in Surrey gangland-style hit." *Vancouver Sun*, May 14, 2005, A1.

———. "Guns seized at wake for slain UN gangster." *Vancouver Sun*, July 28, 2008. B2.

———. "Gang leader's father defends realtor; Slain salesman may have been killed for other reasons, says elder Roueche." *Vancouver Sun*, August 26, 2008, A1.

———. "Reformed UN gangster recalls glory, horror: 'Honour, loyalty, respect' among the 'virtues'—drug addiction among the vices." Canwest News Service, March 2, 2009.

———. "Arrests a breakthrough in fight against gangs: police; 5 charged, more arrests expected in shootings." *Vancouver Sun*, March 4, 2009, A1.

———. "Slain man was part of Pattison kidnap plot: Killed in Argentina." *National Post*, November 5, 2009, A4.

———. "Bacon's isolation breaches Charter rights, lawyer argues; There are no grounds for gang leader's new cell conditions, despite arguments that he is held in separate confinement for his own safety, she says." *Vancouver Sun*, November 14, 2009, A14.

———. "Vancouver man killed in Argentina was wanted in U.S.; UN gang associate allegedly part of a large drug smuggling ring." *Vancouver Sun*, November 14, 2009, B11.

———. "Gang leader's life caught on tape; Clay Roueche boasts of drug connections, talks of buying guns in wiretaps before his arrest." *Vancouver Sun*, December 11, 2009, A17.

———. "Gangsters have a new drug of choice; More and more are popping the painkiller OxyContin to take the edge off their violent lives." *Vancouver Sun*, July 3, 2010, A14.

———. "One man dead, two hurt in Surrey targeted shooting." *Vancouver Sun*, October 24, 2011, A3.

———. "First appearance for B.C. Hells Angels members charged with murder." *Vancouver Sun*, November 21, 2011.

———. "Murder trial begins for two Hells Angels, five others." *Vancouver Sun*, November 22, 2011, A5.

———. "Gang associate convicted after hiding gun in park: Gangster faces a minimum three-year term." *Vancouver Sun*, March 9, 2012.

———. "Gang associate convicted on firearm charges: Judge accepted circumstantial evidence that suspect had hidden loaded gun in booth at baseball diamond." *Vancouver Sun*, March 10, 2012, A13.

———. "Gangster's slaying a sign of rising tensions: Ranjit Cheema was trying to re-establish himself as a major player in B.C.'s drug trade." *Vancouver Sun*, May 3, 2012, A1.

———. "Accused wasn't found innocent: Crown; Malik seeks repayment of $9.2 million in legal fees after acquittal." *Vancouver Sun*, May 30, 2012.

———. "Dhak associate Manny Hairan dead: Jujhar Khun-Khun wounded." *Vancouver Sun*, January 15, 2013.

———. "Moving up the Hells Angels' ranks: Michael Plante is made an 'official friend' and entrusted with a cache of weapons." *Vancouver Sun*, January 30, 2013, A6.

———. "Two men found guilty of running DTES crack operation, working for criminal organization." Postmedia Breaking News, June 6, 2013.

———. "Guilty: gangsters hunted bacon brothers; UN gang members plead guilty to conspiracy to murder their underworld rivals." *Vancouver Sun*, July 9, 2013, A1.

———. "Hells Angels used bat, hammer to beat dad to death, trial hears." *Vancouver Sun*, February 4, 2014, A5.

———. "Two Hells Angels sentenced to 15 years for brutal Kelowna slaying." Postmedia Breaking News, February 5, 2014.

———. "Beating death linked to 'rude' Facebook post: Petty dispute between two families led to fatal assault of Dain Phillips, court hears." *Vancouver Sun*, February 5, 2014, A7.

———. "B.C. Hells Angels under siege; 18 of 100 full-patch members have either been charged or convicted of crimes." *Vancouver Sun*, February 6, 2014, A1.

———. "Son of fatal Kelowna beating victim testifies that all four accused kicked and stomped his dad." Postmedia Breaking News, February 25, 2014.

———. "Targets of weekend shootings belong to rival warring gangs: Police warn young women after reality star Mia Deakin injured." *Vancouver Sun*, June 10, 2014, A2.

———. "Gangster from Iraq ordered deported: But political strife puts movement on hold." *Vancouver Sun*, January 12, 2015, A4.

———. "Accused was working for UN gangster, trial hears: Man allegedly shot at vehicle in attempt to kill Red Scorpion member." *Vancouver Sun*, February 17, 2015, A5.

———. "Drug pipeline: How crime groups infiltrate and exploit our docks." *Vancouver Sun*, May 9, 2015, A14.

———. "More charges for Kelowna gang associate." Postmedia Breaking News, May 27, 2015.

———. "Gang associate cries at his attempted murder trial when he recalls being broke." Postmedia Breaking News, June 16, 2015.

———. "Two men involved in fatal attack by Hells Angels lose appeal." Postmedia Breaking News, January 20, 2016.

———. "Accused in fentanyl lab case has drug conviction in the U.S." Postmedia Breaking News, March 22, 2016.

———. "REAL SCOOP: Gangster charged and convicted in connection with Jon Bacon murder." Postmedia Breaking News, June 3, 2016.

———. "REAL SCOOP: Sean Kelly latest victim of Surrey gang war." Postmedia Breaking News, August 2, 2016.

———. "REAL SCOOP: UN gangster to be deported to Iraq in early 2017." Postmedia Breaking News, September 29, 2016.

———. "REAL SCOOP: Barzan Tilli-Choli sent back to Iraq." Postmedia Breaking News, January 20, 2017.

———. "REAL SCOOP: Roueche wanted out-of-town hitman, trial hears." Postmedia Breaking News, April 22, 2017.

———. "REAL SCOOP: Witness describes UN violence over years." Postmedia Breaking News, May 5, 2017.

———. "REAL SCOOP: Bacon murder took gang war to the streets of Kelowna." Postmedia Breaking News, May 21, 2017.

———. "REAL SCOOP: Judge rules evidence allowed in Bacon murder trial." Postmedia Breaking News, June 21, 2017.

———. "REAL SCOOP: Hells Angel David Giles dies months after record sentence." Postmedia Breaking News, July 3, 2017.

———. "Witness says Dhak contracted gang to kill his enemies; Under Oath: Crown witness identified only as 'B' testifies at murder trial of alleged UN hitman Cory Vallee." *The Province* (Vancouver), October 19, 2017, A13.

———. "REAL SCOOP: Vallee murder trial verdict coming June 1st." Postmedia Breaking News, February 19, 2018.

———. "REAL SCOOP: Watch the surveillance video of Jonathan Bacon's murder." Postmedia Breaking News, May 2, 2018.

———. "REAL SCOOP: Years of violent retaliation before Kelowna plea deal this month." Postmedia Breaking News, May 12, 2018.

———. "Key events in the conflict with the Wolf Pack alliance." *The Province* (Vancouver), May 13, 2018, A13.

———. "Hells Angels still expanding after 35 years in B.C." Postmedia Breaking News, July 19, 2018.

———. "REAL SCOOP: Another murder charge laid in LeClair murder." Postmedia Breaking News, July 31, 2018.

———. "Gangster shot dead in Mexico becomes third Alkhalil sibling slain since 2001." *Vancouver Sun*, October 6, 2018, A3.

———. "Man who killed biker buddy gains release: Langley resident ordered to live in halfway house when out of prison." *Vancouver Sun*, February 3, 2022.

———. "Plasma torch, accomplices helped accused killer escape jail: sources; Two Americans posing as contractors tentatively identified, Interpol alerted." *Vancouver Sun*, July 23, 2022, A4.

———. "Video released of suspects who broke accused killer out of jail." *The Province* (Vancouver), August 10, 2022.

———. "Judge surveys CCTV scene before slaying; Jury to deliberate on Duhre murder case after today's instructions from bench." *Vancouver Sun*, August 26, 2022, A14.

———. "Gangster vanishes while on parole: Two months earlier, associate in middle of second murder trial escaped from Lower Mainland jail." *The Province* (Vancouver), September 23, 2022, A4.

———. "Gangster, killer, escapee: How Robby Alkhalil broke out of a B.C. jail." Postmedia Breaking News, December 7, 2022.

———. "A Murder in Phuket: B.C. gang conflict moves overseas." *Vancouver Sun*, January 20, 2023.

———. "Accused killer Conor D'Monte should be sent to Canada for trial: U.S. Attorney." *Vancouver Sun*, January 27, 2023.

———. "Psychologist didn't factor Hells Angel Larry Amero's messages into his report, B.C. court hears." Postmedia Breaking News, May 16, 2023.

———. "Amero sent tips on hits via texts, Crown says." *Vancouver Sun*, May 18, 2023, A6.

———. "Wolfpack gangster Larry Amero is sorry, court hears at sentencing hearing." *Vancouver Sun*, September 28, 2023.

Canadian Press. "Crown tardy in laying charges: High-profile cases proving tough calls." *Calgary Herald*, May 6, 2004, A12.

———. "Man who infiltrated Hells Angels for police testifies at Vancouver drug trial." September 14, 2006.

Cherry, Paul. "Police officer spooked by suspects during surveillance, court told." *Montreal Gazette*, February 4, 2020, A3.

Desi, Vancouver. "Surrey man gunned down in Delta driveway had Dhak gang links." *Hindustan Times*, January 6, 2015.

Ealand, Nick. "Surrey man with gang links killed in targeted shooting." Postmedia Breaking News, October 7, 2015.

Edwards, Peter. "This gang associate fled to the GTA to avoid rivals. Did a tweeted photo at a Raptors game lead to his murder?" *Toronto Star*, December 26, 2021.

———. "Murders of GTA men highlight Mexico's bloody history with Canadian organized crime." *Toronto Star*, January 24, 2022.

———. "Double murders highlight bloody history." *Toronto Star*, January 25, 2022, A11.

Edwards, Peter with Daniel Renaud. "Canadians tied to Mexican drug wars: Unsealed RCMP report reveals fears of cartels' widening influence." *Toronto Star*, April 19, 2013, A6.

Fraser, Keith. "Accused denies misleading full-patch Hells Angel in attempt to get him involved in petty dispute." Postmedia Breaking News, April 17, 2014.

———. "Gang links were a motivating factor in fatal attack, lawyer tells court." *The Province* (Vancover), May 7, 2014, A8.

———. "Court told alleged shooter boasted he would shoot gang rival in head." *The Province*, February 17, 2015, A9.

———. "Shooting spurred two more conspiracies: Crown tells court killing of Jonathan Bacon prompted accused to commit subsequent crimes." *The Province* (Vancouver), June 29, 2021.

———. "Final arguments in murder trial focus on revenge plots following 2011 killing." *The Province* (Vancouver), July 7, 2022, A3.

———. "Hells Angel convicted in murder case claims trial delay unreasonable." *The Province* (Vancouver), December 13, 2022, A9.

———. "Man convicted in Surrey Six murders has died in prison." Postmedia Breaking News, December 16, 2022.

Fraser, Keith and Kim Bolan. "Gangsters convicted in murder case: Jury deliberated for three days after 14-month trial in brazen public execution of rival in 2012." *The Province* (Vancouver), August 30, 2022, A6.

Global News. "UN gang member pleads guilty to Bacon brothers murder conspiracy." April 16, 2013.

Gurneyen, Kyra. "Canada drug trafficking groups expanding Mexico ties." *Insight Crime*, September 12, 2014.

Hall, Neal. "Body found in Richmond is executed gang member: Raymond Chan is the city's first homicide of 2003." *Vancouver Sun*, May 16, 2003, B3.

———. "Police agent reveals his climb up angels ranks: B.C. Informer says being an enforcer put him in jail, where police recruited him." *Vancouver Sun*, September 16, 2006, B9.

———. "Surrey man gunned down in Delta driveway had Dhak gang links." *Hindustan Times*, January 6, 2015.

Hume, Jessica. "Vancouver gangland shooting injures 10." *National Post*, December 13, 2010, A1.

InSight Crime. "Mexican Drug Gangs Have 230 'Branches' in US, Canada." January 11, 2011.

Keller, James. "5 'Surrey Six' victims were killed to eliminate witnesses: Crown." Canadian Press, September 30, 2013.

Killebrew, Bob and Bernal, Jennifer. "Crime wars: Gangs, cartels and U.S. national security." Center for a New American Security, 2010.

Laws, Jennifer. "Testing the Limits on Abuse of Process: Her Majesty the Queen v. Matthew James Johnston, et al." TheCourt.ca, December 6, 2021.

Lazaruk, Susan. "Hunger strike at pretrial centre: Co-accused in Jonathan Bacon murder among inmates complaining about conditions." *The Province* (Vancouver), October 4, 2015, A3.

McClellan, Wendy. "United Nations gang boss behind bars: Barzan Tilli-Choli, 26, charged with attempted murder." *The Province* (Vancouver), March 4, 2009, A3.

McFee, Jennifer. "IHIT identifies Coquitlam homicide victim." Postmedia News, *Coquitlam Now*, July 12, 2011.

Mercer, Katie. "Gangster leaves town: Man linked to Bacon brothers ordered to move." *The Province* (Vancouver), March 20, 2009, A2.

Michaels, Kathy. "Gang life laid out in Bacon shooting trial." *Lake Country Calendar*, August 17, 2017.

———. "Kelowna was a key location in a Surrey gang's drug trafficking network before a war broke out . . ." *Lake Country Calendar*, August 17, 2017.

———. "Bacon trial: Out of control gang war: Trial into the 2011 murder of B.C. gangster Jonathan Bacon continues in Kelowna." *Abbotsford News*, October 10, 2017.

———. "Bacon shooting: 2011 killing motivated by revenge." *Lake Country Calendar*, May 29, 2019.

Munro, Harold. "Police probe fatal blast, car fire: Surrey RCMP suspect arson, murder after body found." *Vancouver Sun*, May 4, 1994, B1.

O'Connor, Elaine. "Fatal shooting spree 'settling of beefs' between Bacon and Dhak-Duhre gangs, police say." *The Province* (Vancouver), January 20, 2012.

Oliver, Cassidy. "Murder may signal gang's demise: Slaying of Red Scorpions leader may also trigger more gang violence, expert warns." *The Province* (Vancouver), January 5, 2014, A4.

Peacock, Andrea. "Bacon murder trial: Getaway vehicle found torched on remote road." *Kelowna Daily Courier*, June 27, 2017.

———. "Court told of inner workings of deadly Dhak Group at Bacon murder trial." *Kelowna Daily Courier*, August 17, 2017, A13.

Pemberton, Kim. "A promising life that went wrong: For Jimmy Reynolds, the As and Bs turned into stealing cars . . . and then death." *Vancouver Sun*, November 6, 2003, B3.

Proskiw, Adam. "Kelowna gangster pleaded guilty and was sentenced to jail for helping murder Jonathan Bacon." *InfoNews Kelowna*, June 3, 2016.

Ramsay, Matthew. "Bertuzzi's lawyer packs his own mighty punch: 'Formidable opponent' to represent NHLer charged with assault." *Ottawa Citizen*, July 11, 2004.

Ramseyen, Geoffrey. "Gangster killing points to Canada-Mexico criminal ties." *InSight Crime*, May 2, 2012.

Raptis, Mike. "Dhak Gang: Who are they?." *The Province*, February 7, 2012.

———. "Bacon murder trial: Accused killer in celebratory mood after gangland slaying." Postmedia Breaking News, August 15, 2017.

Sher, Julian and Wendy Stueck. "The Rise and Fall of the Bacon Brothers." *The Globe and Mail*, August 18, 2011, A10.

Staley, Roberta. "Body found after fiery blast." *Surrey Leader*, May 4, 1994, 3.

———. "Date set for hearing." *Surrey Leader*, May 24, 1987, 3.

———. "'Dangerous' mental patient recaptured." December 5, 1990, A25.

———. "Surrey man banks on delay to go free." *Surrey Leader*, April 18, 1998, 21.

The Province (Vancouver). "Shooting victim had criminal past, cops say." July 13, 2011, A10.

———. "Squamish murder victim identified as Surrey's William Woo." October 3, 2011.

———. "Timeline of UN–Red Scorpion violence: Referenced at Cory Vallee trial," *The Province* (Vancouver), February 18, 2018, A10.

Wilson, Tim. "The UN Gang, and the Canada-Mexico Connection." *InSight Crime*, January 19, 2012.

REPORTS

"National Intelligence—Global Initiatives Criminal Intelligence Brief, Cartel de Jalisco Nueva Generacion (CJNG) THE FANTASMA Network and Canadian Connections." January 20, 2020.

The part about Barber being mistaken for Jamie Bacon when he was shot dead comes from Keiron McConnell, author of the paper *Vancouver Gang Violence: A Historical Analysis*. Kwantlen Polytechnic University, 2019.

Keiron McConnell's *Vancouver Gang Violence: A Historical Analysis* helped with section on Nikki Alemy, Kevin LeClair, and Randy Naicker.

Commission of Inquiry into Money Laundering in British Columbia, Final Report, June 2022. The Honourable Austin F. Cullen, commissioner.

Criminal Intelligence Service of Canada. *Public Report on Organized Crime, 2023*. Royal Canadian Mounted Police, 2023.

INDEX

A

Adkins, Jesse ("Egon"), 139

Al ("Screwy"), 13

Alemy, Nicole ("Nikki"), 11, 71, 154, 167

Ali, Aram, 70

Alkhalil, Hisham ("Terry"), 20–21

Alkhalil, Khalil, 20

Alkhalil, Mahmoud ("Mac"), 19–22, 26

Alkhalil, Nabil, 20–21

Alkhalil, Rabih ("Robby"), 20, 127–129, 141, 152, 195, 253, 257–259, 272, 276

escape from prison, 267–270

Alkhalil family, 19–20, 26, 28

Amero, Larry Ronald, 26, 44, 68–69, 72, 91, 93, 111, 126–127, 135, 175, 258–259, 274, 278

attempted murder of, 114–119, 122–124, 127, 177, 245, 265

retaliation for, 133, 151–152

Shane charged in attempted murder of, 219

Shane's open letter to, 275–277

B

Bacon, Jamie, 26, 44, 71, 210, 214, 272–273

Bacon, Jarrod, 26, 44

Bacon, Jonathan, 26, 44, 149

murder of, 115–119, 143, 168, 175, 183, 185, 210, 220, 245, 265, 273–274

aftermath, 124, 145, 149–150, 159

police investigation, 154, 178

Shane charged in murder of, 218–219

Bacon brothers, 35, 38, 44–45, 70–71, 228, 252

Barber, Jonathan, 228

Beaver, Sean, 153

Bertuzzi, Todd, 201

Big Circle Boys Asian gang, 37

Black, Lyndsey, 116, 118, 120, 219

Bolan, Kim, 115, 272

Boucher, Maurice ("Mom"), 99

C

California, visitor from, 133–135

Cambie Street shooting, 71

Canada
auto theft in, 13
cannabis legalization, 11
drugs into, 43, 70
immigration to, 2, 20
Mexican cartel branches in, 67
Canadian Security Intelligence
Service (CSIS), 238, 243, 262
Castaneda, Elliott "Taco," 138
"Cell 312," 211–213
Center for a New American
Security, 67
Charlwood, Krista, 207–208, 217,
243–244, 247, 261–262
Cheever, Mike, 207–208, 217,
243–244, 247, 261
Christiansen, Kelly, 97, 144,
149–150, 182
CISC (Criminal Intelligence Service
of Canada), 31
"City guys" gang, 29
Cocks, Norm, 53, 66, 97–101, 134,
276
Collaborators of Justice Unit, 224,
237–238, 240
Coordinated Forces Special
Enforcement Unit (CFSEU), 86
Correctional Service Canada (CSC),
273
Corrections Canada, 165
"Cowboys, The," 84, 141
Crossroads rehab centre, 142

D

Dankoski, Shane
arrests, 11, 13, 96, 131, 165,
183–187, 191, 196, 203, 209, 218
best friend (See Hairan, Manny)
businesses, 51, 56–58
car theft, 10, 13–14, 195
casino ban, 145
childhood, 3–9
criminal charges lists, 203–204,
218–221
detention (juvenile), 7
disappointment with gang, 132,
152, 160
drug dealing, 10–11, 18, 22–24,
27, 30–31, 42–43, 45, 49, 51–52,
60–63, 95, 102–103, 126, 137,
169, 208, 224
drug dealing in prison, 234–238
drug use, 47, 53, 75–76, 94,
100, 114, 171, 176, 186–190,
193–199, 202–203, 205–206,
217, 219, 223, 248–249, 262,
280
abstaining from, 281
Opiate Substitution Therapy
Program, 227, 243
rehab, 142, 203, 208, 249
withdrawal, 187–188
family
aunt (Donna), 3, 5–6, 8, 11
aunt (Kathy), 1–2

cousin (Melissa), 11

cousin (Nikki), 11, 167

cousin (Sheldon), 11, 57, 63–64, 66, 115–116, 163, 167, 181

daughter (Jaida), 281

daughter (Jayla), 281

father (*See* Dankoski, Tim)

girlfriend, 40, 47, 50, 52–54, 82–83, 89, 106–108, 121, 128, 142–144, 149, 154, 166, 177, 182–183, 189–194, 196, 198, 235, 282

grandfather (Ron), 3

half-brother, 195

mother (Darlene), 3–7, 11, 18, 56, 153–154, 166, 192–194, 205, 243

sister (Christina), 3–4, 56, 66, 83, 166, 173, 193, 245

son (Jayden), 53–55, 76, 79, 82, 121, 143, 149, 182–183, 193, 235, 282

son (Jordan), 76, 177, 186, 193, 282

uncle, 74

wife (Alesia), 261–262, 280

fears of vengeance, 270, 273–274

gang sponsor (Jason), 29, 186, 196, 198

Hells Angel ambitions, 124, 133, 135–136, 141, 145, 275

hits on, 172–173

incarceration, 203, 209–217, 247 [*See also* Collaborators of Justice Unit; Kent Institution (maximum security federal penitentiary); Living Unit Five (LU5)]

release, 260

segregation, 233, 235, 244

murders and hits by, 73, 95, 121 (*See also under* Amero, Larry Ronald; Bacon, Jonathan)

new life of, 267, 279–281

nickname "Rooster," 111, 172, 180

open letter to Larry Amero, 275–278

police relationships with, 13, 62–63, 66, 97, 109–110, 112, 120, 131, 168, 174, 177–181, 185–186, 205–208, 219, 221

procuring prostitution, 195–196, 208, 219

rise in gang hierarchy, 39–41, 46–47, 51, 130

rock bottom, 199, 202

schooling, 6–7, 155, 224

self-reflection, 245–246, 248

stress and anxiety, 41, 47, 51, 75, 94, 121–122, 164, 176, 181, 186, 189, 210, 218, 264

suicidal ideations, 243–244, 248

warrant for, 182–183

as witness for the Crown, 200,
204, 210, 217–221, 262–266

Dankoski, Tim, 1–6, 29–30, 54–55,
60, 74, 76, 131, 193, 223–224,
233, 248, 260, 282

David (former classmate), 24–25

Delta Grand. *See* Grand Hotel
and Casino

Dhak, Gurmit Singh, 27–29, 31–33,
35, 37–39, 45–46, 58–59, 69, 92,
127, 139, 158, 230–231

gift from, 198

gravesite of, 129–130, 132, 146

home of, 72, 83

murder of, 77–79, 82, 84–87, 114,
152, 162, 276

aftermath, 88, 90–92, 94, 97,
100, 102, 105, 108, 110, 116,
163–164

Dhak, Sukh Singh, 152, 167, 177,
277

arrests, 93–94, 112

avenging Gurmit's murder,
114–115, 117–119, 121, 123,
128, 148–149

as boss of the United Nations
gang, 19, 26–29, 36, 45–46, 107,
110–111, 127–128, 131, 152,
155, 157–158, 204, 264

dangerous personality of, 18,
32, 37–40, 48, 63, 69, 98, 103,
105–106, 113

drugs from, 42–43

drug use, 114

funeral of, 162–163, 175, 194

aftermath, 164

girlfriend, 103–105

gun running, 44

hit on, 132–133

home of, 72–73, 164

jewelry of, 31

murder of, 161, 175, 198, 269

nickname "Buddy," 129, 132

paranoia of, 37–38, 93, 99,
131–132, 143, 159–160

reaction to brother's death, 79,
81–92, 111

as Shane's boss, 35, 39–41, 47,
50–51, 53–55, 58–59, 65, 73, 75,
77, 83, 94, 99, 130, 139, 147,
220, 245, 275–276

Dhillon, Manjot, 166

domestic abuse, 3–4, 104, 190, 195

"Donkey," 155, 171–172

Doust, Leonard (Len), 200–203,
205, 207–208, 217–219, 221, 233

drugs

cannabis, 10–11, 18–19, 24, 38,
126–127, 158, 213, 217, 235

cocaine, 52, 75, 92, 95–96, 98,
102–103, 123, 134–135, 140,
143, 165, 196–198

crack cocaine, 5, 42, 52, 61,
196–197, 199, 208–209, 219

ecstasy, 23, 93, 95, 112, 147

fentanyl, 171, 196, 235–236, 280

heroin, 94, 114, 171, 176, 184–187, 190, 193–197, 208–209, 214, 216–217, 219, 236, 280

methamphetamine, 98

morphine, 188

Narcan (naloxone), 280

oxycodone, 188, 280

OxyContin, 75, 186

Percocet, 47, 53, 57, 75, 95–96, 171–172

Suboxone, 236–238

super buff, 42–43

Duhre, Balraj, 35, 277

Duhre, Sandip ("Dip"), 34–36, 43, 72, 74, 85, 110–112, 127–130, 146–149, 151–152, 155, 211, 258, 267, 269, 276–277

Dustin (neighbour), 17–18

E

El Chapo, 67

Ellis Street clubhouse. *See under* Hells Angels

Elshamy, Dean Mohamed, 35, 146–147

Eric Dykeman, 205

"Exchange Cowboy," 151

F

Fat Jay, 89

Fitzgerald, James ("Fitzy," "Fatty"), 18–19, 35, 41, 43, 51, 55, 73, 95, 110, 115, 155, 159, 168, 171–172, 179–180

arrest of, 184–185

attack on, 160

Five Rivers Funeral Home, 85

"FOB killers" gang, 29

Fresh, Dougie, 126–127, 177

Furtado, Philip Bettencourt/ Betencourt. *See* Alkhalil, Rabih ("Robby")

G

Gadbahn, Sam, 130–131, 178–183, 185

Gambino crime family, 48

gang lingo, 21, 44–45, 65, 78, 80

gangster code, 30–32, 48–49

Gianis, Kyle, 20–21, 195

Gianis, Nick, 20–24, 195

Giles, Dave ("Gyrator"), 66, 99–100

Gisby, Tom, 44, 69, 92–93, 152–153

Global United Nations Syndicate (GUNS). *See* United Nations ("UN gang")

Godfather, The, 27, 151

Gold, Alan, 266

Goodfellas, 27

Gotti, John, 36

GPS trackers, 44, 46, 78, 87, 115, 172, 179–180

Grand Hotel and Casino, 111, 125, 220

   murder at, 117–118, 120, 131, 133, 182, 265 [*See also* Kelowna shooting ("casino murder")]

Gravano, Sammy ("The Bull"), 48

Green, Audrey, 2

Green, Bob, 2, 107

Guzmán Loera, Joaquín Archivaldo. *See* El Chapo

H

Hadden-Watts, Leah, 116, 118–119, 135–136, 245, 265, 274

   Shane charged in attempted murder of, 219

Hairan, Manny

   attempted hit on, 125–127, 143, 153

   business of, 29

   drugs and, 43, 75, 95

   as friend, 18, 27, 48, 53, 55–56, 67, 74, 89, 93–94, 103, 105, 131–132, 136–138, 141–142, 160, 163, 199

   in gang hierarchy, 38, 41

   as gangster, 19, 28, 58–59, 69, 73, 77, 81, 84–85, 87, 92, 107, 114–120, 122, 127, 130, 155–156, 182, 221

   as informant, 174–177, 279

   jewelry, 31

   mother of, 170

   murder of, 167–171, 173, 176–177, 198, 245

     aftermath, 199

Halbauer, Kyle Darren, 232

Hansen, Airell Dale, 12

Hansen, Duane ("Big Duane"), 12

Hansen, Lance Tracy ("Oddy"), 8, 12–18, 97–98

Hansen brothers, 231

Hansen family, 111

Heed, Kash, 269

Hells Angels, 2–3, 66, 68–69, 84–85, 87, 98, 106, 111, 114, 116, 122–123, 128, 139–140, 145, 165, 181, 197

   about, 14

   conflict with, 32, 111

   Death Head, 52–53, 64, 66, 139

   Downtown Eastside Vancouver chapter, 14–15, 97

   Haney chapter, 274

   Kelowna ("K-Town") clubhouse, 66–68, 99, 133–135, 139, 168, 181, 276

   Kelowna ("K-Town") clubhouse (Ellis Street), 64, 117

   members, 26, 44, 53, 66, 90, 93, 118, 153, 198, 272 [*See also* Amero, Larry Ronald; Cocks, Norm; Giles, Dave ("Gyrator"); Green, Bob; Skreptch,

Joseph Bruce ("Skreppy");
Thomas, Robert)
Richard, 65
Scotty, 141
Tommy the Prospect, 64–65,
117–118, 134
membership to, 99–100, 124
murder committed by,
100–101
patches, 28, 99, 123, 139
Playa del Carmen clubhouse,
139, 141
screening for, 22
Southland chapter (Edmonton),
67
sponsored for, 97–98, 101–102
strip club owned by, 148
titles, 38
White Rock chapter, 68, 117,
127
working with, 137
Ho, David, 201
Hooites-Muersing, Anton, 201

I
Independent Soldiers, 69, 71, 84,
90–92, 108, 114, 116
Integrated Homicide Investigative
Team (IHIT), 207
Interpol Red Notice, 268
"Iraqi Edward," 196
"Iraqi Kurds" gang, 29

"Iraquians," 20
Ivans, Jeffrey Ronald, 138–139

J
Jesse, 213
Johal, Bindy, 34–35, 74
Johnston, Jennifer, 200, 205–208
Jones, Michael, 115, 117, 119–120,
122, 185, 221, 262, 265

K
Kaawach, Ahmet ("Lou"), 138
Kataoka, Adam Naname ("Nam"),
138
Kelowna, BC. *See also* Kelowna
shooting ("casino murder")
business in, 57, 73, 95
condo in, 96
friend from, 197
gang war in, 88, 110–111, 115, 121
Hells Angels in, 64–67, 99–100,
116, 118, 123, 139–140
police in, 97, 173, 184, 202, 218,
221
RCMP detachment building,
264
returning to, 262
Shane's home in, 50–52, 61–62,
75, 77, 79, 82–83, 94, 142–143,
172–173
Kelowna Rockets Junior A, 57, 149,
173

Kelowna shooting ("casino murder"), 122, 125–133, 138, 145, 147, 149, 152, 155, 160, 171, 175, 177, 182–183, 185–186, 210, 219–220, 222, 245, 274, 276–277. *See also under* Bacon, Jonathan; Project E-Nitrogen

Kendall, Gordon Douglas, 138–139

Kent Institution (maximum security federal penitentiary), 38, 240–241, 247–249, 256, 259–260, 262, 271
cell at, 244

Khun-Khun, Jujhar, 38, 41, 81, 83–84, 92, 95, 103, 108–109, 115, 117–118, 120, 125, 131, 155, 160, 174, 214, 216
arrest of, 185
attempted hit by, 180–181
hits on, 132–133, 168–170, 175, 177
letter from, 215
trial, 262, 265
as UN gang member, 221

Krake, Christopher James, 110

Krywaniuk, Larry, 255

K-Town. *See* Kelowna, BC

L

Lal, Corey, 44–45, 230

Lam, Adam, 8–9, 17–18

Le, Quang Vinh Thang (Michael), 230–233

LeClair, Kevin, 70–71

Leone, Stevie ("Tucker"), 18, 39, 73, 77, 103, 110–111, 117, 127, 141–143, 145

Living Unit Five (LU5), 224–231, 233, 235, 237–239, 244, 248

Loft Six nightclub murder, 21, 26

Luxury Holdings, 29

M

mafia, 32, 38, 128

M and H Ltd., 29

Mantel, Thomas, 18, 38–39, 73, 92, 110, 117, 127, 132, 155, 158–162, 164, 175

"Matt the Rat," 95–96, 121

Mayfair Gardens, 8–9, 40

McBride, Jason ("White Boy"), 221, 257
about, 33
arrest of, 185
business with, 58
Gurmit and, 79
as hired killer, 32, 34, 78, 86–87, 115, 117–120, 122, 143, 182, 201
incarceration, 214
trial, 262, 265–266
violence of, 106–108, 201–202

McCarthy Tétrault law firm, 200

McConnell, Keiron, 70

Vancouver Gang Violence: A Historical Analysis, 71

McDonald, Dwayne, 168–169, 173–176, 178, 184, 264–265, 279

"memorabilia seller," 57–60, 73, 114, 163–164, 194, 197

Mexico, 37, 53, 135–137, 141, 143, 177, 197, 242

cartels in, 43, 66–68, 70, 137, 139 (*See also* Sinaloa Cartel)

drug trafficking from, 69, 138

violent crime in, 138–139, 152–153

Missing Women Commission of Inquiry, 251

Moore, Steve, 201

Mounties. *See* RCMP (Royal Canadian Mounted Police)

"Mr. Burns," 171–172

Murphy, Sean, 71

N

Naicker, Randy, 69, 71

National Inquiry into Missing and Murdered Indigenous Women, 251

"newcomer, the," 61–64

New Westminster Supreme Court, 219

North Fraser Pretrial Centre, 267

O

Oak Street restaurant shooting, 87

outlaw motorcycle gangs (OMGs), 32. *See also* Hells Angels

P

Pacific National Exhibition, 39, 132

Palladium nightclub murder, 35

Phillips, Dain, 100

Pickton, Robert ("Willie"), 250–258, 261, 271–272

Plante, Michael ("Big Mike," "Sherman," "Million-Dollar Rat"), 15, 98

Port-Cartier prison, 271

Special Handing Unit, 270

Potts, Randy, 14–15, 98

Project E-Nitrogen, 130. *See also under* Kelowna, BC

Project E-Pandora, 15

psychic, 166–168, 176, 245

Q

Quattro restaurant shooting, 79

R

Ranch Park Elementary School shooting, 110

Raposo, John, 257–258, 269

RCMP (Royal Canadian Mounted Police), 13, 31, 62, 85, 97, 112, 119–120, 130, 137, 149, 168, 178, 184–185, 188, 200, 203,

205, 207, 217, 221, 229, 262, 264–265, 268–269

report on Canada/Mexico organized crime, 137–138

Red Devils, 203

Reddy, Chris, 91–92, 108–110

Red Scorpions, 70, 84, 116, 128, 201, 210, 216, 228, 230–231, 273

religion, 229

Renaud, Daniel, 137

Reynolds, Jimmy, 11

Riach, James ("Looney"), 116, 118–119, 121

Shane charged in attempted murder of, 219

Rich, Bob, 35

Richards, Ryan, 71

Richmond Highway shooting, 84

Ricky Rings, 89

Riverside Crematorium, 162

Robinson, Svend, 201

"Rooster." See Dankoski, Shane

Ross, Rick ("Rozay"), 271–272

Roueche, Clay, 29, 36–38, 44, 70–71, 152

Roueche, Rupert ("Rip"), 37

Rouse, David, 265–266

Russell, Daniel Ronald, 201, 227–228

Ryan (former classmate), 202

S

Sahbaz, Salih ("Sal") Abdulaziz, 152

Shakur, Tupac, 146

"Side Swiper," 152

Sinaloa Cartel, 67, 123, 137

Skreptch, Joseph Bruce ("Skreppy"), 139–140

"Skull Buster," 151

Soomel, Rajinder, 71

Spencer, Doug, 34, 160

Steroids & Silicone (boat), 116, 118

Surrey, BC. *See also* Surrey Six massacre

business in, 29

Cedar Hills, 18

Chevron gas station, 18–19

childhood in, 8, 52, 97

drug transport from, 23, 50, 62, 94

Fraser Heights, 92

gang activity in, 70

Guildford, 155, 195

Holly Park, 20

hospital, 188

mother's home in, 192–193, 198, 208, 257

Newton, 72

pretrial correctional centre, 93, 187, 210–212, 216, 218, 262, 273, 281 (*See also* "Cell 312")

prison break in, 269

shootings in, 35, 109, 120, 132, 142, 147, 153–154, 166, 168, 171

Skytrain Station, 11

strip club in, 89

Sukh brothers in, 73, 75, 77, 82, 84, 104, 131, 152, 160

Thomas Mantel in, 158

Whalley, 11, 72–73, 81, 271–272

Surrey Six massacre, 45, 230, 250

T

Thomas, Robert, 101

Throttle Lockers, 197

Thunderbird Mall shooting, 71

Tilli-Choli, Barzan, 70, 152

Tran, Viet ("Billy"), 33, 58

Triads, The, 231

U

United Nations ("UN gang")

about, 28–30

beads, 28, 32, 34, 36–37, 66, 80, 89, 115, 118, 130, 143, 161, 177, 263

Dhak-Duhre group, 47, 65, 93, 102, 105, 153, 155, 163

drug cooking, 43

founder, 36–37

hierarchy, 41, 74

hits by, 70–71, 73, 84, 87, 105, 119, 138–139, 258 [See also Kelowna shooting ("casino murder")]

members, 201, 203, 225, 227, 257

parties, 53

rivals, 26, 92, 98, 108, 110–111, 141, 154, 157, 230

Shane's sponsor, 186, 198

(See also under Dankoski, Shane)

shirt with logo, 59, 66, 172

signals, 44

tattoo, 231

V

"Valley Side" gang, 29

Vancouver Law Courts, 151, 161

W

welfare, 5, 11, 20, 62

Westerhead, Kyle, 149

Wheeler, Doug, 38, 51, 53, 89, 95, 110, 121, 124, 155, 158, 266

"Where's Waldo," 152

White Boy Posse, 232

Williams, Chris, 13, 97, 109–110, 120

Willock, Tyler, 70

Wiwchar, Dean, 159, 256–259, 267, 276–277

Wolfpack Alliance, 26, 28, 44, 68, 70, 72, 79, 84, 90, 92, 98, 105, 110, 123, 128–129, 133, 154–155, 157, 159, 166, 171, 199, 256, 258–259, 272

Woo, William Lim ("Billy"), 133

Woodruff, Jack, 231–232

PETER EDWARDS is the organized-crime beat reporter for the *Toronto Star* and the bestselling author of seventeen non-fiction books and one young adult novel. His works have been published in four languages. Edwards is a member of Top Left Entertainment, a production development company, and an executive producer for the Citytv series *Bad Blood*, created by New Metric Media and aired on Netflix. His book *One Dead Indian: The Premier, the Police and the Ipperwash Crisis* was made into the Gemini Award–winning movie *One Dead Indian* by Sienna Films that aired on CTV. Edwards was awarded an eagle feather from the Union of Ontario Indians and a gold medal from the Centre for Human Rights. His book *Delusion* (published in Europe as *The Infiltrator*) is on the CIA's recommended reading list for staff and agents.